James Gilmour

Among the Mongols

Elibron Classics
www.elibron.com

Elibron Classics series.

© 2005 Adamant Media Corporation.

ISBN 1-4021-6555-2 (paperback)
ISBN 1-4021-3636-6 (hardcover)

This Elibron Classics Replica Edition is an unabridged facsimile of the edition published by the Religious Tract Society, London.

Elibron and Elibron Classics are trademarks of Adamant Media Corporation. All rights reserved.

This book is an accurate reproduction of the original. Any marks, names, colophons, imprints, logos or other symbols or identifiers that appear on or in this book, except for those of Adamant Media Corporation and BookSurge, LLC, are used only for historical reference and accuracy and are not meant to designate origin or imply any sponsorship by or license from any third party.

HUNTING WOLVES IN MONGOLIA.

AMONG THE MONGOLS.

BY THE
REV. JAMES GILMOUR, M.A.
LONDON MISSION, PEKING.

MONGOL GIRLS.

LONDON:
THE RELIGIOUS TRACT SOCIETY,
56 PATERNOSTER ROW, AND 65 ST. PAUL'S CHURCHYARD.

PREFATORY NOTE.

IN its original form this book had a large circulation, and excited an unusual amount of interest. It was felt that the writer was a man of fervent missionary enthusiasm; it was evident also that he was a man of strong and decided views, fully equal to the task of making those views clear to the mind of the reader.

But Mr. Gilmour possesses also a very marked literary style. In fact the reviewer of the book in the *Spectator* went so far as to compare it to the writings of Daniel Defoe, and to say: "The newness and value of the book consist solely in its Defoe quality, that when you have read it you know, and will never forget, all Mr. Gilmour knows and tells of how Mongols live."

The book is now published in this new and cheaper form in the hope that it may continue to do good. It is full of incidents and adventures, and they are all "real true"; it is full of valuable and novel information; it can be read simply for amusement of a high type; or—and this is the chief end for which it is re-issued—it can be read as one proof out of many that noble, earnest, godly men are bravely fighting heathenism and sin in the dark places of the earth, and should be sustained by our sympathy and our prayers.

It has been thought well to let Mr. Gilmour's own account of his book stand, and so the original preface follows this note. Mr. Gilmour is now (1888) living among his Mongol friends, and striving to heal both their bodies and their souls.

PREFACE TO THE FIRST EDITION.

THIS book aims at representing to the western reader whatever is most noteworthy and interesting in the home life, manners and customs, occupations and surroundings, modes of thought, superstitions and religious beliefs and practices of the Mongol tribes who inhabit the eastern portion of the plateau of Central Asia lying between Siberia on the north and China on the south.

It is not a missionary's report nor a traveller's diary, nor a student's compilation, but has for its source things seen, heard, and experienced by me while travelling with natives through the desert, sharing with them the hospitality of the wayside tent, taking my turn in the night-watch against thieves, resting in the comparative comfort of the portable cloth travelling tent, or dwelling as a lodger in their more permanent abodes of trellis-work, and felt while engaged first of all in learning the language and acquainting myself with the country, and afterwards in the prosecution of my missionary duties.

Starting from Peking as head-quarters, I first saw the plain in August, 1870, and during most of the intervening years have spent the summer months itinerating among the tribes to the west, north, and east of Kalgan; and have had the opportunity during the winter months in Peking of meeting Mongols who come to that great centre on Government duty from nearly all the tribes scattered over the vast extent of desert territory which acknowledges the Chinese rule.

Knowledge of the language and familiarity with the people, combined with carefulness of observation and caution of statement, lead me to believe that the information contained in the book is correct and reliable.

With regard to the Buddhism spoken of throughout the work generally, and especially treated of in the eighteenth chapter, it should be remembered that this is not the theoretic system of that ancient religion, but the development of it which now obtains in the practical life of the present-day Mongols, namely, the old doctrines mixed up with extraneous beliefs and superstitions native and imported, and for which perhaps the best name would be Lamaism.

The engravings which are described as native sketches are the work of a Chinese artist in the border town of Kalgan, and his pictures, though a little at fault in some minor details, are correct enough in the general impression they give of the scenes represented.

CONTENTS.

CHAPTER I.

FIRST ACQUAINTANCE WITH MONGOLIA.

Landed on the plain in the dark. Morning on the plain. Boiling tea. Russian soldier's adventure with dogs. Fellow-travellers arrive in the night. Start in morning. Midday halt. Parting feast. Russian manner of adieu. Fairly away into the desert. Members of the caravan. Order of march. Difficulty of intercourse. Pocket-dictionary. Shooting ducks and geese. Commissariat department. Fresh camels. Urga. North of Urga mountainous and wooded. Cross mountain range. Accident. Kiachta in sight. Devotions in Russian church. Mongol lama's present . . . . . . 19—28

CHAPTER II.

PICKING UP MONGOLIAN.

Mongolian Phrase-book. Mongolian teacher in Kalgan. Mistaken sentence. Note-book and pencil in Buriat tents. An object of suspicion. Buriat teacher in Kiachta. Progress unsatisfactory. Take to the plain. Lama at his prayers. Mongolian lodgings. Suitability of the tent. Manner of study. Progress. Lessons not a success. Purity of the language in the tent. Corrupt nature of general Mongolian conversation. Mode of life in the tent. "Steam of the cold." Tea. Porridge for "Our Gilmour." Dinner. Tripe. Bed. Charcoal. Wood fuel. Tent on fire. Snow and ice melted for water. Lama host goes home. New Mongol lodgings. Quarrel between father and son. Night alarm. Flight. Lodgings in South Mongolia . . . . . 29—45

CHAPTER III.

THE BAIKAL IN WINTER.

The Baikal regarded as sacred by the Russians. Date of freezing. Affects the felt cold of the atmosphere. Marine boiler. Snow near the Baikal. Ridges and hills of ice. Ice on edge. Transparent ice. Thickness of the ice. Track across the lake marked out by trees. Restaurant on the middle or the lake. Boats on the beach. Customs barrier. Baggage searched. Irkutsk. Curious honey casks. Chinese in Irkutsk. Irkutsk in a thaw. Snowstorm on the Baikal. Racing on the ice. Change of horses. Sledge upset. Expansion and contraction of the ice. Effect of thaw on the Baikal. Change of season troublesome in crossing the Baikal . . . . 46—55

CHAPTER IV.

TRACES OF THE OLD BURIAT MISSION.

Tombs at Selenginsk. Tombs at Onagen Dome. Log-built mission houses. Siberia of the present day. Devotedness of the missionaries. Russians think the missionaries dirty. Russians do not understand religious enthusiasm. Modes of carrying on mission work. Translation of the Scriptures. An energetic Buriat. The mission closed by order of the Emperor. Converts compelled to join the Greek Church. Results of the mission . . . . 56—72

CHAPTER V.

LEARNING TO RIDE.

First lessons. Mongols ride with short stirrups. A six hundred mile ride. Buying a whip. The start. Crossing the Tola in flood. A Mongol's exhortation. Camping out. Dreams. Fall. Rat pits. Mending harness. Mode of journey. Hospitality of the poor better than that of the rich. Inhabitants. Influenza. Animals in tents. We prefer to camp out. Guide bewildered at his native place. Find a trail. Guide's home. Character of guide. Reputation among his countrymen. New guide. Rainless district. Change to camels. Camels and horses compared. "Have you a revolver?" Mending a camel's foot. Gobi. A hill with one side. A thirsty ride. Stones of Gobi. A tent at last. Tea in the desert. Enchanted land. Stony illusion. Recollection of Gobi like a nightmare. Progress in learning to ride. Snatches of sleep. A green land. Miss our way. "What shop do you belong to?" Kalgan . . . . 73—98

CHAPTER VI.

A NIGHT IN A MONGOL'S TENT.

A dust storm. Tents. Hospitality. Quarters for the night. A reading lama. Reading the gospel by fire-light. "Yes, I have spent a good night" . . . . 99—103

CHAPTER VII.

BUYING EXPERIENCE.

Preliminary preparations. Waiting for a Mongol. My first camel. Load up and start to look for a servant. Upset. A Mongol manufacturing gunpowder. Hire a servant. Chanting prayers for the dead. A runaway camel. Fit out and start. Camel driver incompetent. Camel sticks. Put back and lightened. Dog carries off mutton. Camels unsuitable for my purpose. Sell off. Poetical justice. Ox-carts. Oxen. Camels and oxen compared. Tents. Mongols thoughtless and careless . 104—117

CHAPTER VIII.

HOW TO TRAVEL IN MONGOLIA.

How Mongols travel. On camels with a tent. On horseback. In ox-carts or horse-carts. On foot. Incidents *en route*. How Chinamen travel. Camel cart travelling for foreigners generally. Requisites. Scenes on the plain. Pleasantest part of the ride. Customs to be observed by travellers. Mongols hospitable and desire reciprocity . . . . 118—129

CHAPTER IX.

DINING WITH A MONGOL.

The invitation. My host preparing himself for dinner. Conversation under difficulties. Arrival of a congenial companion. Dinner ready and served up. The piece of honour. The proper custom. The second course. Early hours. Why the rump is the piece of honour. Paying a Mongol in his own coin. A live dinner . . . . . 130—134

CHAPTER X.

APPEAL TO A MONGOL MANDARIN.

The use of a passport. Hiring horses. Stopped on the highway. A horse left on our hands. Asking advice of a local mandarin. The mandarin's settlement of the case. Another quarrel over a horse. A broken head. Fight in the tent. "He would leave his coat with me." "Ne exeat regno." Asking a mandarin's advice. His official utterance. His private opinion. Nothing private in Mongolia. Reconciliation. Tit for tat . . . . 135—144

CHAPTER XI.

LAMA MIAO.

Situation. Meaning of name. Trading centre. Man being starved to death. The cage. Demeanour of the criminal. Tantalising the sufferer. The "*Mirth of Hell.*" Jeering of the crowd. Death. Hardheartedness of the Chinese . 145—149

CHAPTER XII.

URGA.

Religious capital of Mongolia. Situation. Mongol name. The "Green House." View from behind the Russian Consulate. Wind. The Chinese trading town. Chinese cash currency introduced. Chinese not allowed to take their wives to Urga. Temples in the Mongol settlement. Praying-wheels at street corners. Worship by prostration. Mongol reason for it. The open market. Audacious eagles. The priestly part of Urga. The trade of Urga. Tea agencies. Beggars in the market-place. Wickedness of Urga . . . 150—158

CHAPTER XIII.

WU T'AI SHAN.

The great sacred place of Mongol pilgrimage. Advantages secured by pilgrims. Surrounding scenery. "The hamlet in the bosom of the mountains." Temple on hill-top. Beauty of scenery. Temple above a gateway. Three hundred praying-wheels. Immense praying-wheel. P'u Sa T'ing. Pneumatic praying-wheel. "The ice that never melts." Shrines on hill-tops. Hardships of Mongol pilgrims. Worn-out pilgrims escorted home. Expeditions of lamas from Wu T'ai to Mongolia. System of granting annuities . . . . 159—171

CHAPTER XIV.

KALGAN.

Meaning of the name. A table-land eaten away by water. Picking the bones of the skeleton. Picturesque rocks. "Heavenly fish." Houses perched on the hillside. Difficult entrance. Custom of dismounting at the gate. Upper Kalgan. Lower town. Building land scarce. Falling stones. Thunderstorm at dark. Kalgan a great market for Mongol wants. The Chinese trade. The tea trade. Tea villages on the plain. Transport of tea to Siberia. Imports. Soldiers' quarters. Government offices. American missionaries . . . . 172—184

CHAPTER XV.

DOCTORING THE MONGOLS.

Mongol doctors numerous. Mostly priests. They live in their patient's house. Mongols make good patients. Belief in water cure. Almost all Mongols suffer from disease. The missionary swamped in the doctor. Mongol admiration for the missionary doctor. The successful eye operation. Mongol suspicious of morning walk. About an evening ride. About writing. Missionary must not be a sportsman. Diseases prevalent in Mongolia. Religious element in medicine. Feeling the pulse. Swallowing medicine for external application. Patients duped by Chinese traders. Curious cases. Dying Chinaman. Mongol views on the galvanic battery. Divination. The doctor taking his own medicine for example sake. Medical knowledge helps to gain the good-will of the people . . . . 185—208

CHAPTER XVI.

THE GOSPEL IN MONGOLIA.

Halt at tents. Scripture pictures. Books. Utility of tracts as compared with Gospels. Difficulty experienced by a heathen in understanding Scripture. Bibles and tracts should be sold together. Mongols despise our Scriptures as small in extent. Buddhism not to be successfully attacked through its deficient astronomy and geography. The hope for Christianity among the Mongols . . . . 209—215

CHAPTER XVII.

MONGOLS' DIFFICULTIES ABOUT CHRISTIANITY.

Christianity regarded as superfluous. The grandeur of Buddhism. If Christianity is true, Buddhism is false. The various forms of Christianity. Paucity of Christian Scriptures. No liturgy in our Bible. The Trinity. Resurrection. Suffering. How do we know our Bible to be true? Mongols as a rule admit that they are sinners. Counting beads. Buddhism says a man can save himself. Thinks Christianity too easy. Finds Christianity too difficult. Answers to prayer. Some of the objections are earnest, some are frivolous. Answer to many objections. Material difficulties in the way of Mongols willing to accept Christianity . . . . 216—227

/ CONTENTS.

CHAPTER XVIII.

MONGOLIAN BUDDHISM.

Buddhism as it exists now in Mongolia. Power of Buddhism over its votaries. Noble ideas it has given the Mongols. Immortality of the soul. Ten black sins. Five *Zabsar ugwei* sins. Rewards and punishments. Humanity. Heaven and Hell. Power of prayer. Adaptation to the capacity of its votaries. Motives are recognised. Resemblances between Buddhism and Christianity. Buddhism hinders material prosperity. By the number of lamas. By its arrogant self-sufficiency. Hinders learning. Oppression exercised by the lamas. Deceit practised by them. The living Buddha system. The lama system a curse. To the lamas themselves. To the people generally. Buddhism has no intelligent worship. Buddhistic worship is debasing. Buddhistic good works often do harm. Buddhism makes men sin in actions which are indifferent. Buddhism fails to produce holiness. Buddhism is a usurper . . . . . . 228—261

CHAPTER XIX.

THE FIRST OF THE WHITE MONTH.

Preparations. Mongol mode of eating. Amazement at the size of foreigners' noses. Seven dinners on the last day of the year. Reflections suitable to the season. Embracing. Salutation. "Lucky airt" for the year. Duration of the feast and time of ceremonies . . . . 262—270

CHAPTER XX.

NORBO'S MARRIAGE.

Making a mistake. All hands at work. The silversmith. Broken-legged brother of the bride. Cart-load of ladies. Bridegroom and party arrives. Fight. Adorning the bride. Ceremony at starting. A true weeper. Bridegroom's tent barricaded. Homœopathic remedy . . . 271—279

CHAPTER XXI.

FRIENDLY MONGOLS.

Mongol dogs. Snuff-bottles. Running the gauntlet. Furniture and appearance of tent. Swallows' nest in tent. Common sense *versus* Buddhism. White food. Home-made fiddle. Mongol song. Pleasant recollections. A suffering inhabitant. 280—289

CHAPTER XXII.

THIEVES IN MONGOLIA.

A dangerous man. Successful thieves respected. Difficulties of cattle-lifters. Famous locality for thieves. Bold daylight theft. Pilgrim's horse stolen. Strange adventure. A bow at a venture. Hiding cattle. Way of transgressors is hard. A good word for the Mongols. Buddhism does not repress stealing . . . . 290 – 297

CHAPTER XXIII.

A MONGOL COURT OF JUSTICE.

"Have you medicine good for wounds?" Mental tonic wanted. The justice-tent. The court opened. Onlookers. A row of prisoners waiting trial. Punishment. Manner of counting the lashes. Various cases. Conditional confession. The Governor-general. Fatality about confessing. Departure of the judge. Defiant prisoner . . . . . 298—307

CHAPTER XXIV.

A MONGOL PRISON.

Deputation from patients in prison. The staff of prison officials. A prison with open doors. Arrival of turnkey with candle. Appearance of turnkey. Chess-playing. Thunderstorm. The dungeon. Mongol prisoners not in danger of escaping. A feast in prison. Parting ceremonials. Irksomeness of confinement to Mongol prisoners 308--316

CHAPTER XXV.

WHISKY IN MONGOLIA.

"Have you caught the mares?" "Is the *airak* good?" The taste of *airak*. The distillation of whisky. Milking of mares not profitable. Leads to drunkenness. Fewness of teetotallers. Behaviour of a *good* man when drunk. Evils of drink. A whisky-loving living Buddha . . . 317—323

CHAPTER XXVI.

THE MIDSUMMER FESTIVAL.

Summit-spring temple. Worshippers and traders encamped. Carrying sacred books round the temple. Chinese traders. Chinese restaurant. Arrival of worshippers. The *Dault*. My turns comes. The *Ch'am* described. The *Ch'am* is a representation in pantomime of the early history of Buddhism. Passing under the *Sawr*. Carrying forth the *Sawr*. The Babel of dispersion. Thunderstorm. Carrying round Maitreya . . . . 324—337

CHAPTER XXVII.
MONGOL TOILET.

Difference between the dress of men and women. A Mongol's robe is his room. Slovenly appearance of women's dress. Dressing. Washing. Mongols do not bathe. Snuff-bottle. Women's hair ornaments. Men's dress very becoming. 338—343

CHAPTER XXVIII.
ÆSOP IN MONGOLIA.

The hare and the lion. The tortoise in the well. The seven lice and the flea. The trader and the madman. The crow and the lama. The parrot and the king. The reformed cat. Pebbles for jewels. The mouse and elephant. The pearl-borer. The bad-tempered monkey. Fox and bird. The painted fox. Strain at a gnat and swallow a camel. The frog and the two geese . . . . . . 344—354

CHAPTER XXIX.
MONGOL STORIES.

The recluse. The good king and the bad king. The wizard. The painter and the joiner . . . . . . 355—365

CHAPTER XXX.
WOLVES IN MONGOLIA.

Sometimes not seen for a long time. Adventure. Wolves fear Mongols. Wolves attack Chinamen. Encounters with wolves. Wolf hunts. Oxen heading off a wolf. Wolves in the fold. Wolves called *"wild dogs"* . . . . . 366—374

CHAPTER XXXI.
THE MONGOLS IN PEKING.

Attractions offered to Mongols by Peking. Resident lamas. Temples in Peking. Book-shops. Mongols come to Peking on Government duty, on pilgrimages and to trade. The Wai Kuan and the Li Kuan. Christian books. Duration of the Mongol season. . . . . . . 375—383

LIST OF ILLUSTRATIONS.

	PAGE
Hunting wolves in Mongolia	*Frontispiece*
Russian soldier pursued by dogs	22
Mongol knife and sheath	44
The sledge race	54
Selenginsk	57
Sheep crossing the Tola	75
A Mongol camp	82
Catching horses on the plain	85
Women gathering fuel	91
Approaching the Great Wall by night	95
A runaway camel	110
Travelling tents	115
Mongol cart with shafts fastened to poles borne by two riders	120
Travelling in a camel cart	124
Mongol mandarin and attendant	138
Pilgrims approaching a temple	160
Mongol pipe and pouch	175
Mule litter for mountain travelling	179
Going for the doctor	187
Mongol charm	230

Praying-mills driven by wind	238
Mongol Lama of high rank	245
Lama's cap when officiating	251
Mongol wooden image of Buddha	254
Mongol Lama	264
Scales for weighing silver	272
Narrow escape of the little dog	282
Mongol girls	286
Mandarin of rank travelling in sedan carried by four horses and preceded by his seal-bearer	306, 307
The Yellow Temple, Peking	332
Mongol tents and camels	378
Camel caravan *en route*	382

AMONG THE MONGOLS.

CHAPTER I.

FIRST ACQUAINTANCE WITH MONGOLIA.

Landed on the plain in the dark. Morning on the plain. Boiling tea. Russian soldier's adventure with dogs. Fellow-travellers arrive in the night. Start in morning. Midday halt. Parting feast. Russian manner of adieu. Fairly away into the desert. Members of the caravan. Order of march. Difficulty of intercourse. Pocket-dictionary. Shooting ducks and geese. Commissariat department. Fresh camels. Urga. North of Urga mountainous and wooded. Cross mountain range. Accident. Kiachta in sight. Devotions in Russian church. Mongol lama's present.

It had been dark some hours, and though late we were still travelling on, when suddenly a great outcry of several voices was heard on our right, then the cart could be felt diverging from the road on to the grass, and a few minutes later we came to a standstill. Crawling to the mouth of the cart and drawing back the curtain, there could be seen dimly in the darkness a Russian soldier on his knees blowing at a smoky fire which now and then emitted a feeble flicker of flame, just enough to reveal for a moment the face of the soldier and a gleam of the white inside of the half-erected tent behind him. A number of people speaking Mongolian in a loud voice gathered round the cart; and as the eye became more accustomed to the surroundings it was possible to discern the dark outline of camels and baggage lying around in confusion. My Chinese carter, in place of taking me to a Chinese inn, as had been arranged, had taken me out on to the open plain, and unhitching his two mules, went off and left me in the encampment of the caravan of Mongols who were to take me across the desert.

We had left Kalgan shortly after noon, and travelled without stopping for refreshment. Part of our road had been over a lofty mountain pass, where the keen air gave edge to a keen appetite; and after it was too dark to read, the imagination had conjured up a very charming picture of the array of dishes with which it would be proper to celebrate the hospitality of the last inn I could hope to see for a month. It was a surprise to look out and see, not the courtyard of an inn, but a caravan encamped on the open plain. The visionary feast vanished, I was to have no more to do with inns, I had already entered on the desert journey.

I had come fully equipped with provisions and cooking utensils, and though everything was among the baggage of the caravan it was not easy to find things in the darkness. In addition it was already very late, and the fire was slow to burn up. The rest of the caravan had not dined, so that rather than cause delay I declined the use of the fire which was offered me, and accepted the invitation to share in the common meal. This settled, we gathered round the fire to watch the progress of the cooking. The large shallow iron pot that was produced was new, and the first process was to clean it, but this cleaning was performed in such an unsatisfactory way that I gave up the idea of sharing the food cooked in it, bethought myself of a cold chicken, with which a missionary lady, herself experienced in the exigencies of Mongolian travel, had kindly and thoughtfully provided me, ate part of it by the light of the fire, and leaving the Mongols and the Russian soldier filling their wooden cups from the pot which had just been lifted from the grate, retired to my cart for the night. The cart was long enough for a man to lie stretched out at full length, and the fatigues of the day and the strange surroundings of the place were soon forgotten in sleep.

Next morning, on putting my head out of my cart, I found that the sun was high in the heavens, the Mongols were sitting round the fire watching the same pot I had left them engaged with last night, this time filled not with rice but with tea, the furious boiling of which they were moderating by dipping it up and pouring it back again from a height; the camels were dispersed at no great distance, grazing among the profusion of vegetation and flowers that covered the plain; a little way off were some Mongol tents; behind was the green range of hills over which we had come last night; before, the open plain over which we were to start to-morrow. It being the middle of August, the weather was at its best, and the plain in all its glory.

The day was Sunday, and as no one had anything to do but wait for the arrival of the travellers who were to complete the number of our caravan, all spent a day of delicious repose. At one time the repose was suddenly broken by a stirring incident. A great cry made us look towards the Mongol tents, and there we saw our Russian soldier running full speed, pursued by the dogs of the place, which were rapidly gaining on him. For a moment the issue seemed doubtful, but the distance was not great, and he had time to dart in at the low door before the baffled brutes overtook him.

RUSSIAN SOLDIER PURSUED BY DOGS.

He had sauntered carelessly towards the tents with no thought of danger, when the dogs, which had been a little way off on the plain, suddenly spied him and gave chase. But for the friendly warning of some one who had noticed them, they would have been upon him before he was aware. As soon as the pursued made good his escape, the feelings of spectators, natives, and the pursued himself found vent in laughter; but the adventure, though trivial in itself, was useful as teaching, in a very graphic manner, the care that a stranger must exercise in approaching Mongol habitations.

The evening came, but not our expected travellers, and it was not till some time during the night that their arrival broke the slumbers of our company.

The following day, after early breakfast, some friends, who had come to convoy the Russian family in whose company I was to cross the desert, went off for a forenoon's shooting, while the Mongols set seriously to work to arrange and load the camels for the first half-day's march. Soon after we had encamped for the mid-day halt, the sportsmen turned up, a feast was prepared and discussed, the final adieus were said, the parting being made all the more impressive by the Russian men kissing each other, and, about an hour before sunset, the separation took place, our friends turning southwards towards China, we turning northwards towards Russia; and feeling much as if on board a ship starting on a voyage when the pilot has just left taking letters with the last salutations to our friends.

We were now fairly started on the journey of a month, which was to take us from Kalgan, a town on the north frontier of China, to Kiachta, on the south frontier of Russia, a distance of about eight hundred and forty English miles.

The caravan consisted of the Russian postmaster, who had been stationed some years at Kalgan, and was now with his wife, four children, and a soldier—who spoke of his master as the "Commandant," returning to his native Siberia—myself, and four or five Mongols, to manage the camels and camel-carts.

The postmaster had two camel-carts for the personal accommodation of himself and family, and several camels carrying his provisions and goods. I had a camel-cart and one loaded camel. The Russian soldier perched himself upon a camel load, and there were in addition a string of camels carrying grain, the private trading venture of the Mongols whose camels we hired.

The order of march was nearly as regular and monotonous as the features of the desert itself. At sunrise all got up and cooked and ate breakfast. Then the march began and lasted usually till noon, when, at some favourable camping place, a halt was called, the camels turned adrift to pasture, the main meal of the day cooked and eaten, and a fresh start made about an hour before sunset. This night march was the longest continuing usually till after midnight, sometimes even till dawn of next day. The desert roads for the most part are not rough, and the motion of the cart did not often disturb our sleep, but it was remarked that we usually awoke when the cart came to a stand, just as passengers in a steamer at sea wake up when the screw stops.

As we travelled long stages, and were a good deal occupied during the halts,—the Russian father and mother with their children, I with my cookery, having no servant,—we had scant leisure to faternise with each other. Even when we had time and opportunity, we could do little in the way of conversation. The Russian lady knew no language but her own, of Russian I knew nothing, so exchanges of courtesies between us had to be conducted in dumb show. Her husband, the "Commandant," knew some Chinese, of which I also knew a very little, and sometimes, when our Chinese failed, the soldier was called upon to make a vain attempt at communicating with me by means of Mongolian, of which I know even less than of Chinese.

Almost the only time of day the postmaster and I had for attempts at conversation was between sunset and dark, when the children being quiet he and I would walk together in the cool alongside of the caravan, and hold what intercourse was possible. In desperate extremities he had one resource. Diving into the depths of his trouser-pocket, he would produce from that receptacle a Russian-Chinese phrase-book, turn over the leaves, and point out to me the Chinese characters, hoping that I might recognise them. Sometimes I recognised them, sometimes I did not.

The postmaster, like most Russians that came to Kalgan, was a sportsman and a very good marksman, and frequently gave a pleasant variety to our table by shooting wild ducks and geese. On one occasion he bagged four out of a flock of geese that had alighted on the bank of a small river. This was all the more to his credit as he was short of shot, and had taken to gathering minute pebbles from the road with which to eke out his failing ammunition.

In the matter of provisions we each had our own supply, the only real difficulty being meat. In starting for Kalgan I had a stock of dried mutton, the postmaster had a crateful of chickens. The chickens and the dried mutton ran out simultaneously, when we bought sheep as we found necessary, the postmaster taking the largest share for his numerous family, a smaller portion being alloted to me, and the Mongols coming in for the entrails, which they seemed to consider a great delicacy.

After travelling about three hundred miles, the Mongols made a detour from the straight road to their own home, and furnished us with fresh camels and men, who took us on to Urga, about six hundred miles from Kalgan, where their contract ended. Here, through the kindness of the postmaster, I was hospitably accommodated in the consulate premises for the two days that elapsed before Mongols and camels could be found to take us the remaining third of our journey, to Kiachta.

North of Urga the aspect of the country entirely changes. In place of a great plain destitute of trees, we found a mountainous region clothed with forests, and intersected with streams running through fertile valleys. On leaving Urga we had to provide ourselves with bricks of tea for the purpose of hiring oxen to drag our carts over a mountain pass too steep and too lofty to be accomplished by camels. The loaded camels got over the pass without much difficulty, but so steep were the hills that our carts proved a heavy pull for the strong oxen even that are kept and hired out to assist travellers in crossing the mountains. The whole journey was accomplished in nearly the stipulated time and without serious misadventure.

But lesser accidents were not wanting. One night I woke up feeling involved in a kind of chaos. My cart had upset, and I was mixed up under most of the things that were inside. It took me some time to scramble out, and when I succeeded I found the Russian soldier making a vigorous assault on the Mongol by whose carelessness the accident had happened. Seeing the "Commandant" coming up to reinforce his subordinate, I hastened to interpose, and found I was none too soon, for the Mongol had proved no match for the Russian, and had already been severely handled.

One morning, at the end of the stipulated month, we suddenly emerged from a belt of pine forest, and straight before us, seemingly at no great distance, on the other side of a broad, shallow valley, stood Kiachta. The most prominent feature visible was the church, the dazzling whiteness of whose lofty dome is seen from a great distance, and is the first indication to a traveller crossing the desert from China that he is again nearing civilisation.

Kiachta and its white church seemed near, but the distance was greater than it seemed, and some additional delay was caused by a stream in the bottom of the valley, which had too soft a bed to be crossed by camel-carts, and had to be circumnavigated. When Kiachta was at last reached the whole caravan drew up in front of the church, and all the Russian travellers entered to pay their devotions. This done, we marched about a couple of miles into Russian territory, to Troitsko Safska, a town of some three or four thousand inhabitants, where my travelling companions put up at the quarters there prepared for Russian officers on travel. In a few days they continued their journey to some inland part of Siberia.

After the Mongols had been paid and dismissed with suitable presents, one of them, a lama,[1] came back and presented me with a Russian copper coin. The coin was of little intrinsic value, but I was pleased with the gift, taking it as an indication of the man's gratitude for what had been given him. A friend, however, construed the action differently, regarding it not as an

[1] A lama is the Mongol name for priest.

acknowledgment of what had been given, but as an advance towards friendship on the part of the Mongol which I would be expected to meet by returning a silver coin. The conduct of the lama seemed to agree with this supposition, and as he had already received more than he deserved, I made an end of the case by returning him, with many gestures of politeness, his own copper coin. He took it and departed, seemingly not in the least disconcerted or annoyed by the rejection of his gift.

CHAPTER II.

PICKING UP MONGOLIAN.

Mongolian Phrase-book. Mongolian teacher in Kalgan. Mistaken sentence. Note-book and pencil in Buriat tents. An object of suspicion. Buriat teacher in Kiachta. Progress unsatisfactory. Take to the plain. Lama at his prayers. Mongolian lodgings. Suitability of the tent. Manner of study. Progress. Lessons not a success. Purity of the language in the tent. Corrupt nature of general Mongolian conversation. Mode of life in the tent. "Steam of the cold." Tea. Porridge for "Our Gilmour." Dinner. Tripe. Bed. Charcoal. Wood fuel. Tent on fire. Snow and ice melted for water. Lama host goes home. New Mongol lodgings. Quarrel between father and son. Night alarm. Flight. Lodgings in South Mongolia.

BEFORE leaving Peking I had been presented with a "Road Map of the Route from Peking to Kiachta." Between Peking and Kalgan this map was useful, but beyond that its use ceased, for the simple reason that of the many roads from Kalgan to Kiachta the map delineated one, and our caravan followed another.

On the margin of the map, however, were printed little groups of Mongol words and phrases, designed to assist the studious traveller in holding communication with the natives of the desert. These served as my first phrase-book of Mongolian. During the two weeks' delay that occurred in Kalgan before Mongols and camels could be found for the desert journey, I took lessons from a Mongol who occupied the post of teacher to the American missionary whose guest I was. In addition to these two helps—the road map and the Mongol teacher—I had paid some attention to Schmidt's Mongol grammar. Before leaving Kalgan I had, through the medium of Chinese, got the Mongol teacher to drill me in the Mongol sentence equivalent to "I don't speak Mongolian; I am learning it;" and I hoped this would serve me as an introduction to such Mongols as I met, and would perhaps induce them to tell me the words for the common objects and actions of everyday life. These words I was prepared to secure by means of a pencil and a small note-book, always at hand for the purpose. With these slender preparations, linguistic and material, I entered on the desert, eager to pick up any words I could find.

I soon found good reason to remember my Mongol teacher. As I began to understand more of the language, I became aware that in using the sentence which he had given me, and which I had been in the habit of repeating with great satisfaction to most of the Mongols who saluted me, I had not been expressing my desire to *learn* the language, but had been telling all and sundry that I knew and spoke Mongolian!

Of the words on the margin of the map some proved useful, some the Mongols could hardly recognise from my pronunciation, which was not to be wondered at, considering the difficulty of representing their words by English spelling; while some phrases there given were idioms current among a distant tribe, but not commonly used in the native place of the Mongols with whom we were travelling.

The first month after arriving in Siberia was spent in a Buriat-speaking district. I lived in a Russian house and tried to pick up the language by the help of a teacher, and by going about among the people with a note-book and pencil. In this latter department my success was varying. Some days I picked up many useful words and phrases, on other days I was less successful. I used to enter the tents of the Buriats, who are Mongols settled in Siberia, and, though for the most part politely received, I was in some places regarded with suspicion.

One snowy day I entered a tent, and was getting on well, taking down a number of words from the frank young Buriat who was the owner, when three or four dark-looking men entered, said something to my host, tried to question me, and produced such an impression on the young Buriat that when I attempted to resume the work which their entrance had interrupted he would make no reply but "Don't know." It was quite evident that something was wrong, and finding I could do nothing more in that tent, I rose to go. I was aware that my movements were observed, but thought no more of the matter till some time afterwards, when my host came home with a good story of how some Buriats having fallen in with a nondescript individual, who would give no account of himself, had been on the point of seizing him and forwarding him to the governor of the district. They had not ventured to carry out their intention, but communicated with the local authority, describing the man and stating their own suspicions. He, being aware of my presence in the district, was able to set their minds at rest. I experienced no more suspicion in the course of my word hunting, and on some days I came home more proud of half a pageful of words and phrases than ever was sportsman of a good bag of game.

After a month spent thus I returned to Kiachta, established myself in lodgings, and pursued the study of Mongolian, turning my attention mainly to the reading of the Scriptures, which had been translated into Buriat by Messrs. Stallybrass and Swan. But it was difficult to find a competent teacher, and the incompetent teacher who could be found could come only at an inconvenient time of the day, when he himself seemed exhausted and half asleep. Notwithstanding severe application, it was evident I was not making satisfactory progress.

Matters came to a crisis one night when a friend, after hearing me talk with two lamas who happened to call, remarked that if he had studied Mongolian as long as I had he would have spoken better than I did. I had for some time been dissatisfied with hard work and little progress, and this remark, though made laughingly and without any purpose of influencing my movements proved the last straw that broke the camel's back.

Next morning, taking my "Penang lawyer,"[1] to defend myself from dogs, I set out for Kiachta, crossed the frontier into Mongolia, and, after a two hours' walk, reached the tent of a lama whose acquaintance I had made some time before. As I approached the tent I heard the sound of the lama's voice, and when I entered he still continued his devotions, interrupting himself only to say "Sit" and, with his hand, motion me to a seat. I sat down, and no further notice was taken of my presence for ten or fifteen minutes, when, having

---

[1] A "Penang lawyer" is a heavy walking-stick, supposed to be so called from its usefulness in settling disputes in Penang.

finished his prayers, he hastened to salute me as if I has just entered.

After tea had been produced and we had talked some time, I told him the object of my visit, namely, that I wanted to live in his tent and learn Mongolian from him as my teacher. He was quite willing, his main difficulty being that his tent was a poor one; he was afraid that I would freeze, and that he could furnish me with nothing better than Mongol fare, which he supposed I would not relish. In reply to his question when I would begin, I said "At once," and receiving his assent I felt that I was established as an inmate of a Mongol tent.

Next morning he accompanied me to my lodgings in Kiachta, that I might bring some bedding, etc., and on the road we came to an arrangement as to terms. He agreed to board, lodge, and teach me for a sum that amounted to a little over one shilling a day. From that time I used to divide the week between my Russian and Mongolian lodgings, spending three, or four, or five days in the tent, and the remainder in civilisation.

Everything about the tent was wonderfully suited to my needs. The lama who owned it was some two hundred miles from home, so we were not troubled by superfluous members of his family. He was only temporarily located there, and had no dog, so I could go out and in as I liked. He was rich, so could afford to keep a good fire burning, a luxury which could not have been enjoyed in the tent of a poor man. His business required him to keep two or three men servants about him; and as a man of his position could not but have good tea always on hand—a great attraction in the desert—the tent was seldom without conversation going on in it between two or three Mongols.

This last—conversation carried on by Mongols just as if no one had been listening—was exactly what I wanted, and I used to sit, pencil and note-book in hand, and take down such words and phrases as I could catch. Exclamations and salutations made by and to persons entering and leaving the tent; remarks made about and to neighbours and visitors; directions given to servants about herding, cooking, and mending the fire, were caught in their native freshness and purity and transferred to my note-book. In the quiet intervals of the day or evening, I would con over again and again what I had caught.

Learning the language in this way, I soon could speak a good deal more than I could understand or my teacher could explain to me. Though I could not parse the phrases, nor even separate out the words of which they were composed, much less understand the meaning of what I said, I knew when and how to use them, and could hardly help having the accent correct, and could not avoid learning first those words and phrases which were in most common use. Thus, with only a fraction of the labour I had spent over books, I soon began to feel that I was making good progress.

I fear that my teacher did not find my conduct at all satisfactory. I had anticipated great benefit from his instruction, and one of the inducements that took me to his tent was the fact that I knew him to be a good Mongol scholar, able to read, write, and explain well. He too had conscientious ideas of the duty he owed me as teacher, and a few days after taking up my residence with him, he called upon me to receive my first formal lesson. This and the one or two following attempts that were made did not prove a success. As soon as he began to teach me he spoke in such a stilted fashion that I could make nothing of it; my not understanding annoyed him, his insisting in speaking in that style annoyed me, we both got vexed with each other, and had to give it up. Subsequent attempts proved no better, and after a few such lessons I avoided them. Whenever I saw him getting ready to teach me, I used to pick up my "Penang lawyer" and go for a two hours' walk. By the time I returned he either was busy or had forgotten his intention, and I escaped for the day. To those who had mastered the colloquial there could not have been a more efficient teacher of the written language, but his attempts then to teach me the mysteries of writing were premature and labour spent in vain.

A slight drawback to learning a language by repeating everything that any one happens to say, is that some of the phrases so picked up are not very choice. As the language begins to be understood any impropriety in a phrase soon becomes apparent, and can be avoided. It is something to say for the purity of the ordinary conversation carried on in that tent, that of all the numerous sentences thus learnt indiscriminately, I found only two, on fuller acquaintance with the language, to be unfit for use. Of these the more objectionable was after all very harmless, and the other was more absurd than objectionable, while both were perfectly free from any taint of impurity.

Yet it would be a great mistake to suppose that the ordinary conversation of Mongols is pure. Very far from it. In addition to a great many sayings and expressions that would shock civilised ears, but which are due more to the unsophisticated nature of their manners and customs than to any impurity of mind and thought, there is in daily use a vast amount of impure language for which no excuse can be found, and which is simply the expression of corrupt thought. Often in after years, when hearing loathsome language, I have wondered how it was that I heard so little of it when living in the lama's tent. One reason doubtless was that vile conversation frequently hides itself under inuendo, and for the most part is indirect, so that a learner would not be likely to catch it sufficiently clearly to be able to write it down. Another reason may have been that seeing there was "a chield among them taking notes," they were somewhat on their guard. But both these reasons taken together are not sufficient to account for the purity of their talk, and I am fain to believe that it was mainly owing to the good sense and decency of my lama host, whose general bearing and presence were a rebuke to such iniquity, and who ruled his house better than to allow its inmates to indulge in the sin of wicked conversation.

A few words about our mode of life in the tent will illustrate the manners and customs of the northern Mongols. At dawn the serving-lama rose and lit the fire. As soon as the flame blazed up, slow streams of white mist became visible converging towards the fire from holes and seams in the felt sides of the tent. The Mongols called this the "steam of the cold," and they were correct enough, for this phenomenon was visible only in the intense cold of the depth of winter. The question is, what caused it? Had it been *vice versâ*, the vapour in hot air condensing in colder air, it would not have been at all mysterious. In Kiachta, when the door of a warm room communicating directly with the cold atmosphere outside is suddenly opened, the hot air is seen to flow out like a cloud of steam, and this is just what might be expected; but why should cold air entering a tent condense its moisture to the point of visibility? It was remarkable too that this phenomenon was never witnessed except in the morning, and lasted only for a few minutes, say ten or fifteen, after the fire first blazed up.

As soon as the fire had somewhat warmed the tent, the other inmates got up and dressed. Meantime, the servant put the pot on the fire, and placed in it a block of ice or a pyramid of snow. When this had melted, the scum and sediment were removed, and the water thus purified put on to boil, a handful of pounded brick tea being thrown on the surface. After ten or fifteen minutes' hard boiling, kept in check by occasional use of the ladle, the tea was poured into a pail, the pot swept out with a wisp of the hairs of a horse's tail, a little fat melted in the pot, the cracklings carefully removed, enough meal added to make the compound into a kind of porridge, after a time more meal added and well stirred till the mass seemed brown and dryish, then the tea, cleared from the sediment, poured in and boiled up, and the "meal-tea" was pronounced ready. This rather elaborate process of adding fat and meal was gone through to supply the lack of milk. The lama had no cows with him, and I think that during the whole of that winter I saw milk in his tent only once, when some one presented him with a frozen piece of it, looking very much like a small cheese.

This meal-tea in the morning, and again at noon, was the only food partaken of by the Mongols till sunset, and the only exception I had them make in my favour was to secure for myself a cupful of the flour when it had reached the stage in which it resembled porridge. This they called "Scotland," and set aside for the use of "Our Gilmour."

About sunset the servant, glancing up to the hole in the roof as to a clock, would say, "Shall I make dinner?" The lama, nothing loth, would say, "Make it." The servant needed no urging, and I as guest looked on with interest. Outside the tent was a strong dog-proof kind of cage, into which had been put the whole winter's stock of beef, mutton, and tripe. There it needed no salting. The frost kept it perfectly fresh, and so hard that the portions used for each meal had to be hewn off with a hatchet. Enough to serve the wants of the lama and myself was hewn off and boiled, then fished out with the fire-tongs and put into a basin or on a board. My host and myself appropriated pieces, which we ate by the help of a knife only, in true Mongol style.

While we were thus having our first course, some millet was thrown into the pot in which the meat had been boiled, in a short time was pronounced cooked, and formed our second course. The meat was frequently tough and difficult to manage, but this second course of millet boiled in soup and served up rather thin was always grateful, and I have seldom before or since tasted any preparation of civilised cookery that proved so delicious. The excellence of this soup consisted, I suppose, not so much in itself as in its surroundings. Among the most ordinary articles of civilised diet it would, I doubt not, rank low indeed, but with desert hunger, one meal a day, and everything else dirty and badly cooked, this well-cooked millet was indeed a delicacy,

As soon as our meal was over the servants set about theirs. A huge mass of tripe, wrapped up in the stomach of a sheep and frozen solid, was brought in from the outdoor larder, attacked vigorously with a hatchet, and the detached fragments put on to boil in the pot. To see what it was like, I insisted one evening in taking my dinner with the men, but I must say it did not prove a very satisfactory adventure. The men, poor fellows, seemed to relish it greatly, and used to devour large quantities.

However cold the weather might be, these evening dinners were always a hot time both for master and men. The fire was piled up to give light, the food taken was excessively hot, and under these circumstances it was not easy to keep cool. A Mongol, indeed, does not seem to suppose that he receives full benefit from his dinner if the eating of it does not make him perspire profusely.

Most Mongols retire to rest immediately after the evening meal, but my host was a great exception to the rule in this respect, and used to sit by the fire till ten or eleven o'clock, sometimes even till midnight. When at length he did go to bed, it was the duty of the servant to see him snugly tucked into his sheepskin coat, and it used to sound strange to hear the master indicating, in Mongol fashion, by the points of the compass, the places where the tucking in was deficient.

After the master had been properly tucked, and I had drawn on sheepskin boots, buttoned up my greatcoat to the chin, tied down the ear-flaps of my fur cap, and been covered up with a couple of Scotch plaids, the last act of the day was performed. The tent was closed above, the door was made fast, and a large jar filled with charcoal was produced. The charcoal was made by the care of the men throughout the day, who, during their spare time as they sat by the fire, kept rescuing and quenching the glowing embers of the wood as it burned in the grate. Each piece, as it was quenched, was thrown into this jar, and after everything was made fast at night the whole contents were piled in one heap on the fire. In a few minutes there was a splendid glow, and, for the only time perhaps in the twenty-four hours, the atmosphere of the tent was really hot. Every one used to lie and look at it with a glow of satisfaction and gradually drop off to sleep. In a room such a proceeding would have been dangerous, but in our tent danger there was none. Even after every exertion to stop draughts and close up holes, there was more than sufficient ventilation to have frustrated a much more determined attempt to produce asphyxia.

Argol, the dried dung of animals, is the common fuel of Mongolia. In our tent wood was used exclusively, because we were near a forest, and my teacher, having men and horses at command, could have the wood carted more easily than he could have had the argol gathered. Wood is in some respects nicer to use as fuel, but it has one disadvantage—it gives off little explosions, which drive sparks on to the clothes of those sitting around, and even sometimes sets fire to the roof of the tent.

One night, when a stranger lama, who was our guest, was talking with me about Christianity, I had occasion to point upwards, and in a moment the whole tent was in an uproar. Following the direction indicated by my hand, they had looked up and seen that a spark had ignited the roof, and spreading over the soot-covered felt, had made a glowing patch as large as a man's hand. The fire was rapidly spreading, and every one instantaneously proceeded to put into execution a method for extinguishing it, at the same time shouting lustily to the others to hand him such things as he wanted. Unfortunately, all the Mongols present were short of stature, and, though the tent was not a tall one, none of them could reach the burning spot, all the more so, as it was directly over the blazing fire. Several attempts made at extinguishing it had been ineffectual, the glowing patch was rapidly spreading, and the excitement in the tent every moment increasing, when our lama guest in the confusion seized a ladle and began to dash water on the sooty roof. For the most part he missed his aim, and the inky water descending in a shower drove everybody else off the field, and sent them cowering into the sides of the tent, uttering shouts of protestation, and vainly endeavouring to protect their clothes. The burning soot was finally scraped down with a stick, and the lamas again resumed their places round the fire, regarding with rueful looks the black marks spattered all over their red coats.

The water used in the tent throughout the winter was procured by melting ice or snow. As the snow is gathered at no great distance from the tent, it is liable to contain all manner of impurities, and sometimes at the bottom of the pot in which the melting has taken place are found things which anybody but a Mongol would consider very objectionable.

The ice-water is much more satisfactory. It is usually brought from some lake where the water is clean, and being transparent any piece containing impurity can be seen and rejected. One of the pretty sights to be seen in the courtyards of Chinese places of business in Kiachta is the great square stacks of clean, transparent, crystal-looking ice, piled up in the shade of some wall, and forming the water supply of the firm during winter.

Russians out of doors, and Mongols always, protect themselves by wearing skin robes. I neglected this precaution, and, even in the Mongol tent, deemed warm underclothing and a great-coat sufficient. I had to pay for my temerity afterwards, and should have spared myself much discomfort if I had only followed the sensible advice and example of Russians and Mongols, and encased myself in a sheepskin. Even in my noonday walks a damp handkerchief would freeze in the pocket, and I would return to the tent with beard and moustache a mass of icicles, formed by the congealed moisture of the breath. The nights were of course much colder, but in their great sheepskin robes and shaggy goatskin overcoats the Mongols seemed to stand it well, and might be heard singing cheerily in the middle of the night, as the long strings of tea-laden camels defiled past our tent, crunching the frozen snow under their broad feet.

Towards spring my lama teacher finished his business, broke up his establishment and returned home. Circumstances prevented me accepting his invitation to accompany him to Urga. I was very sorry not to be able to go with him, but it was well I did not. I learned afterwards that they had an exceedingly hard journey, and, notwithstanding their skin coats, suffered much from the cold. It is needless to say that had I accompanied them without furs I would have suffered much more

A FAMILY QUARREL.

We parted with deep regret and kindly feelings; we had all got to like each other, and I have no doubt that the Mongols often look back to that winter with pleasure, and tell with glee doings and sayings of the foreigner whom they always spoke of as "Our Gilmour."

After experiencing how easy it was to get on with Mongolian by living in a Mongol tent, I could not rest till I had installed myself in another. The circumstances and surroundings of this second tent were much less favourable for my purpose than those of the first, but after all I had not much reason to complain, when an unlooked-for incident put an end to my residence there, and sent me back to Kiachta.

My teacher was a young layman, who held some small appointment in the *yamen*,[1] and lived in a tent close to the father who had adopted him. The two did not get on harmoniously. The wife of the father stirred up mischief, and, primed from this source, the old man would come into his son's tent and scold him by the half-hour together. Though unpleasant in one sense, this was not without its benefit for me in helping me to acquire the language, and during those scenes I used to enrich my note-book with a number of energetic phrases and sentences.

One night the quarrel assumed a more serious shape, the father was more excited and determined, and because the son refused to manœuvre matters in the yamen so as to let the father have some advantage about an old horse, he declared he would not leave his son's tent, but live there and be a burden to him, and pointing to the dinner cooking in the pot, declared his intention of beginning by eating that.

[1] Yamen is the Chinese word for Government office.

Just when the dinner was ready he got up and left, threatening, however, to come back and end the quarrel by means of the knife. I thought that it was all empty bravado, but the son was alarmed, said I did not know his father, and assured me that the old man was in earnest, and meant what he said. Under these circumstances the meal went off so poorly that it would have been small loss if the father had remained and carried out his threat of eating it. After dinner the young man could not rest, but kept pacing about on a little piece of felt, talking most seriously and philosophically about death and its consequences. By-and-by he settled down, and, as things seemed quiet, we all retired to rest.

MONGOL KNIFE AND SHEATH.

We had not been long in bed when the stillness of the night was broken by a great uproar in the tent of the father—he had got his knife, and was coming to finish the quarrel, but was meantime being detained by the females of his household, who clung to him and shrieked with all their might. Instantly the son sprang up and darted out, and I, thinking that the infuriated Mongol with his knife in his hand in the small tent, and without a light, might mistake me for his son, soon followed him. Without waiting for my boots—the only particular in which I was undressed—I rushed out, and found my companion standing in a fierce north wind, with no covering but a sheepskin, and, as the uproar still continued, I started at a run for the nearest tents, which were not far off. Before I had gone far I became conscious that some one was behind me, and could not make out whether it was the son following my example, or the father mistaking me for his son. As soon as I reached the tent, in place of entering, I ran round to the back of it, and waited till my pursuer came up. He called to the inmates, and, recognising the voice as that of the son, we entered together. A skin was offered me, my boots were brought, and I was soon asleep. In a little while I woke up to hear the voice of the father in the tent. He was borrowing an ox and cart to move his tent and goods. In the morning I learned that the son had gone into hiding; and when, in the afternoon, I came with a conveyance to remove my things, I found that the father had carried off his tent and all his belongings, and disappeared from the neighbourhood. In this abrupt way closed my second term of tent life in Mongolia.

After I began making evangelistic tours, I had good opportunities of picking up further acquaintance with the language, while yet enjoying the comparative cleanliness and comfort of my own travelling tent; but these opportunities are not for a moment to be compared to those that I enjoyed as a silent listener in another man's tent.

CHAPTER III.

THE BAIKAL IN WINTER.

The Baikal regarded as sacred by the Russians. Date of freezing. Affects the felt cold of the atmosphere. Marine boiler. Snow near the Baikal. Ridges and hills of ice. Ice on edge. Transparent ice. Thickness of the ice. Track across the lake marked out by trees. Restaurant on the middle of the lake. Boats on the beach. Customs barrier. Baggage searched. Irkutsk. Curious honey casks. Chinese in Irkutsk. Irkutsk in a thaw. Snowstorm on the Baikal. Racing on the ice. Change of horses. Sledge upset. Expansion and contraction of the ice. Effect of thaw on the Baikal. Change of season troublesome in crossing the Baikal.

ANY one living at Kiachta may learn that the Russians of Siberia hold Lake Baikal in great veneration, and ascribe to it something of a sacred character, speaking of it as the Holy Sea! During the winter the Baikal is sometimes referred to in a way that makes it difficult, especially for a foreigner, to regard it with veneration. Though rivers generally in the region about Kiachta are sealed up and frozen strongly enough to be crossed even by cattle and carriages on the first of November, the Baikal, 150 miles distant, resists, it is said, all the cold, and keeps obstinately open till about the twenty-seventh of January. The consequence is that the moisture rising from this great sheet of water imparts a dampness to the air which much intensifies the feeling of cold. As soon as the Baikal freezes over the air gets dry, and the cold, though perhaps quite as intense as before, is supposed to be much more endurable.

In travelling from Kiachta towards the Baikal, the first sign of navigation which met our eyes was a great gaunt house-looking spectre, which loomed through the twilight before us on the road one morning at early dawn. At first we could not guess what it was, but coming up close to it, we found that it was the boiler of a steamship, evidently intended for the steamer on the Baikal, and said to be *en route* from England *viâ* the Amur to that distant inland sea. One of the four wheels of the great truck on which it rested had given way, and its escort, carrying off all the movable fittings of the car, had for the time being abandoned it where we saw it.

As we drew near the Baikal we found the country so deeply covered up with snow that we had to leave the tarantass and take to the sledge. The south shore of the lake was a confused mass of ice heaped up in ridges and hills, evidently the work of a storm which had blown from the north after ice began to form on the surface. A little further on we found more evidence of the action of the wind in a part of the lake covered with thin ice broken up, and for the most part on edge, looking exactly like the tops of walls that are defended by having pieces of glass set in lime. Through this a road must have been cut before horse or sledge could pass. After a little we came to ice smooth but covered with snow; and it was not till we were well out that we came upon pure transparent ice, on which one could stand and feel almost insecure, as if nothing but water was underfoot. The thickness of the ice can be seen by the great cracks that run down through it, and appeared to be ten or twelve feet.

The track over the lake is marked out by a line of young Scotch fir trees, about five feet high, fixed upright as if planted, a precaution necessary for the guidance of the sledge drivers, not only during the night, but also in the daytime, when a blinding snowstorm may descend at any time and obliterate all traces of the road. I had heard that about the middle of the lake there was a restaurant for the refreshment of travellers, and had pictured to myself a neat inviting little place, snugly furnished and tempting to passengers. In due time we reached it, but the reality was very different from the picture. It was a hut of boards, and the accommodation was designed to supply the wants of sledge drivers employed in the transport of goods, rather than meet the fastidious tastes of the romantic traveller. On entering we found it a mere hovel, kept by two disreputable-looking men, and filled with brawling carters, who were busy drinking tea and devouring black bread. One corner was a little better than the rest, and retiring to that we were supplied with a leaking samovar, drank a hasty tea, and continued our journey.

The ice towards the north shore was clear of snow, and admitted of rapid travelling; and though the road does not go straight across, but slopes away westward, the whole distance from shore to shore can be easily accomplished in about three hours, exclusive of the delay which takes place while the horses are being rested at the half-way house. On the north side, high up on the beach, were some boats whose appearance would excite the mirth of a British sailor, but which were doubtless well calculated to meet the exigencies of the ferry traffic on this great high road of Central Asia. After crossing the lake the post route follows the shore for two stages, which were done on the ice.

Leaving the ice, we were transferred to a very small and very uncomfortable tarantass; and the open water, marking the point where the Baikal discharges its surplus waters into the Angara, had begun to be visible, even in the darkness, when our attention was directed to a closed barrier in front of us. We were at the customs house, our things in the carriage were pulled about by Cossacks, the straw rummaged, and the key of my portmanteau demanded. On my suggesting that if they wanted to examine my luggage at midnight, it should not be done out on the highway, but in the station house, a procession was at once formed, and my things led captive. Arrived there, a group gathered round to see the contents of my portmanteau, and such a thorough and minute search was made that I suggested the searcher had better look into the letter packet also! This settled the case, it was hastily closed up, the officer declared himself satisfied, I was escorted back to my carriage, and not troubled to open my hand-bag, which also had been carried in for inspection.

As it was my first experience of passing a customs barrier in Russia, I thought the proceedings both unnecessarily rude and high-handed, but was convinced that no disrespect was meant to me, when I saw a Russian officer subjected to exactly the same treatment. Nothing contraband was found, the signal was given, the barrier, painted with stripes like a barber's pole, which had hitherto blocked the road, was raised, and we went on our way, and saw no more of the Baikal for some days.

It is not needful to say much of Irkutsk, the capital of Siberia. It looks well in the distance, with its numerous and imposing public buildings; it bears close inspection, with its trade, its stores, its streets, its carriages for hire waiting at the stands, and its public market, the most curious, at least to unaccustomed eyes, sort of goods exposed for sale in which are sections of the trunks of trees hollowed out and filled with honey, coming, it is said, from the Amur. In the museum a set of brass idols were pointed out to me, procured from the Buriats, who, it is said, had piously stipulated that their lamas should be allowed to visit them and offer them worship from time to time. In the streets I met three Chinamen engaged in the paltry business of peddling sweetmeats. My visit being near the end of March, the streets of Irkutsk were in a deplorable state with the cold slush of melted ice and snow. Many of the poorer Siberians are but poorly housed, clad, fed, and shod, and it is not surprising to learn that this beginning of the return of spring, giving damp feet and thawing abominations that have been frozen up all winter, is signalised by the increased prevalence of disease.

Having fallen somewhat into Russian habits of travelling, we left Irkutsk at nightfall, untied, after a little, the tarantass bell, which, on approaching Irkutsk, had been silenced out of respect to the dignity of the governor resident there, and after a night's journey, against the dangers of which we had been warned in vain, arrived in safety and at an early hour at the station on the shore of the lake. As the journey along the northern shore of the lake in going had been made in the dark, I hoped to perform the return journey in daylight. My wish was gratified, and more too, for I was destined to see this part of the lake not only by daylight, but under a furious snowstorm. The sledge used in that part of the country is simply a deep box, in which the passengers recline on their bedding and luggage, and it proves moderately warm, as no part of the person is exposed but the head, and in a storm even that can be covered up.

At the first station on the lake we had seen a Russian and his wife start out on a sledge some little time before us, and by avoiding all delay on the way, and using all expedition at the second station, we got off in our sledge at no great distance behind them. After some good running in the snowstorm we overtook them, and had drawn a little way ahead, when we were met by two sledges, with which both our own sledge and that of our competitor changed horses. We thus lost the small advantage we had gained, and the race began afresh. We both were anxious to be first at the station from which the crossing of the lake is made, fearing that whoever came in second might have to hire outside horses, which, in so long a stage, would entail a very considerable extra expense. The passengers were thus eager in the race, and the drivers well knew that the winner was likely to have a larger gratuity than the loser, so they were fully as eager as the passengers. So away we went with our fresh horses over the smooth surface of the lake, caring nothing for the storm, and meeting trains of goods-laden sledges, moving slowly in long lines, apparently as regardless of the snow as ourselves. Occasionally the one driver would shake out his reins, give the suppressed wolf-like howl peculiar to the Russian coachman, and, with horses at full gallop, dash ahead of his opponent; then the other driver would shake out his reins, utter his suppressed howl, and shoot ahead. We were happy in having the best horses, and had finally taken and kept the lead, but the other sledge was slowly overtaking us, the station-house was not far distant, both teams were flying at full speed, the passengers were eager, the drivers excited, and the horses warmed to their work, and with blood thoroughly up seemed to enter into the spirit of the contest as heartily as the men, the pace was already furious, and the final effort was about to be made, when one of our number uttered an exclamation, and looking back we saw the sledge behind us had upset and scattered the Russian, his wife, and their belongings over the frozen and snowy surface of the deep. Happily no one was hurt, but the race was over, and soon after we reached the post-house, the Russian entered smiling at his misfortune and defeat, called for the samovar, and when last we saw him he was seated with his wife at the tea-table stirring up a tumblerful of hot tea, the strong deep colour of which was all the more striking from the melting lumps of loaf-sugar that shone white as they were driven round in the glass.

In crossing the lake we had a strong wind behind us, and felt warm enough as long as we kept running, but the cold felt very piercing whenever our driver had to stop at some of the great cracks, and probe with a pole for firm footing for his horses among the crushed ice. These great rents and the crushing of their edges were said to be caused by the ice expanding and contracting as the temperature varied. They were not numerous, but in some cases were difficult of passage.

THE SLEDGE RACE.

Going northwards I had crossed the Baikal on March 23, returning southwards on March 28, and there was visible a great change, which had been wrought by the few days of thaw which had intervened. The ice had lost its clear black appearance, sharp angles were melted down, and the general surface looked weather-beaten and mouldered.

The Baikal when frozen is passed rapidly by sledge, when free from ice is crossed easily by steamer, and in either case causes little hindrance to traffic and passengers. The troublesome times are before the ice is safe to cross and after the thaw has broken it up without melting it. In both these cases the traffic has to pass round the south end, thus increasing the length of the journey very considerably.

CHAPTER IV.

TRACES OF THE OLD BURIAT MISSION.

Tombs at Selenginsk. Tombs at Onagen Dome. Log-built mission houses. Siberia of the present day. Devotedness of the missionaries. Russians think the missionaries dirty. Russians do not understand religious enthusiasm. Modes of carrying on mission work. Translation of the Scriptures. An energetic Buriat. The mission closed by order of the Emperor. Converts compelled to join the Greek Church. Results of the mission.

"A MISSION among the Buriats, a Mongolian tribe living under the authority of Russia, was commenced by the Rev. E. Stallybrass and the Rev. W. Swan, who left England in the year 1817-18. The mission was established first at the town of Selenginsk, and afterwards also on the Ona; but in 1841 the Emperor Nicholas broke up the mission, and the missionaries retired from the field."

Such is the brief official record which the London Missionary Society is wont to produce, when occasion arises to refer to its first endeavours for the conversion of the Mongols. The history of this most interesting mission has never been written,—probably never will be written. No attempt at a history is made here; but as this old mission is often asked about, perhaps the few particulars that have in various ways come to the knowledge of the present writer may have interest for some of his readers.

REMAINS OF THE MISSION.

Among the traces of this mission may be mentioned the *tombs of the dead*. On the banks of the Selenga, and within easy reach of the town of Selenginsk, is a substantial stone-built inclosure containing four graves, —those of Mrs. Yuille, two of her children, and one of the Rev. E. Stallybrass. There is also inside the protecting wall a stone pyramid of decent height,

SELENGINSK.

with a Latin inscription, so obliterated as to make it impossible to discover whether it marks the resting-place of Mr. Yuille, or merely commemorates the erection of the monument by him. In 1871, the wall, the pyramid, and the graves, were in a state of good preservation.

About three days' journey from Selenginsk, at a place called Onagen Dome, are other two tombs. Originally they had been surrounded by some inclosure, but latterly all traces of the inclosure had disappeared, and the tombs stood in the open field unprotected from the cattle, which used to come and rub themselves against them. They were simple brick erections, two or three feet high, and covered with full-length cast-iron plates, the one bearing a Latin, the other a Russian, inscription. The Latin inscription runs as follows:—

```
        IN   HOC SEPULCHRO  CONDU
        NTUR  RELIQUIAE  MORTALES
              SARAE STALLYBRASS
        UXORIS   CARISSIMAE   FIDE
                LISSIMAE  QUE
        EDUARDI         STALLYBRASS
        EMISSARII    A    SOCIETATE
        LONDINENSI    PRO     EVAN
        GELIO     INTER    ETHNICOS
                PROPAGANDO
        OBT   FEBRUARII   10    DIE
          A    S    H    1833
                 AETAT    49
        UBI    EST   MORS   STIMU
                         LUS  TUUS
        UBI      EST     SEPULCHRUM
                  VICTORIA ATU
```

The grave with the Russian inscription is that of another Mrs. Stallybrass, who died in 1839, aged 32.

Both at Selenginsk and at Onagen Dome the mission houses stood close to the graves; the graves in fact being within the inclosures of the premises. Two or three years ago, the mission house at Selenginsk was standing, in good repair, and occupied by a Russian official. The house at Onagen Dome had been sold to some one, who removed it to another locality.

Some miles from Onagen Dome stood another mission house, which, when the missionaries left, fell, I think, into the hands of a Buriat chief. It was finally acquired by the Russian government, and transported to Onagen

Dome, where it served for the parish school and schoolhouse; the teacher, not long ago, being a young Buriat who was proficient in both the Mongolian and Russian languages.

These houses, built and inhabited by the missionaries, were the ordinary dwellings used by the Russians in Siberia. They are log-built, the seams being caulked with moss. Such houses are very strong and substantial, and well calculated to resist the violence of the earthquakes which are said to visit the country. An earthquake occasionally shatters a brick-built church, but a log house is as safe as a basket, and could scarcely fall in, though it were pretty well tilted on its side. It is no uncommon thing to see houses, whose foundation has given way, leaning over in an alarming degree; but beyond looking laughable, they are as good as ever, and the inhabitants go in and out as if the house were newly built and square up. This log structure of the houses affords exceptional facilities for removing the building. The logs are merely taken down one by one, carted to the new site, and a few Buriat carpenters soon put them up again as they were. The mission house, after being removed to Onagen Dome, was in all particulars the same as it had been when standing in its original place.

Both at Selenginsk and at Onagen Dome the missionaries displayed great good taste in the selection of localities. At Selenginsk their abode looked straight out on a reach of the river, where they could see the broad flood flowing away from them. Close to the house on the left hand was a huge bluff; away to the right they looked up the river. On the other side of the river was a broad expanse of field and forest, gradually rising up towards the mountains, which formed the background and bounded the view.

At Onagen Dome also, the main feature of the landscape seen from the mission house was the river winding along the level bottom. There was a broad expanse of level land, and the scene was finely shut in by well-wooded hills. Any one who had to live in Siberia could hardly have made a better choice of scenery.

But the missionaries, though perhaps they had an eye for the beautiful when they decided on the exact site of their dwelling, were evidently guided by the interests of their work when they selected the locality. Selenginsk was a conveniently central situation, and a missionary could hardly have done better than settle on the wide and well-peopled (for Siberia) plain at Onagen Dome.

And there they were, those heroic men, and more heroic women, fifty years ago; for the gospel's sake, making their homes in the country to which Russia banishes her criminals. There they lived, there they laboured, and there three of the ladies died. Banishment to Siberia! Exile in Siberia! Death in Siberia!

Siberia, nowadays, and under some circumstances is not at all a bad place to live in. A Russian peasant or a Buriat thinks it rather a fine country. The climate is severe, the winters are hard and long; but there is plenty of work, good wages, and abundance of cheap food. The distances are great, there are tracts of bleak desolate country, the forests are gloomy, and people few; but these things the natives are used to, and do not seem to mind them. Even educated and refined Russians find the country quite tolerable now. There are telegraphs reaching to every large town; there is a complete and cheap postal system; and travelling is more easily accomplished than perhaps in any other country not possessing the facilities of railways. These things at the present date make Russian existence in Siberia quite tolerable.

But the missionaries were not Russians, and lived, not in the ameliorated Siberia of to-day, but in the old dismal Siberia of half a century ago. To be in Siberia then was to be pretty well out of the world; and for Englishmen and Scotchmen to be there meant a degree of isolation and solitariness that must have been hard to bear. No telegraphs then, and postal facilities were very meagre. They were foreigners in a strange land, looked on with suspicion by the government, the ecclesiastics, and the people; and, above all, were utterly beyond the range of Christian sympathy. And there they were year after year, learning the language, translating the Scriptures, preaching the gospel, and instructing the ignorant adults and children.

They had gone to Siberia, not to seek to bring men over from the faith of the Greek Church, but to seek the conversion of the Buddhistic Buriats; so, remembering their aim, they removed themselves as much as possible from the Russian inhabitants, and surrounded themselves with, and sought friendships among, the Buriats. This was severing the last link that bound them to the civilised world, and rendering their isolation nearly complete. There was some romance in their situation, but the sustaining power of romance is feeble when it is a year or two old; they had a noble aim and a strong enthusiasm, which no doubt sustained them well; but even then there must have been times when they thought fondly of their native lands and home friends, and when the depressing effect of their intercourse with the degraded Buriats, and the bleak gloom of the desolate distances of Siberia, must have weighed down on their spirits like a millstone.

To the ability, devotedness, and perseverance of the missionaries good testimony has been borne, even by those who had no sympathy with them in their endeavours to convert the Buriats. One of the missionaries, after spending a term of years in Siberia, revisited his native land. When he returned to his field of labour, he did not go alone, but was accompanied by a youthful bride, who had been reared in the enjoyment of all the elegances and refinements of one of the most refined of British cities. Turning her back on so many things and friends that were dear to her, she set her face towards Siberia, and arriving there in due course, so mixed with the people, and so applied herself to the acquisition of the language, that not only could she speak it well among the natives, but could read and write it, so as to be able to conduct a correspondence in it, upwards of a quarter of a century after the missionaries had left the country at the command of the Emperor Nicholas.

A strange spectacle were those missionaries in Siberia to the Russians who dwelt in the various towns. The Russians could not understand them, and seem never to have been weary of talking about them, and wondering and laughing at them. One curious instance of how the missionaries were misunderstood has reached us. The Russians declared they were not clean,—that they liked to be dirty! Now, to understand the full meaning of this charge, it must be remembered that most Russians in Siberia now, and perhaps a greater portion then, would not be by any means considered models of cleanliness. The peculiar wooden architecture of the houses, the moss packing between the logs, the cracks and chinks in the timber walls, combined with the universal lack of plaster, puts the housewife at such a disadvantage, that, in most cases, she seems to give up the contest with enemies to domestic comfort, whose appearance in a clean English home would cause a war of extermination or a change of quarters. The Russians, perhaps partly from necessity, accept the situation very placidly, and this gives rise to a state of matters that causes not a little astonishment to Englishmen who happen to go into Siberia, and take their native ideas of cleanliness with them. This is only one particular, but it is perhaps enough. And yet these Russians, so deficient in cleanliness themselves, used to think that the missionaries were not clean! It seems strange at first, but the cause is not far to seek.

Remembering that they had come to Siberia for the sake of the Buriats, they, as far as possible, discarded Russian servants, employed Buriats about them, and cultivated the society of Buriats. Who—a Russian would ask—would prefer to live with Buriats rather than with Russians? And who but a man that loves dirt would rather frequent dirty Buriat huts than drink tea and vodka and play cards in an elegant Russian house? And so it came to pass, that people who hardly knew what the rudiments of cleanliness were, decided that the missionaries were not clean enough to please them!

Another thing also must have told against the missionaries: namely, the inability of the Russians to understand religious enthusiasm or earnestness. Religion with them is taken very easily. It seems with most to consist of the observance of saints' days, attendance on services, crossing before pictures, etc. They may be bigoted enough, and hold firmly enough to the rites and ceremonies of the Greek Church, but thousands of idolatrous Buriats about them would not disturb them much. They are Buriats, why should they not be and remain Buddhists? Is not their religion as good for them as ours for us? To be a Buddhist is to be a Buriat, to be a Christian is to be a Russian; if the Buriats want to become Russians, let them be baptised and take a Christian name; if they do not, let them be as they are,—who cares? "Was born a Buriat; became a Russian," is a phrase sometimes used to denote a converted Buriat.

Loyalty to Christ,—love to Jesus,—a feeling of anxiety in one's own heart because men do not trust in Christ for salvation,—an earnest desire to bring men to Christ; these are emotions such as perhaps most Russians do not understand for themselves, and would be slow to credit others with the genuine possession of. There may be happy exceptions, but it is to be feared that this is true of the great mass of the Siberian adherents of the Greek Church.

What then were they to make of the missionaries? Unable to understand their motives, could they do anything but misconstrue their aims and actions? And so it happened that evil reports were continually finding their way to the authorities, who, perhaps, were not so far ahead of the people in enlightenment of ideas and friendliness of feeling toward such intruders as English missionaries in Siberia.

But the missionaries had come authenticated from St. Petersburg itself; and though they might think and speak evil of them, none could interrupt them. And so things went on for years.

Of their modes of carrying on mission work there is not much to say particularly. They travelled much, as might be supposed, seeing that the Buriats live scattered, a few here, a few there, over a wide space. Medicine they used, perhaps because they could hardly help it. Doubtless the Buriats then, like the Mongols now, credited them with the possession of medical skill; and the little that an unprofessional foreigner may happen to know about a few cures is often a wonderful improvement on native means and methods. At any rate, their fame as doctors got established, and long journeys were often undertaken in the hope of being benefited by their treatment.

Daily services were held at each of the stations, consisting of singing, reading the Scriptures, exposition of the same, and prayer. Thirty to forty were often present at these meetings. Schools too were established, with the hope of raising up an instructed Christian generation.

But the great work which they ever returned to, as their other missionary duties permitted them, was the translation of the Bible into the language of the Buriats. This was no light task for two men to accomplish; but they did complete it, and printed and published the Old Testament in Siberia, under an imperial licence dated St. Petersburg, 1840.

The New Testament was not published till 1846, and then it was done in London. The type with which the Old Testament was printed is of the proper Mongol shape; but the New Testament was printed with Manchu type adapted. The Manchu type does well enough; though very different in appearance from real Mongol type, it is yet quite as legible as the true Mongol shape. But to return;—the Old Testament had been printed and published in Siberia, and the missionaries were proceeding with the preparation of the translation of the New Testament. They were in good spirits, and were more hopeful than they had been.

One man, a Buriat, had opposed them and their doctrine much. He was a man of intelligence and of great energy. Many were the long arguments and contentions he had entered into with the missionaries about their religion and his. Many a stern duel had he challenged them to in controversy, and in most, if not all, of these contests he considered himself, if not victor, at least not defeated, and certainly not convinced. One man of this stamp counts half a host. Suppose a Buriat had half resolved to become a Christian, perhaps one of his most serious obstacles to open declaration would be the thought of this man. If the missionary hardly silenced him, what could he, the feeble convert do? And so one man may keep back a large number of would-be converts. Doubtless this man did.

At length this man of a thousand showed signs of giving in. He was a man of no half-measures, and, if he became a Christian, would help as energetically as he had opposed. Well might the missionaries be glad and hopeful. They had gathered a few converts about them already; could they but secure this man for a Christian, his thorough-going temperament would be a strength to them, and the mission, which had progressed so laboriously slow, might now be expected to begin to reap in joy.

About this time, one day a notice was sent from the local government office, summoning the missionaries to hear an imperial order from St. Petersburg read to them. It had come at last;—they were ordered to leave the country.

The order was not couched in respectful language, nor was it in any sense complimentary to the missionaries; it certainly did not order them out of the country in so many words; not at all, it only said that they could not remain where they were, except they bound themselves not to teach religion! I think—but cannot be sure about this—there was even mention made of the fact that they might remain so long as they confined themselves to secular instruction and efforts directed towards the social elevation of the people; but Stallybrass and Swan had come to preach the gospel of salvation, and if not permitted to do that, could not remain. Sorrowfully they settled their affairs, packed their things, took tearful farewells of their few converts, and feeling that they were leaving them as sheep in the desert without a shepherd, entered the sledge, and were driven stage by stage Europewards, over hills and desolate plains, and through hamlets they were never again to be allowed to visit; —banished from Siberia.

Besides Stallybrass and Swan, there was a Mr. Yuille connected with the mission. John Abercrombie, a Kabardian who had been rescued from slavery by the Scotch missionaries and trained in their printing office, joined the mission as printer in 1834. He also left with Stallybrass and Swan in 1841. A traveller passing through Selenginsk in 1863 heard of Mr. Abercrombie having been in that neighbourhood. He was known as the Englishman, probably because he could speak English. Mr. Yuille, who had charge of the press, remained in Siberia after his colleagues had returned to England. The convert Shagdur, in a letter written to Mr. and Mrs. Swan, a year after their departure, speaks of having met Mr. Yuille at Udinsk, and says he had no intention of leaving soon. He was pledged not to teach religion; but to work for the education and elevation of the people; but after a short time he too was withdrawn, and so ended the labours of the missionaries in Siberia.

The few Buriat converts had, *nolens volens*, to join the Greek Church; and the energetic Buriat who contested and held out so long, but gave in at last, and who, bold as ever for his convictions, declared himself for Christ,—if I mistake not, *after* the order removing the missionaries came, had to be dealt with specially. His energetic character and name were so feared, that he was ordered by the paternal government to remove from the neighbourhood, and take up his abode at quite a distance. It was not expressly stated that this banishment was in consequence of his having become a convert; but both he himself and everybody else knew all about what it meant. His determination and influence were so dreaded, that it was thought safer to send him out of the way to a place where he was not likely to do any harm; and there he remains till this day, or at least did remain till a recent date.

What argument was advanced against the continuance of the missions perhaps cannot now be known, but one thing can be mentioned, which may have something to do with it. Even a quarter of a century after the missionaries left Siberia, all converts were spoken of as belonging to the English, or rather as being Englishmen. The converts themselves knew better; but the mass of the people, Russians and Buriats, seem to have regarded conversion to Christianity as a desertion of Russia and a going over to England. It is easy to see how powerful an argument this could become in the mouth of a person inimical to the mission, and how ready a Russian ruler would be to listen to advice which urged him to quash the beginnings of an English faction in Siberia.

It is hardly probable that the mission was broken up from religious motives on the part of the Russian government. A government which, at least, provides for the religious wants of its subjects according to requirement, managing, controlling, and providing for the appointments in the Greek, Lutheran, Roman Catholic, and Buddhist Churches, could hardly have very serious religious scruples about a few Protestants more or less. Perhaps, though, it may be that one element of aversion to the mission was the fear that, at some future time, there might be another added to the many sects, for which the government would have to provide worshipping facilities in Siberia.

Despotic governments do not usually burden themselves with giving extended reasons for their actions; so, in its own summary way, Russia spoke the word and the mission ceased in 1841.

It may be asked then, what did all the zeal, labour, and ability of the old missionaries accomplish? The answer is,—a score or so of converts, the translation of the Bible, and an indefinite moral influence.

As to the converts, some remain to this present day members of the Greek Church, and apparently good, warm-hearted, intelligent Christians. As to the original number, perhaps there were not so many as twenty; perhaps there were more. But even though there were a few more than the larger number, that were a small harvest to reap after twenty years labour of two or three men.

The translation of the Bible into the Mongolian language opened up the sealed book of the Scriptures to the Buriats of Siberia and to the Mongols of Mongolia. No small result this. The translation is not by any means perfect, partaking of the imperfections of all first versions of the Bible in any language; but the work has been well understood in Siberia, and, for the most part, quite serviceable in the various regions of Mongolia in the Chinese empire.

Superficial judges have sometimes condemned it, because frequently a Buriat or a Mongol will look at it, read a little, shut up the book, and hand it back saying he cannot understand it. A little more experience often leads to the conviction that it is not the language that is the difficulty, but the subject-matter. This is not the place to enter on a discussion as to how far the Bible without note or comment is likely to reach the understanding of a previously heathen people. There are perhaps instances which can be quoted, in which the Bible alone, unassisted, unexplained, has done, and done well, its wonderful work of convicting and converting men, and even of originating a little company of devout Christians. These instances, it is said, can be quoted, but they are rare; and perhaps the old Siberian missionaries would have done better, had they first prepared and published (that is, if the Russian government would have allowed them) some little compendium of Christian truth and doctrine, couched in the common language of the people. The peculiar relation in which they stood to the Russian government may have something to do with determining them to seek first the translation of the entire word of God.

The New Testament has been circulated quite extensively in Mongolia. Now and again, in out-of-the-way places, an English traveller may be informed that so and so has a foreign book; and when it is called for, out comes a New Testament in Mongolian by Stallybrass and Swan. On inquiry, it frequently turns out that the said copy has been brought from Kiachta on the Russian frontier, by some friend who had gone there with camel-loads of goods. In not a few cases,—perhaps in all where the book has come from Kiachta—the English title-page has been torn out.

In addition to the gathering of a few converts, and the great work of translating the entire Bible, the Siberian missionaries have exerted a moral influence of no small extent. The picture of these men away among the remote tracts of Siberia, searching out the few and scattered inhabitants, and seeking to impart to them the truths of the gospel, is well calculated to sustain flagging missionary zeal in other less difficult fields. This of itself is a good deal; for such pictures are not usually lost on the world.

But the most practical outcome of this influence seems to be the fact, that the Greek Church has started mission work for the Buriats. About the extent or nature of the work no details are forthcoming; but that it exists at all is something; and the great probability is, it owes its origin to the example set by the English missionaries, who began their work in Siberia more than half a century ago. It is a pity that the Buriats who embrace Christianity should be under the necessity of embracing, at the same time, all the many errors and superstitions with which the Greek Church has adulterated the truth. On the other hand, many good things can be said of the Greek Church; one is that she extends the open Bible to her followers.

It is a matter for devout thankfulness, that she can hold out to the Buriats who join themselves to her, the complete word of God in their own language.

The other missionary labours of the translators were condemned and stopped long ago; they were not allowed to preach and teach; they had to leave the country; but this enduring monument still remains. In time to come it may be revised, corrected and improved, as all first versions have to be; but still, after all, it will be essentially their work; and perhaps the time may yet come, when there shall be many Mongol-speaking Christians to bless the labours of the early missionaries, and read the Bible translated by them.

CHAPTER V.

LEARNING TO RIDE.

First lessons. Mongols ride with short stirrups. A six hundred mile ride. Buying a whip. The start. Crossing the Tola in flood. A Mongol's exhortation. Camping out. Dreams. Fall. Rat pits. Mending harness. Mode of journey. Hospitality of the poor better than that of the rich. Inhabitants. Influenza. Animals in tents. We prefer to camp out. Guide bewildered at his native place. Find a trail. Guide's home. Character of guide. Reputation among his countrymen. New guide. Rainless district. Change to camels. Camels and horses compared. "Have you a revolver?" Mending a camel's foot. Gobi. A hill with one side. A thirsty ride. Stones of Gobi. A tent at last. Tea in the desert. Enchanted land. Stony illusion. Recollection of Gobi like a nightmare. Progress in learning to ride. Snatches of sleep. A green land. Miss our way. "What shop do you belong to?" Kalgan.

As a traveller in Mongolia must be something of a horseman, I was eager to take lessons in riding, and a Mongol friend used to indulge me occasionally, by causing to be caught and saddled for me such an old quiet beast as the aged grandmother or the very young children of the family were in the habit of riding.

In a country where children are sometimes expert riders soon after passing the age of infancy, a *man* who could not ride was considered a great novelty, and when the steed was led up, the whole community would turn out to enjoy the spectacle of my awkwardness in mounting. As the Mongols ride with the stirrup straps so short that a foreigner's legs became cramped, I used, when practicable, to have them lengthened, and then their wonder was not that I should find difficulty in mounting, but that I should be able to mount at all.

These occasional rides, however, did not go far towards making me a horseman; so being at Urga, and under the necessity of crossing the desert to Kalgan, I got a Mongol to contract to convey me thither on horseback, hoping, among other things, that a ride of this length, six hundred English miles, would do something towards making me feel comfortable in a saddle.

My Mongol contractor was to provide a saddled horse, but I had to find my own whip. Giving a lama a brick of tea, I sent him out to the market to make the best bargain he could. He soon returned with a heavy club-looking piece of wood, about twenty inches long, tapered a little, with a cowhide lash attached to the lighter end and a loop of light thong running through a hole in the heavier end. The hand is thrust through the loop, and, when not in use, the whip hangs from the wrist, leaving the hand free. When the whip is wanted it is thus always ready, simply close the hand, and the whip is grasped.

I was a little astonished at the weight of the thing at first, but the Mongols assured me it was all the better for that. Should a robber come, I was just to grasp the lash and the thick end of the whip, give him a good crack on the head, and the robber would have the worst of it. They were not far wrong. One good blow, delivered as directed, would almost have smashed a man's skull.

SHEEP CROSSING THE TOLA.

After many delays everything was declared ready for the start, the horses were led out, I scrambled up, and we rode slowly off, among the last words I heard uttered being expressions of opinion from the spectators to the effect that, if I could not mount a horse better than that, I was not likely to reach Kalgan by horseback. We soon reached the north bank of the Tola, and found that river in flood, not very high, however, flowing with a beautiful clear stream, but rather cold to the touch, as most of the increase in its volume was caused by the melting of snow. The ordinary ford was a little too deep, so we went a little higher up, to a place where the river was broader and more rapid, and therefore shallower. Here we found a flock of sheep being transported over the river in a fashion truly Mongol, but perhaps the only way possible under the circumstances. They were tied two and two, dragged a little beyond the centre of the river by a man mounted on a camel, then let go. They drifted rapidly down with the current, but struggled towards the bank, and were finally secured dripping and shivering. After looking to our saddle-girths, and drawing up our feet till we were almost kneeling in the saddle, we pushed in. The water came high up the horses' sides, but my guide was used to such things, and I got on very well by keeping my horse close under the lee of his. As soon as we got over we dropped our feet into the stirrups, laughed at the adventure, and rode on, knowing that, whatever difficulties we might meet, we had no more rivers to ford for the rest of the six hundred miles.

That evening we had dinner in the tent of a mutual friend, who escorted us for some miles in the dark, and then proceeded to take a most affectionate and pious farewell of us, exhorting me to pray to my God, and he would pray to his. When in his tent my contractor had vainly endeavoured to buy horses, and when our friend impressed upon him the necessity for prayer and its helpful nature in a journey like that on which we were entering, adding that he would pray for us, the disappointed man turned himself round in his saddle, and said, with great energy, "If you had sold us a couple of horses cheap, it would have helped us on our journey a great deal better than praying."

In the contract, which had been carefully drawn out and signed, it had been stipulated that my guide was to find tents in which I could sleep at night. We rode on till about eleven o'clock, when suddenly my guide's horse left the road and began to describe a semicircle. On my calling out and asking what all this meant, it appeared that the rider had been fast asleep in the saddle; he woke up with a start, looked about him in a bewildered manner and asked, "Where are we? From what direction did we come?" A little after we came to a knoll near which was some good grass. Here I was called upon to dismount, the saddles were taken off, the horses fettered, and thus, sheltered from the north wind, we were to sleep out on the wild. The proper way of "retiring to rest" in such circumstances is to place the saddle for a pillow, set up the saddle-bags as a screen from the wind, spread the saddle felt for a mattress, put on all warm gloves, cravats, etc., that come to hand, cover up with any rugs you may have, and wish for the morning.

A hungry man, it is said, dreams of feasts; I was a cold man that night, and my dream was of a nice warm bedroom with a good bed and a cheery fire. So real was the vision that I awoke saying, "If I had only had this some time ago coming from Urga." I looked about, and saw the dim horizon over the distant mountains, heard the horses grazing near, listened to the snoring of the Mongol, and realised that we were out on the desert.

When daylight came we caught our horses and started, but had gone only a very short distance when my horse's fore-feet sunk into the earth, and as we were going at a smart pace and down hill he was unable to recover himself. For some yards he staggered along and then came down, throwing me on my head with a shock that was all the more painful on account of the chill and stiff state I was in, through not having got warmed up after the cold of the night.

The fall was occasioned by my having allowed my horse to ride over a hollow piece of ground. These treacherous parts are the trouble of riders in Mongolia. A little rat-like animal excavates galleries under ground, and a horse passing over one of these must go through. These dangerous spots are usually distinguished by a different colour and appearance from the rest of the ground, but sometimes even a practised eye may be at fault, and a few moments' inattention is enough to bring down the best horse and rider.

Just before spring, sometimes, large tracts of the desert are fired accidentally from the unextinguished fires left by passing caravans, and purposely by the natives, that the new grass may grow up better and free from the old. In these burnt tracts it is almost impossible to distinguish the hollowed spots, and a few days later in this ride, while passing over a burnt district, my guide had his fall. He was before me, and we were going at a rapid rate when, all of a sudden, I saw his horse with its head towards me, its four feet in the air, and its rider undermost. My guide was a large man, and was considerably crushed, but it is strange that he was not more hurt by so bad a fall. Both the saddle-girths were burst, but, true to his Mongol instinct, the rider held fast to the halter, and did not let his horse go.

After a little he recovered from the effects of his fall, picked up his scattered belongings, and set about repairing his broken saddle-girths. As we had no spare strings or straps with us, and were far away from human habitations, I wondered how he would make good the damage. I was not left long in suspense; without hesitation he at once took a handful of hair from the tail of his horse, twisted and plaited it together, and in a few minutes the straps were as strong as ever. As the tails of the horses are allowed to grow to the ground, a Mongol horseman on a journey is never at a great loss for a string; careless in the extreme, he is apt to forget anything that can be left behind, but when needed the tail of his horse is never far to seek.

For some days we rode on, sleeping out on the plain, dismounting about midnight to feel the grass with our hands, hobbling our horses, and "turning in" as soon as we found good pasture. About dawn we resumed our journey, drawing up at some tent about sunrise for our morning tea. Later on we stopped at some tent for breakfast, and towards evening again halted for dinner. With about two exceptions we were treated with great kindness. The "pot and ladle" were put at our service, and in most cases our tea made and our food cooked for us, no remuneration being expected, asked, or given, beyond a little tea, or the leavings of our meal, which, with this object in view, was always more abundant than was necessary to supply the wants of two travellers. We found that we fared much more economically, and were better treated, and received with a much warmer welcome, in the tents of the poor than in the abodes of the rich. A rich man would make us wait his convenience, and expect us to make extra good tea or a meal which, both as regards quantity and quality, would be in keeping with his dignity and status, and even then we left feeling that our visit had been something of an intrusion. In the tents of the poor, on the other hand, we were warmly welcomed, our tea or food was prepared at once and in all haste, our animals were looked to as they grazed, the share of food which we left in the pot was considered a rich reward, and when all was over we were conducted forth and sent on our way again with many expressions of friendship and good wishes for the prosperity of our journey.

Some of these tents at which we put up seemed very poor and very lonely. One contained almost nothing but the skins of sheep which had died through hard weather; another was the abode of a man suffering and bent down by a spinal disease, but who had a quick and eager mind, which made him welcome us, as sources of information and news about the places we had come from and passed through; many of them were the abodes of women whose husbands were away on distant caravan journeys, while they themselves remained at home caring for the children and a small flock of goats, the kids of which, finding nothing to satisfy their climbing instincts in the flat desert, kept continually leaping on to the roof of the tent, only to be chased off

A MONGOL CAMP. [*From a Native Sketch.*]

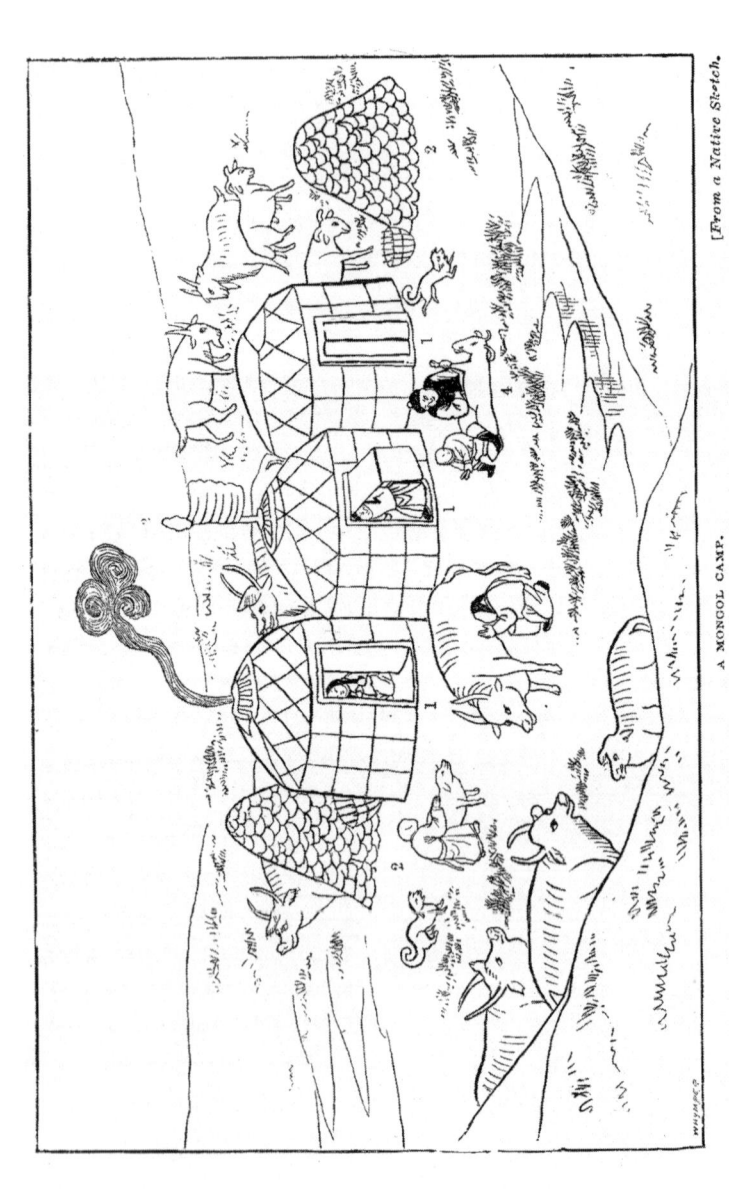

1. Mongol tents.   2. Fuel heaps.   3. Prayer flag.   4. Killing a Sheep.

by one of the children; and almost all of the poorer sort seemed destitute of tea, a want which they sought to supply by boiling again the spent remains of the pounded leaves and twigs of which brick tea is composed.

In one district we had to ride a long stretch of many miles without entering a tent. As often as we drew up at a tent a woman or man would come out and say, "Dismount at my tent at another time, we have the cough." This cough seemed to be a kind of influenza much dreaded by the Mongols. As far as I can learn, it seldom proves fatal, but travellers are careful to avoid it, and no one would think of using the "pot and ladle" of a family suffering from this sickness.

We slept a few of the nights in tents, but I soon ceased to find fault with being compelled to sleep out in the wild. Every day took us farther into summer, and fifty or sixty miles nearer to the equator; the weather was mild, and the temperature soon became sensibly warmer. There is, moreover, one phenomenon of tent life which is not agreeable to a foreigner—the presence at night of calves, lambs, and kids. A poor Mongol shares his tent at night with the young of his animals, and, for the most part, finds it agreeable. With them the tent is warmer, and he and his family can sleep with less to cover them, and so little repugnance seems to be felt towards them that the tents of the rich even are seldom without two or three young calves tethered near the door, which seem quite at home, and spend most of their waking hours in licking everything within their reach. In cold and stormy weather any tent, even with calves, lambs, and kids, is better than outside, but in summer, with no rain and a mild temperature. a traveller moderately provided with warm clothing finds the coolness and freshness and freedom of the open plain preferable, at least for the few nights he is engaged in crossing it. This feeling grew as the journey went on, and towards the end of it, on the southern side of the desert, I was quite as enthusiastically in favour of outside lodgings as my guide.

After five days' ride we reached the native place of the lama who was conveying me through the desert. We did not arrive till nearly midnight, and though, as it afterwards proved, we were within about a couple of miles of his tent, we narrowly escaped sleeping out in the wild. A day or two before we had been rescued from a similar difficulty by the bark of a dog, but though we shouted no dog would answer, the night was dull, and we could find no mark of any kind that indicated where we were or where we should go. To make matters worse, we had left the great road in the afternoon, and for some time had been running across country. Though close to his own home, the lama was quite bewildered. In Gobi no wood grows. The Mongols have, therefore, to buy in Kalgan or Urga the long fishing-rod-like birch poles used in catching their horses. As these poles are too long to carry on a camel, it is usual to tie them up into a bundle, fix one end to a camel, and let the other trail on the ground. A day or two before we had noticed a caravan with such a bundle of rods, going south, and the Mongol, as he rode hither and thither in the dark, detected in the sand the trail of this bundle of rods, and shouted out, with great glee, that we were all right, he knew all about it. Taking his bearings from that slender trail, we set off at full speed, and were soon in his home, the lama the centre of a rapidly increasing company, which hastened to greet him on his return from a lengthened residence in the temple in which he held office in Urga, I drinking milk fresh from the cow, to the amazement of the on-lookers, who here, as everywhere else, were loud in the expression of their astonishment that any

CATCHING HORSES ON THE PLAIN. [*From a Native Sketch.*

one should drink milk "raw," and not boiled, as their universal custom is.

We had been but a few minutes in when the lama told me he was done up, that he could not go farther with me, and that he would send me on in the care of his younger brother, who was not a lama, but a "black man," as the Mongols denominate a layman. I called upon him to produce the man for my inspection, when he arrived drew him close up to the fire till the light fell full on his face, asked him a few questions, and, amid the laughter of the whole assembly, pronounced him "passable," and said I was willing to go on under his care.

This change of guides was directly contrary to the expressed terms of the contract, in which it had been stipulated that the lama was himself personally to escort me all the way to Kalgan. Though I had, for the sake of appearances, to grumble a little at this open violation of the bargain, I was secretly so exceedingly glad of the change that I could with difficulty conceal my satisfaction.

Soon after leaving Urga I had, thinking to expedite matters, on one occasion caught and saddled my horse myself. From that time onwards the lama took it for granted that I would in future make no calls upon him for help in the many menial attentions that have to be paid to a traveller's horse.

When we happened to stop for tea or a meal at tents with the inmates of which he was acquainted, he would relate to them how he had bought at Urga for them tea, tobacco, matches, etc., but that through my niggardliness he had been compelled to part with them in bartering for horses to carry us on our journey, always taking care in his narrations to let it seem as if his taking me through the desert was not a commercial speculation, on which he had ventured in the hope of making a profit, so much as a deed of charity which he was performing for my benefit.

Most Mongols are in the habit of lying more or less, but this man seemed to have so steeped himself in untruth as to be unable to suppose that any one else spoke the truth in circumstances where a lie would be advantageous. Before leaving Urga I had provided myself with a pair of spectacles, pieces of common blue glass set in wire gauze, poor cheap things that even in remote regions, such as Kiachta and Urga, cost only a trifle, but which are of great use in shading the eyes from the glare of the sun on snow or desert. For convenience sake I carried them fastened with their elastic band on to my hat. Soon after leaving Urga, either in a fall from my horse, or in a tent where we had rested, the spectacles were lost. I was grieved at the loss, and the firece glare of the sun on the sandy soil was so strong that it brought on an affection of the eye that did not leave me for months after the ride was finished.

My lama had tender eyes and suffered a good deal on the ride. He called for the spectacles. I told him they were lost. Measuring me by himself he supposed that I was merely telling a lie to avoid lending them to him, and throughout the remainder of the time that we were together he lost few opportunities of complaining to people of the badness of the man he had with him, asserting that I had in my baggage a good pair of spectacles which I would not lend him though I was not using them myself. From the frequency and earnestness with which he repeated this tale, I have no doubt that he sincerely believed it, and after a few remonstrances I gave him up and let him believe his own lie. By telling this story perhaps he secured the sympathy of the listeners, and he had such a fund of falsehood with which he used to set himself off in a good light, that any hearer who believed one half of what the lama said could hardly help having the feeling which one of them gave expression to when he remarked, "There goes a meritorious lama."

It might be supposed that a man like this would soon be seen through and despised by his countrymen, but, on the contrary, it seemed that he was held in high esteem. He was ignorant and uneducated, so much so that he could not sign his own name in Mongolian, or even in Tibetan, though every lama pretending to any standing at all is supposed to be familiar with the latter language, yet he held quite an honourable office in a temple in Urga.

I was glad to hear that I was now to part company with this man who had made himself so disagreeable; and realising the fact that I had ridden out one Mongol, and was in the morning to continue my ride pitted against a fresh man, I called for silence in the tent, ordered a sheep to be bought, killed, and put into shape for carrying, fixed the hour at which we were to start and turned in to sleep.

Next day I was careful to render no assistance to my guide in the matter of managing the horses, and I was glad to find that throughout the journey he never expected me to do anything but allow myself to be looked after and cared for. I soon found, however, that another article of the contract was to be infringed. It had been stipulated that horses alone were to be used, but no rain had fallen in Gobi, and it was pleaded that, not having foreseen this, it was impossible without suffering great loss to cross Gobi with horses. With my consent, therefore, camels were procured, and mounted on these lofty steeds, we for some days and nights paced slowly through a dry and barren land, where no new grass had grown, where there seemed little old grass.

and where the cattle gladly picked up such stray pieces of withered grass as were blown about over the desert, and collected in hollows and little ravines.

The camels were very sure-footed, so much so that though they frequently stumbled they never once fell, even when they sunk into a rat-gallery; and, though the motion was unpleasant and the progress slow, they were very comfortable at night. Unlike horses, camels do not feed at night, so when we wanted to go to sleep we had only to draw them up broadside to the wind, make them lie down, and lie down ourselves on their lee-side, sheltered by their friendly protection.

My first guide had been much annoyed at what he believed to be the lie I told about my spectacles; my second guide soon complained of what he believed to be the truth which I told about my revolver. I had none, and, whenever asked, said frankly that I travelled unarmed. My guide being timid, remonstrated with me for thus betraying my defenceless state to all inquirers, and urged me to tell a lie about it and say that I was armed. On my declining to do this he rode on for a time in silence and apparently in deep thought, then proposed, as the result of his cogitations, that when asked if I had a revolver I should reply, "Supposing I have, what then? supposing I have not, what then?" I saw no harm in this form of answer, agreed to use it, and have often since staved off in the same manner impertinent questions of troublesome Mongols.

I have no doubt that by frankly saying I had no revolver I reaped the full advantage of protection that the possession of firearms is supposed to confer on a traveller in the desert. Most Russians whom the Mongols meet carry revolvers, and when the Mongols heard me denying that I had one, most of them supposed that I was simply following their custom, and telling a lie to avoid the trouble of showing it, or to escape being importuned to give them powder; and one man, in whose tent we drank tea towards the close of our journey, made an earnest and persistent attempt to overcome what he regarded as my reluctance to oblige him by supplying him with foreign gunpowder.

After the camels had travelled some days the soles of their feet began to wear through to the quick in one or two places, and had to be mended! The animal was thrown over on his side his feet put up on a low stool, and the tender part covered by a patch of leather, which was held in its place by thin thongs drawn through the adjacent callosities of the sole. The animal's foot was mended very much as a cobbler mends a shoe.

Before dismissing Gobi a few words of description may not be out of place. One day as we rode along we found a high hill straight in front of us. The summit seemed a good way off to look at, but proved even more distant to reach. Near the top were some women gathering argol, and it appeared rather strange that they should be so occupied so high up above the plain. When the top was reached it was found that there was no descent on the other side; by this sudden rise we had ascended to a table-land, and it was explained to me that we were now in Gobi.

I saw Gobi under the most disadvantageous circumstances. No rain had fallen, no grass had grown, there was nothing but sand and stones with last year's grass dried and brown, and very little even of that. Here and there were the ghost-like remnants of last year's growth of spear-grass, scorched with the sun and bleached with the weather; and the general desolation of the scenery was, if possible, enhanced by the appearance of black rocks which cropped up in perpendicular layers.

Not only was the dryness of the season apt to leave an unfavourable impression of the place, but, through the mismanagement of my Mongol guide, our ride over

WOMEN GATHERING FUEL. [*From a Native Sketch.*

the part which remains most vividly imprinted on my memory was performed in great discomfort.

We had eaten no food and drunk no tea since the day before, and found ourselves, late in the morning, riding from one scene of desolation into another, if possible, still more desolate, and hour after hour we seemed to be coming no nearer the end. The sun mounted higher and higher, till, blazing in his strength, the heat became oppressive. My sun-hat was a protection from above, but from the grassless gravel and sand beneath there glared up a fierce light and heat from which there was no protection. Stretch after stretch of country we passed, but still no wells, no tents, no inhabitants. At last we left all traces of man and beast, left the road even, and entered on fresh scenes of more intense desolation, passing among rocks rough and black that broke through the ground in all directions, rugged and frowning.

Emerging from this we suddenly came upon a stretch of ground almost literally covered with the far-famed stones of Gobi. The prevailing colour was a kind of misty, half-transparent white, exactly like arrowroot or cornflour prepared with water only. Besides these were stones of other colours, including, if I remember aright, red, green, and blue. It was like a fairy scene. The stones were strewn almost as thickly as they could lie. Seen under other circumstances we might have brought away samples of them, but, as we then were situated, neither of us cared a straw for them. The Mongol muttered something about a place where better stone could be found. This he did, I suppose, afraid lest I should dismount to pick up specimens. If so his device was superfluous. It was not stones I wanted, but the delicious dirty Mongol tea. Just when I began to fear that the utmost limit of endurance was almost reached, having drunk nothing for eighteen hours, the roof of a tent was espied at last, and we were soon seated inside drinking tea.

To any one who has not experienced a long-continued, fierce, burning, desert thirst, it is quite impossible to convey any idea of the relief that tea brings. Its virtues are wonderful. It is itself wretched stuff. No civilised man in any civilised country would drink it. But in the desert it is a different thing. The frank welcome and the tea, which is given unasked and as a matter of course, seem to revive nature's exhausted powers, and speedily put to flight the remembrances of a painful ride. It may seem strange that a hungry man should sit down and drink mere tea, "empty tea," as the Mongols would call it, without bread or accompaniments of any kind, but it is the proper thing to do. It removes fatigue, restores vigour, and takes off the rage of hunger without imparing the appetite. In China or Mongolia a traveller exhausted by a long stage, and suffering from heat or cold, should never think of sitting down to a meal, but should address himself to a teapot filled with hot tea. By drinking away at this he soon finds himself veering round into a comfortable frame of mind, and is enabled not only to wait patiently till his dinner is ready, but also to do ample justice to it when it comes without danger of unpleasant consequences afterwards.

There is another element that goes to compose my recollections of Gobi. One morning, when we must have been in Gobi or near it, we found ourselves in a land that seemed enchanted. It abounded with boulders which, in size, shape, colour, and often in arrangement, so closely resembled human habitations, that we were sometimes puzzled to distinguish between stones and houses. Riding up to what seemed the abodes of men, we would find that we were in a solitude among rocks! At other places where it seemed as if we were alone, we would behold people moving about and disappear into what we had supposed to be grey boulders!

Another morning at early dawn we had a similar but more perfect deception. Ahead of us there appeared a tent with a flock of camels lying beside it. We congratulated each other on finding so convenient a place for our tea, and rode up to it cheerily, when, to our amazement, we perceived as we neared it that what we had seen was neither tent nor camels, but a group of boulders, among which was one larger than the rest.

The weird feeling produced by climbing a high hill and finding it had only one side, and of riding among what seemed to be habitations and finding that they were rocks, and then coming upon what looked like rocks and finding that they were human habitations; the depression produced by riding over long stretches of country with nothing but a desolation of rough rocks surrounded with barren sand mixed with gravel; the lonely feeling of travelling through a land in parts destitute of inhabitants, and the pity that could not but be felt on discovering that most of the few and far between dwellers of that sparsely peopled region were at that particular time suffering from influenza; commiseration for man and beast living in a land where no rain had fallen, where no grass had grown, and where, consequently, many of the natives with their flocks and herds were travelling about in search of pasture and water; and the great fatigue of travelling that arose from the unnatural and scorching heat produced by the drought; the combination of all these feelings conspired to leave an unfavourable impression of Gobi, and it was with great joy that at length we found ourselves

APPROACHING THE GREAT WALL BY NIGHT.

beyond the bounds of that afflicted country, and once more journeying over a land green with grass and herbs, where we could dismiss our camels and take again to horses.

South of Gobi the journey was uneventful. Rain had fallen, the plain was green, inhabitants were plenty, and, for the most part, gave us a hearty welcome. The only adventure worth recording was at the close of the journey and at night. We were following along the road when, dark in front of us, rose a great black ridge. I asked my guide what that was. He replied it was a mountain. A nearer approach showed that it was the great wall of China. It was such a marked feature of the landscape that no one who had once seen it could forget it, and on questioning my Mongol I found that he had never been to Kalgan or to China before. Previously he had said that he had been to Kalgan and knew the way, now it appeared that he knew less about it than I did. We passed the wall at a gateway, and followed the road till we found ourselves on a lofty pass, and so surrounded with yawning precipices that came to the very edge of the road and went sheer down into the darkness that it was dangerous to go on without light. We lay down and waited for the dawn, when pursuing our way we descended into China along the dry bed of a mountain torrent, and found that somehow or other we had taken the wrong road, came over the wrong pass, and given ourselves some ten miles extra travelling.

We reached Kalgan in due course, and in such good time that my conductor was entitled to quite a little sum of money as reward for ending the journey before the stipulated date. After a few days' rest he went home with his well-earned money and his worn-out steeds. For days afterwards I indulged in copious draughts of tea, and ever since this pretty thorough lesson in riding have never had any difficulty in performing, either with an attendant or alone, such journeys in the saddle as have been entailed upon me by the prosecution of my missionary duties.

CHAPTER VI.

A NIGHT IN A MONGOL'S TENT.

A dust storm. Tents. Hospitality. Quarters for the night. A reading lama. Reading the gospel by fire-light. "Yes, I have spent a good night."

WE had been travelling, uncertain both as to the time of day and the proper direction of our route. If we could have seen the sun, we should have known both the time and the points of the compass; but the air high up was loaded with very fine dust, which hid the sun and covered the earth with a dull twilight. At last the darkness began to thicken, and we knew night had come, and a short time afterwards we struck the great road, and my guide assured me we were not far from tents. Both our camels and ourselves were fairly tired out, and the hope of rest soon seemed pleasant; but on and on we went, and still no tents.

My guide, being mounted on a swift young camel, kept so far ahead of me that I could just distinguish a dark mass away before me. After following the road a long time, I urged my camel on, overtook the guide, and asked him where these tents were; he simply pointed forward, and said, probably they were there. This was little comfort, but it was all that was to be had; his swift camel soon drew ahead again, and left my old animal far behind. Still no tent; still the distant black mass loomed in the darkness before, and I felt convinced that my guide knew little more about the tents than I did. Suddenly the black mass seemed to become broader. Was it the camel with his length across the road? Then it moved a little to the right. Had my guide spied tents? A very little urging now brought my camel alongside his swifter companion.

We had left the road, certainly, but where were the tents? Some distance off there was a streak slightly blacker than the rest of the darkness. The quick eye of the Mongol had noticed this. As we approached it, dogs began to bark, tent doors opened, and fires gleamed. We had found inhabitants at last. We were soon seated by the bright fire of a lama's tent. The lama was about twenty-seven years of age, and lived with his mother, an old woman over fifty, and another little lama, about fifteen. They were just at dinner, which seemed to consist of boiled millet, flavoured with a very acid kind of sour milk. The old woman urged the two lamas to finish their dinner quickly, that she might heat some tea for the two travellers. After snuff bottles had been exchanged, and the customary questions asked and answered about the personal health and comfort of our host, and the peace and prosperity of his flocks; and he, on the other hand, had been informed who we were, where we were going, and how our cattle stood the journey, my lama guide ventured to ask if there would be room for us to sleep in his tent.

Our lama host did not seem altogether pleased at the request, and answered, "*I am afraid not.*" His fear seemed quite natural. The tent was small, and pretty well filled up round the north part with boxes, and the altar on which a butter-lamp was then burning. Most of the west side was taken up by a lamb-fold, and the east side, in addition to the usual quantity of pots, water-holders, milk-vessels, that cumber that part, had a thriving calf tied up, which for lack of something better to do, kept licking with evident relish everything it could reach. There seemed to be little enough room for three people to sleep, how then could other two find room?

My lama, nothing daunted, replied that I was not proud or troublesome, and could do with very little room; and it was finally settled that I should sleep where I was, and my guide should sleep in a neighbouring tent. This arranged, we drank our tea, the neighbours came in to see us, our host soon thawed, and he and I engaged in conversation, while my guide superintended the cooking of our dinner.

Our host proved more intelligent than lamas usually are, and could read Mongolian—a very extraordinary thing for a priest. When I produced my satchel of gospels, catechisms, and tracts, he handed me a book he had been reading just before dinner. It was not printed but written in a small character, and much thumbed and worn. It was some old historical legend, and the lama pointed to the place where he had been reading, and asked me a word in it he could not make out. He next asked me to read the whole passage, which I did.

It ran thus:—"The hero (I forget his name) stuffing the mouth of the hole with his white bonnet, took a large stone, and 'toong, toong,' beat the ground above

The fox alarmed, rushed out, and ran off with the white bonnet on his head."

I had got thus far when a neighbour came in to let me see a Mongol prayer-book, used in presenting offerings to the god of the fire. I had to read a piece of this also, and then our dinner was ready.

While we ate, our host applied himself to the Gospel I had given him, and he could make it out very well indeed. He asked many questions about Christ and our religion, and this gave ample opportunity of explaining to him and to all in the tent the way of salvation through Christ.

After a good deal of interesting conversation on this subject, the time for sleep arrived. My guide went off to the other tent, and my host pointed out my place of rest between the lambs and the fire. I rolled myself in my sheep-skin blanket, and found that the place given me was just large enough; no more. I could see no place for the lama to sleep; and on asking him what he meant to do, he said he had to sit up and watch a cow that was expected to calve. The cold is so great, even in April, that a newly-born calf exposed all night is frozen to death. The lama settled himself on the southeast of the fire, took the Gospel in his one hand, and with his other hand from time to time kept throwing argols on the fire to keep up light enough to read with. Though very tired, I could not sleep except for a few minutes at a time, and always when I woke up there was the lama reading slowly away at the Gospel, and always adding a few more argols to keep up the light. Happily, the book was printed from wooden blocks by a Chinaman in Peking. This made it less neat than movable type would have been, but at the same time made it much larger and rounder, and much better adapted for the bad eyes of the Mongols and the dim light of their tents. All night through this man kept reading, going out at intervals to see his cow; and when dawn began to come, and people from the other tents began to move about, he went off to sleep, and we got up and prepared to depart.

While the old woman was boiling tea for us, I read a chapter in Mongolian, and when I had finished this, and we were drinking our tea, the lama roused himself and asked why we called the Gospel "the Joyful News." The reason, I told him, was that all men are sinful. This he admitted at once. I then reminded him of how the Mongols sought to wipe away sin, and escape hell by penance, pilgrimages, fastings, offerings, and other difficult works. Now this book says that when a man wants to get rid of his sin, he has only to look to Christ, and his sin clears away; that when he wants to escape hell, he has only to come to Christ and Christ saves him by making him meet for heaven. Is not the book, then rightly named "the Joyful News"? He at once assented, got up, expressed many friendly wishes, escorted us beyond the range of the dogs, and made me promise that if I came back that way I would call on him. As I left his friendly abode I could not help feeling that notwithstanding the cold reception at first, the lambs on the one side, the fire on the other, and the sleeplessness, I had spoken the truth, when, in reply to the pleasant Mongolian salutation on waking, I replied, "Yes, I *have* spent a good night."

CHAPTER VII.

BUYING EXPERIENCE.

Preliminary preparations. Waiting for a Mongol. My first camel. Load up and start to look for a servant. Upset. A Mongol manufacturing gunpowder. Hire a servant. Chanting prayers for the dead. A runaway camel. Fit out and start. Camel driver incompetent. Camel sticks. Put back and lightened. Dog carries off mutton. Camels unsuitable for my purpose. Sell off. Poetical justice. Ox-carts. Oxen. Camels and oxen compared. Tents. Mongols thoughtless and careless.

HAVING picked up some knowledge of the language, taken a long lesson in riding, furnished myself with a box of medicines necessary for the treatment of a number of the diseases most common in Mongolia, the proper cures for which had been pointed out to me by the kindness of a medical missionary in Peking, and packed a box with such Scriptures and tracts as I found ready to my hand in the depôts of the British and Foreign Bible Society and the Religious Tract Society, I found myself the guest of an American missionary located in Kalgan, a Chinese town, situated on the south frontier of Mongolia.

My plan was to get a tent, buy camels, hire a Mongol servant, and travel about the country, camping here and there at inhabited places, in the hope that I might be enabled to dispense medicine and preach the Gospel to the natives who would be attracted to visit me.

The first thing was to find camels; but I could get none for hire or sale, and at last had to give up the attempt and endeavour to wait quietly the coming of a Mongol friend, who was expected to arrive in a few days. *Endeavour* to wait quietly, I have said, for I don't think the endeavour was very successful; and I may here remark that of all the things I have had to do in connection with Mongolia and Mongols, waiting has been that which proved most difficult. When performing hard journeys, when baffled in attempts at mastering the language, when poorly lodged and badly fed on native fare, when treated with suspicion, and even when openly opposed, there is comfort and stimulus in knowing that perseverance will end the journey and conquer the language, that endurance will make up for deficiencies in board and lodgings, and that openness and effort will overcome unfriendliness and hostility. Any one in good health and spirits can get through such difficulties well enough. But to have to sit down and simply wait the coming of a day, or a man, whose advent no effort can hasten, this to me has always proved the hardest task that could be set, and it is one that has often fallen to my lot in connection with Mongolia.

The day came, and so did the man at last, and, learning what I wanted, in a very short time he reappeared, blocking up the gateway with a tall, gaunt camel, the first of that tribe of cattle which I was destined to possess. In a day or two he found me another, but that was all he could do for me; duty called him away, and he had to go on to Peking in the service of his government. Before going, however, he furnished me with the name of a man whom I might find it possible to hire to act as my servant. This man lived away in Mongolia, and could be reached only by taking a journey of about a hundred English miles; but anything was better than inaction, and having procured the felts and frames that compose the uncouth camel pack-saddle, I loaded up one of my two recent purchases, led him clear of the Chinese town, and, after an unsuccessful attempt in which, to the great mirth of the Chinese spectators, I came down by the run, succeeded in perching myself on the top of the load, and took my way northwards to find my possible servant.

The journey took four days, and was uneventful, with the exception of an upset which happened on the first day, and an adventure which closed the third day. Shortly after entering Mongolia proper, my camel insisted on disregarding my attempts at guiding him, and walked along a sloping bank wet with water, which ran from some snow that was melting higher up. As might be expected, his great broad flat feet slipped from under him, and, with a scream, he landed on his beam ends, where, held down by his load, he lay entirely unable to recover himself. I managed to tilt him up, there was no material damage done, and we continued our journey.

The third day, misdirected by a Mongol, whose intentions were doubtless honest and friendly enough, I got into a country I knew nothing about, and had to put up for the night at a tent where I was a stranger, and whose inhabitants seemed a rather rough set. The unsatisfactory feeling I could not help entertaining about my surroundings was increased by the fact that a young man was busy manufacturing gunpowder in an iron pot close beside an open fire. He was grinding it with a stone, and as long as it was moist there was no danger. As it got dry and the process was nearly finished, it was alarming to see how reckless he was; and his rashness at last reached such a pitch that the women of the community remonstrated and compelled him to remove to a safe distance from the fire. Though their looks and surroundings were against them, this family proved honest enough, treated me well, and next day set me on my way again with such correct and clear directions that I had no difficulty in reaching my destination.

The man whom I sought was at home, received my offer cautiously, took a day to think of it, came to report his acceptance of the situation and got very drunk, an example which was followed by my landlady, an old woman of about sixty.

Having bought another camel I proposed to start back to China, but my servant would not hear of it. He was a lama, and at that time was engaged with others in chanting prayers for the good of the soul of a well-to-do neighbour who, when drunk, had met his death by falling from his horse and breaking his neck. My servant, though he could absent himself for a day or two from the prayers, declared his intention of waiting till the final day of the services, when he, in common with the other lamas, would receive the presents of money, or goods, or both, that would reward them for having assisted, as was supposed, in forwarding the soul of their dead neighbour to a place of freedom from suffering.

After a short delay my lama got his gratuity, and we set out on our return journey. On the second day, when encamping for our midday halt, one of our camels got alarmed by the load becoming loose, began to jump and kick, persevered till it kicked itself clear of everything, and started homewards at a smart trot. In a short time it was a long way off, and had I not paid a Mongol to mount a horse and bring it back, we might never have seen it again.

Arrived in China, a few days sufficed to procure a tent and all the other things necessary, and our caravan of three camels, one lama, and one missionary, set out for Mongolia. We had gone but a short distance when I discovered that, through improper loading, the boxes were rubbing through the camel's skin, and on having this pointed out to him, my servant admitted that he was not used to camels, and did not know how to load them. Having been assured that he knew all about camels, I had left the arrangement of the loads to him; but now, finding that he knew nothing about them, I took the thing into my own hands, and soon had the burden fixed up more satisfactorily.

All went well till we came to the foot of the great pass that has to be crossed to reach the plain. It is a high mountain, scaled by a rough road which owes more to the wheels of carts than to the tools of road-makers, and is very steep in some parts. As soon as we came fairly in sight of this pass, one of the camels stopped and refused to go on. Urging it produced nothing, and we finally put up for the night at a Chinese inn. An attempt made the following day was not more successful, and for another night we had to put up in the same inn. It was now apparent that the camel, originally a poor one, had been over-exhausted on the preliminary journey undertaken to find my Mongol servant, and was not in a condition to travel.

I made another discovery at the same time, namely,

A RUNAWAY CAMEL.

that my camels were too heavily laden. I had loaded them up to about what I had learned was the usual amount of a camel's burden, but I now found that, to travel well, such animals as I had would not carry above half of their present load. To get on at all, I was under the necessity of completely reconstructing my whole appointments, and, in place of three camels with full loads, I had to arrange for journeying with two camels with half loads. The disabled camel was left behind, as was also the greater part of my goods; and, following my reduced caravan on foot, we again faced the pass, got over it all right, and at length had the desire of my heart gratified by finding myself encamped in my own tent on the plain, healing the diseases of the Mongols and telling them of salvation through Jesus.

One of the first nights that we spent in Mongolia, a dog entered our tent and carried off a leg of mutton, nearly our whole stock; and from this adventure I learned always to hang up mutton at night beyond the reach of these prowling thieves, who seldom failed to pay us nocturnal visits.

In the course of two summers I gained a good deal of experience of camels' flesh, and came to the conclusion that camels were not the animals best suited to my travelling needs. The main difficulty was that great part of my travelling was in summer, the season of the year when camels are generally disused, and turned loose on the plain to pasture, and gather up a supply of fat and strength, which is essential to their endurance during the rest of the year. So, after having owned quite a number of these animals, which some one has described as "deformed in the very structure of their being," and having performed a number of journeys with them, I had become fairly well acquainted with their capabilities, their excellences, their defects, and the proper method of treating them. Finding, however, that I could do better with other means of locomotion I sold off the whole lot, and have never owned one camel since. It would seem that a kind of poetical justice attended the issue of this final selling off, on my part, of my whole interest in Mongolian camels.

During one of my journeys I had been under the necessity of hiring for a short period two camels from a wealthy Mongol. The bargain had been concluded by the Mongol who was then my servant. Through some oversight or carelessness on his part, some of the terms of agreement had been left rather indefinite, and when I came to give back the animals, their owner not only seized the opportunity to interpret these indefinite terms to the full to his own advantage, but, in order to force me to accede to his demands, treated me in a manner that was an outrage on all justice and uprightness. I had no resource but to submit, and, acting on the principle of never taking offence at the conduct of a heathen, however bad it might be, parted from him on terms of perfect amity. This same man, hearing that I wanted to sell my camels, and evidently encouraged by his former transactions with me, came forward as a purchaser. The price was soon agreed on, and this time, making the bargain myself, the terms were definitely settled. I took the money. He took the animals and departed. Report says that the half of them died, so that in place of making a good sum of money by them, as he intended, he barely realised the sum he had paid for them. If he had been a poor man he would have merited some commiseration on the disappointment of his hopes, but he was wealthy, and it was some consolation to me to think that though in our first business transaction he had over-reached me badly, he had, though quite unintentionally, in this case paid me the full value of my camels.

Having given up camels, my next travelling experiences were with ox-carts. These carts are very rude affairs, and, with the exception of two small pieces of iron, are made entirely of wood, the price of cart and wheels, brand new, varying according to quality from two to three taels, that is, from eleven or twelve to sixteen or eighteen shillings sterling. Each cart is drawn by one ox, and carries a load of about five hundred catties, or between six and seven hundred pounds. The wheels are fixed to the wooden axle, which revolves with them, and the two pieces of iron are small plates of cast metal let into the wood of the cart-frame exactly over the axle, which thus in contact with iron, turns more easily and with much less tear and wear than would be possible if subjected to the friction of wood to wood.

The construction of the carts and especially of the wheels is ingeniously simple. Into one thick beam, called the *skull*, are let, cross-wise, the smaller woods called *arrows;* to each of the six extremities of these three pieces of wood is fixed a felly, everything is driven tightly home, and held in its place by wooden wedges, and the wheel is complete. When both wheels are completed they are firmly wedged on to the axle, and the whole fabric is held together by the power of water. As soon as the wood gets dry the wedges get loose, and the separate pieces of the wheel are in danger of falling asunder. As long as the whole thing is kept damp it keeps moderately well together, and an essential preliminary to starting on a march is to see that the wheels are wet. It was some time, and not till after some misadventures, that I came to know the "points" of a cart.

On the whole my experience of oxen was very favourable, and I learned to admire their strength, powers of endurance and docility. The camel is doubtless *the* beast of burden in Mongolia. There are regions where without the camel travelling would be well nigh impossible; there are seasons of the year when the camel alone is available, and for the rapid transport of goods at all times and places the camel is indispensable. Yet over almost the whole of Mongolia, oxen and ox-carts are largely used, and between some of the large trading centres by far the largest part of the traffic is carried on by ox-carts, the merchants being able to afford the higher rates of camel-freight on only a small proportion of the goods which their business makes it necessary for them to transport.

There were also a few things to be learned about tents. The ordinary travelling tent of the Mongol is shaped exactly like the roof of a gableless house, and is made of two thicknesses of Chinese cloth, being white inside and blue outside. The tent has no door, its "*mouth*," as it is called, standing open night and day. Moreover it is so constructed that it does not reach quite to the ground, but leaves a space of a few inches all round, by which the wind blows through at pleasure. The first improvement that suggested itself was to stop the draught by sewing a fringe of cloth all round the bottom of the tent; the next was to make a cloth door which could be buttoned up at night. Later on, in place of two

TRAVELLING TENTS. [*From a Native Sketch.*

tent poles three were used, which added much to the apparent size and real capacity of the tent by leaving the centre space unincumbered; and the final and crowning device was to have two ridges and a double roof, by which means the excessive heat of the tent, during the cloudless blazing days of summer, was very much reduced. So fierce was the sun that its rays pierced the double Chinese cloth, and penetrated so strongly that opaque objects in the tent used to cast distinct shadows on the floor; but with two roofs separated by a sufficient air space, the brightness and heat were much reduced and the interior of the tent rendered cool and pleasant.

The only drawback connected with these improvements arose from the remarks of some of the Mongols, who seemed to think that any one who took trouble to make a travelling tent comfortable must be very careful of himself. Many of the Mongols admired the double roof as a device that they had not been clever enough to think of for themselves, but some few men seemed to bestow a sort of commiseration on a man who was afraid of sun and wind. One would almost rather broil in the sun and shiver in the wind than be considered effeminate by a Mongol. It was manifest, however, that notwithstanding any remarks Mongols might have to make on this subject, they were very glad of the good shelter afforded by the tent, and some of them would pay me long visits and be very slow to leave, simply because they liked the coolness of the tent on hot days, and the warmth of the tent when a cold wind was blowing.

Any one but a Mongol would perhaps have given me hints that would have saved much trouble on these points; but, thoughtless in their own concerns and careless of their own interests, it was perhaps too much to expect that my servants should be thoughtful and careful about my affairs. Hence it came to pass that not only in the things mentioned, but in many others, having the example of no predecessor, and receiving little aid from the natives, I could only be guided by what seemed feasible, and had no other way of gaining experience but by buying it.

CHAPTER VIII.

HOW TO TRAVEL IN MONGOLIA.

How Mongols travel. On camels with a tent. On horseback. In ox-carts or horse-carts. On foot. Incidents *en route*. How Chinamen travel. Camel cart travelling for foreigners generally. Requisites. Scenes on the plain. Pleasantest part of the ride. Customs to be observed by travellers. Mongols hospitable and desire reciprocity.

MONGOLS usually travel on camels with a tent. This is their usual mode when they are numerous enough to form a company, and when the journey is to some distant place. Northern and Central Mongols, going to Wu-t'ai or Peking, to worship at the famous shrines there, usually travel thus. A spare sheep-skin coat for bedding; a few calf-skin bags (looking like the original calves themselves), with provisions; a small blue cloth tent, black with smoke and a good deal patched; a pot, a grate, two water buckets, and a few odd pieces of felt, are about all the things that are needed. When they go thus lightly encumbered, with no goods to barter, they can travel quickly, the exact length of the daily march depending a good deal on the condition of the camels, the season of the year, and the power of endurance of the travellers themselves. One hundred and twenty *li*, or forty English miles, would be a good day's march; sometimes more would be accomplished,—

often much less. The Mongols like to be careful of their camels, even when they are fat and strong, and would rather lengthen the journey by a good many days than spoil their animals.

But a Mongol is always glad when he can get down from a camel and mount a horse. The motion of a horse, they say, is pleasanter, and then too a horse goes so much faster. They often perform journeys on horseback. The drawbacks to this kind of travelling are, that on a horse they can take only a few pounds of luggage if the journey is at all long, and the horse needs a good deal of care. It is not as in China, where you get into an inn, buy so much fodder, and let the animal munch away at it half the night. In Mongolia you come to a tent and get lodging readily enough, but the horse must be turned adrift to shift for himself. In summer he must not be let loose while the sun is hot; allowing him to eat then would make sores on his back, they say; in the evening and in the early morning he must be allowed time to feed. Then again the pasture in the neighbourhood of tents is usually poor, being eaten down by the cattle of the place.

A common and comfortable way of horseback travelling, is for a horseman to join himself on to a camel caravan. The caravan has its own tent, camps away from settled habitations in the midst of good grass, and the horse finds pasture without trouble.

The carts commonly used in Mongolia are simple and rude in construction, and though a little clumsy, are light. Carts for passengers are roofed in with a frame covered with felt or cloth. Inside there is room enough for a man to sit or lie down and sleep. Horses travel at a moderately good speed, but are seldom used

MONGOL CART WITH SHAFTS FASTENED TO POLES BORNE BY TWO RIDERS. [*From a Native Sketch.*]

in carts for long journeys. Long journeys are usually performed by oxen, and of all means of locomotion in Mongolia they are the slowest, sometimes not accomplishing much more than ten miles a day.

The Mongols like above all things to ride, but many of them cannot find steeds, and a vast deal of foot travelling is done. A large proportion of the travelling on foot is that of poor men who go on religious pilgrimages. Foot-travellers, for the most part, trust to the hospitality of the inhabitants of the districts through which they pass for lodgings, but occasionally they carry a tent with them. On one occasion in the south of Mongolia, I found two men encamped in a tent which weighed only a very few pounds. The frame of the tent consisted of a ridge pole supported in the centre by a stake about the height and strength of a walking-stick. They had a little pot, a little water bucket, a ladle, a piece of felt and a skin. One of the two inhabitants had received medicine from me the day before; so when I presented myself at the tent door to ask for my patient, one of the two hurried out and invited me to enter. There was no room for three, so he remained outside till I left. There was no room to sit up, and certainly no room to stretch oneself out in it; but these two lamas lived in it, and seemed well pleased with their accommodation. They belonged to Urga, and had been to Wu-t'ai; at least they said so. They had been some months on the road, and were then about five or six hundred miles from home. The tent and fittings seemed so unique that I have ever since regretted that I did not buy it all up as a curio.

At another place I fell in with four men going to Ando, a place somewhere to the south-west. They had a tent and travelled heavily loaded. They had been a month on the road, and still had about three or four months' travel before them. They were all young, about twenty-four, and were going west to study at some famous seat of learning, hoping to come back with their degrees and a reputation for scholarship, that would secure them rank and position among the lamas of their native place. As they intended to be away some years, they doubtless had each a store of silver in the baggage, but their travelling expenses cost them little, as they begged most of what they needed. They evidently had the sympathy of the people with them, and found little difficulty in getting gifts. They fared plainly too. I saw them set on the pot, fill it up to the brim with water, and proceed to add the requisite quantity of millet. The cook on this occasion was evidently the hungry man of the party: so, chuckling at the absence of two frugal lamas of the company, he coaxed his companion into a laughing consent to add a little more millet than usual, on the pretext that the particular millet in question "*did not swell*." They were preparing to dine on millet and water, but a small piece of poor cheese having been obtained, a few slips were thrown into the pot to give a flavour.

Lamas and laymen sometimes go hundreds of miles on foot to famous shrines, and occasionally break down on the way. In such cases they usually apply to the temple for assistance, and not unfrequently get it. On one occasion, some men from the Sunite country started for Wu-t'ai on foot, and arrived there foot-sore and weary. They applied to the temple, and as some men from their quarter of the country were on the temple roll, for handsome donations given some years before, the worn out travellers were well treated and sent home on horses. Of course the travellers thus assisted were expected to make some return, and doubtless this example of kindness won for the temple a good many adherents and a good many subscriptions.

Chinamen travel in camel carts. This is the common method adopted by rich merchants. The camel cart is closed in all round, is long enough to sleep in stretched out full length, and is just as broad as you like to set the wheels. It is very comfortable. The camel caravan usually does a good part of its travelling at night, that is no affair of the traveller's; he goes to bed and sleeps till morning

Ordinary travellers find the camel cart the most comfortable mode of transit. After securing cart and camels, the next thing is to lay in a stock of provisions and get other requisites together.

For the cart it is necessary to have a small wicker jar of oil with a brush to apply it to the wheels; an iron lantern, a stock of Chinese candles to burn in it, a few extra sheets of paper to renew its coverings; and two little pieces of wood fastened together by a cord to block the wheels when the camel is taken out of the shafts, and the cart is left resting on the support in front with which it should be furnished.

Travelling in Mongolia has many pleasures, but ordinary travelling is so slow that the tedium threatens to swamp them all. Horseback travelling does away with the tedium as far as possible, and presents the greatest number of new scenes and circumstances in rapid succession. Night and day you hurry on; sunrise and sunset have their glories much like those seen at sea; the stars and the moon have a charm on the lovely

TRAVELLING IN A CAMEL CART. [*From a Native Sketch.*]

plain. Ever and anon you come upon tents, indicated at night by the barking of the dogs,—in the daytime seen gleaming from afar, vague and indistinct through the glowing mirage. As you sweep round the base of a hill, you come upon a herd of startled deer and give chase, to show their powers of running; then a temple with its red walls and gilt ornamented roofs looms up and glides past. Hill-sides here and there are patched with sheep; in the plains below mounted Mongols are dashing right and left through a large drove of horses, pursuing those they wish to catch, with a noosed pole that looks like a fishing-rod. On some lovely stretch of road you come upon an encampment of two or three hundred ox-carts, the oxen grazing and the drivers mending the wooden wheels, or meet a long train of tea-laden silent camels. When the time for a meal approaches and a tent heaves in sight, you leave the road and make for it. However tired the horses may be, they will freshen up at this. They know what is coming, and hurry on to rest.

The greatest pleasure attending such a ride is the finish. After ten days or a fortnight of discomfort, fatigue, sleeplessness, and hard fare, to take a bath, change clothes, sit down to a foreign meal spread on a white table-cloth, and go to sleep in a comfortable bed, is a luxury that can be fully appreciated only by those who have performed the ride.

In connection with travelling, it may be in place to speak of the proper manner of entering a tent. Some travellers, from mere ignorance, make grave blunders, and though the Mongols are the first to forgive people ignorant of their ways, yet it is better to know some of the more important customs to be observed.

From whatever side the tent is approached, be sure to ride up towards it from the front. If you come upon it from behind, ride round it at some distance, so as to come up in front. If on foot it is more important still to observe this rule. When within a short distance,— say speaking distance,—of the tent, stop and shout *nohoi* (dog), and if the dogs have not come out against you before this, they will be pretty sure to come and come in force now. But the *nohoi* is not meant to challenge the dogs to combat, but to warn the people in the tent to come out to restrain them. The Mongol dogs are very savage, and without the protection of the tent people it would be rash and dangerous to attempt to advance. At the cry of *nohoi*, or *nohoi hurae*, the people in the tent are bound by law to come out and protect the traveller. Until they receive this protection, horsemen remain in the saddle; foot travellers keep the dogs at bay as best they can with a couple of sticks. The idea of the two sticks is, I suppose, that when one of them is laid hold of by a savage animal of the pack, there is another stick still left free to lay about with. Two or three women and children probably come out, scold off the tamer animals and sit down on the fiercer ones, while the traveller hurries in. He should be careful, however, to leave his sticks or whip outside the door. This is a universal custom in Mongolia, as far as I have observed, and is seldom or never violated by Mongols. So far is it carried, that a child who brought the stalk of a tall reed into the tent where I was visiting, and played by striking the ground with it, received a severe reprimand and narrowly escaped chastisement.

The idea of leaving the sticks and whip outside, as explained by the Mongols themselves, is that any one who comes into a tent carrying a whip or stick, insults the inhabitants by conducting himself as if he had come to whip or beat them like dogs. "What use have you for your whips and sticks inside the tent? Outside you keep off the dogs; here are you going to beat us in our own tents?" Having left his stick outside, then the traveller, on getting through the low doorway, may say *mendu* to the people inside, and proceed to sit down on the left side of the fireplace, about halfway between the door and the back of the tent. If no demonstration is made, the traveller may sit there; but if asked to go higher he can either accept the honour or decline it, as may seem best to himself. It is not usual to take off the hat on entering, but most roadside Mongols are used to the foreign custom of uncovering, and it does not shock them. If the hat be taken off, it should be laid *higher*,—that is further up towards the back of the tent, —than the visitor himself. Either this, or it may be laid on the top of a chest, but in no case should it be laid towards the door. The traveller should sit cross-legged; but if he cannot do this, he should be careful to stretch his legs towards the door. The feet pointed inwards towards the back of the tent would be considered great rudeness, even in a foreigner. The next thing is the interchange of snuff bottles. A Mongol visitor offers his first to the host and the people of the tent, and receives theirs in return; but foreigners do not carry snuff generally; so the Mongol host offers his to the foreign visitor. The bottle should be received in the palm of the right hand, carried deferentially towards the nose, the stopper should be raised a little, then a sniff, the stopper may be readjusted, and the bottle handed slowly and deferentially back to its owner. Those who speak the language, while receiving and returning the bottle, make and answer inquiries about their host's and their own health. People who don't speak Mongol can make a few nods and give a pleased smile or two, which will be taken as an equivalent for the customary phrases of politeness.

Meantime the women have been warming tea, and soon a little table is set before the visitor; then he is handed a cup of tea, which he should receive with both his hands. He may set it down on the table for a little, or he may drink it off, if it is not too hot. Tea in Mongolia is not the mere formality it often seems to be in China. The visitor is expected to drink it and hand back his cup, with both hands as before, to have it refilled several times. When he has had enough he should say so or indicate it, that the cup may not be refilled. While he has been drinking tea, a plate of white food is usually set on the table or handed to him, to be received with both hands. As a rule, this is not expected to be eaten, but must be tasted. Taking a mere crumb is sufficient; then the plate should be deferentially delivered back with both hands.

On leaving the tent there are no very special formalities to be observed. The Mongols do not usually have any custom equivalent to our hand-shaking and "good-bye." A bow and a smile outside the tent door before mounting will be sufficient.

As to entering tents on the plain, there need be no bashfulness. Any traveller is at perfect liberty to alight at any village he may wish and demand admittance; and any Mongol who refuses admittance, or gives a cold welcome even, is at once stigmatised as *not a man but a dog*. Any host who did not offer tea, without money and without price, would soon earn the same reputation, the reason being, I suppose, that Mongolia has no inns, and all travellers are dependent on private houses for shelter and refreshment. At first sight it seems rather exacting to leap off your horse at the door of a perfect stranger, and expect to find tea prepared and offered to you free; but probably the master of the tent where you refresh yourself is at the same time sitting likewise refreshing himself in some other man's tent some hundred miles away; and thus the thing balances itself. The hospitality received by Mongols in travelling compensates for the hospitality shown to travellers.

Not a few tents are at one time or other under prohibition. Sickness, a newly-born child, the children being inoculated, and a few other things happen to make it impossible to allow strangers to enter. In the case of a single tent standing alone, the traveller under such circumstances would have to go on; but in a village, not more than one or two tents are likely to be forbidden at the same time, and shelter can be found in the others.

Mongols sometimes complain of the Chinamen, who come to Mongolia, enter their tents, and receive their hospitality, but who, when their Mongol friends go to China, will not let them enter their dwelling-houses. Sometimes when I am among them in their tents, they ask incredulously if I would let them enter my house, and I of course say I would, and keep my word to such as visit me at home. Mongols in Peking, who have entertained foreigners in Mongolia, sometimes complain of the manner in which they are driven away from the gates of foreign residences in Peking.

CHAPTER IX.

DINING WITH A MONGOL.

The invitation. My host preparing himself for dinner. Conversation under difficulties. Arrival of a congenial companion. Dinner ready and served up. The place of honour. The proper custom. The second course. Early hours. Why the rump is the piece of honour. Paying a Mongol in his own coin. A live dinner.

ONE afternoon towards evening, when sitting in my teacher's tent, a horse-herd appeared inside the door, and said that the mandarin desired my company to dinner. On asking when I should go, the reply was "Now," so I got up and accompanied the messenger back. I was ushered into the presence of my host, and found that the dinner was only a semi-official one, and as such was to take place in the second-best tent. The mandarin was preparing himself for the repast by drinking, out of small cups, Chinese whisky, which he heated by inserting the conical metal wineholder into the fire, or standing it in the boiling pot. How long he had been so employed, or how much whisky he had thus consumed, was doubtful, and he seemed so intent on imbibing more, that he did not care to talk much.

When he did speak it was only to ask formal questions which he had asked and heard me answer before, and when I attempted conversation, he, for the most part, simply stared at me in a blank manner, and, if he replied at all, uttered little more than monosyllables. Frequently when I spoke, he would look at me intently till I had finished, then, gulping down the whisky which he had meantime been holding in his mouth, he would utter an inarticulate grunt by way of assent, and busy himself heating or pouring out more whisky.

In the face of such a display of intelligence it was useless to prolong attempts at conversation, and I was about to follow the example of my host and relapse into silence, when his married daughter, a comfortable-looking, plump, broad-faced matron, who happened to be home on a visit, came to the rescue, and attempted to interest her father by showing my watch, and questioning me about our foreign marriage customs. But it was all in vain. The man seemed to have no capacity for or interest in anything but Chinese whisky.

Having invited me to dinner, I was a little surprised that he made no attempt to entertain me with conversation, and we were feeling a little awkward (by we I mean all the occupants of the tent except the host, who seemed quite happy as long as his whisky held out), when a neighbour, a poor old man blind of one eye, came in and seated himself between the fire and the door, the humblest place in the tent.

The mandarin commanded a servant to supply the new-comer with a measure of warm whisky and a cup, when the poor old man's tongue was loosed at once, and, to our great relief, so was the mandarin's, and these two men, dissimilar in everything but their love of drink, had a long and lively talk together. There was no need to force a conversation between them, and for a long time they rattled away speaking of horses, cattle, and the general affairs of the country-side. The children, both of the house and of the neighbouring tents, got out dice and had a regular game, which I watched till dinner was almost ready. When that time arrived a Tibetan lama, who happened to have come that evening, was sent for. He came and shared the place of honour with me. This yellow-coated individual was to me what the poor tippler was to my host. He was intelligent and inclined to talk, and we did talk together, and I was feeling quite at home, till some food was brought in for the mandarin's inspection,—my lama's half-uttered sentence was left unfinished, his countenance became fixed, his gaze abstracted, his whole attention centred on what was in the great man's hands. I seemed to have faded altogether from the region of his consciousness, and our conversation came to an end.

But the silence did not last long, for soon the mutton was pronounced "done," and the serving lama who held the keys and acted in general as butler to the mandarin produced two great brass flat dishes. One of these he heaped up with meat for his master. The other was filled with one huge piece of mutton, the hinder part of the back bone, including the great, broad, fat tail, several smaller portions, such as ribs, etc. We set to work, the lama explaining that to present the rump and tail was the highest honour that a host could offer a guest at a feast.

Armed only with a knife, we soon made havoc of the steaming mass, when the mandarin remarked that evidently I was not aware of the proper custom. The lama explained that a portion should be given to all in the tent, which was now nearly full of neighbours and children who had collected for the occasion. At my request, he kindly undertook to perform the office of dissection and distribution for me. His knife knew all the joints and turns among the bones, and in a short time all in the tent were eating. While we were going on with this first course, millet was added to the water left in the pot in which the mutton had been boiled, and by the time that we had finished the tail and picked the bones the millet was ready, and was dealt out to all who could hold out a cup. As soon as the millet was finished, cushions were talked of, and I was politely invited to sleep where I was. The lama had gone a few minutes before, and I took the hint and departed, leaving the family going to bed at half-past six o'clock.

Setting the rump and attached tail before a guest is honouring him, because a sheep having but one tail, the presentation of this dish necessitates the slaying of a sheep, and it must also be a good one, for none but a fat one has a tail that is fit to be seen. It is rather awkward for a foreigner to feast comfortably, having to attack, with no assistance but that of a knife, a great expanse of fat mutton spread on a brass dish nearly two feet in diameter; but I used to feel that I had quite repaid my Mongol hosts in their own coin when, in Peking, I invited them to take their place at my table and wield a foreign knife and fork.

The multitudinous dining appliances of civilisation are as bewildering to a Mongol, as their absence is embarrassing to a foreigner in a tent feast; and perhaps the guest in each case fares about the same, and feels that the feast ministers more to his dignity than to his appetite.

In the case of a lady a tent feast is not a success. On

one occasion a Mongol who had been a guest at our table in Peking, wishing to feast my wife and myself at his own home, and yet not knowing how to make food that we could enjoy, solved the problem in a very sensible way. He sent us the sheep alive, apologising for his ignorance of cookery, and requesting us to dress it in the way that we liked best.

CHAPTER X.

APPEAL TO A MONGOL MANDARIN.

The use of a passport. Hiring horses. Stopped on the highway. A horse left on our hands. Asking advice of a local mandarin. The mandarin's settlement of the case. Another quarrel over a horse. A broken head. Fight in the tent. "He would leave his coat with me." "Ne exeat regno." Asking a mandarin's advice. His official utterance. His private opinion. Nothing private in Mongolia. Reconciliation. Tit for tat.

IN travelling in Mongolia it is necessary to be furnished with a passport, in order to be able to satisfy suspicious mandarins as to who and what the strange traveller may be, and, in case of trouble, to be able to claim the good offices and assistance of the local authorities. I never had my passport demanded by suspicious magnates, but I had, on two occasions, to ask advice from Mongol officials. The first case was as follows: Having intimated that I wanted to hire a horse for a journey, a Mongol came to my tent, bargained and settled as to the price, and arranged definitely to let me have it if, on inspection, I found it suitable. The horse was away on the plain feeding, and was to be shown when the drove was brought home in the evening. When the drove came I deputed my Mongol servant to examine the animal, and he reported it as quite unfit for use.

Hearing this I told my servant to bargain for some one else's horse; he soon returned to say he had found another, and, supposing the matter all right, we retired for the night.

Early next morning the horse was brought, my servant mounted, and hearing him ride off I put my head out of my tent to see how he looked on his steed. It was a misty morning, and he was already some distance away, but I could see that he was pursued, and finally overtaken and stopped by a horseman, who, with a deal of shouting and noise, accompanied him back to my encampment. The cause of the trouble was soon explained. The hindering horseman was the owner of the horse first bargained for, who, eager for the hire, insisted on his horse being taken. It was explained to him that his horse was hired only on condition that, on inspection, it proved suitable, and that, being found to have a sore back, it had been rejected and another hired in its place. A great amount of talking ensued, the upshot of which was, that the owner of the horse with the sore back sullenly and silently agreed that the other horse should be taken, and my servant accordingly departed.

The disappointed man remained at our encampment, and, seeing him look unhappy, I spoke to him in a friendly way. He seemed pleased enough at first, but suddenly changed his manner, said, "You hired my horse, I have brought him, here he is, ride him or not ride him, you must pay for him, I leave him with you tied here," and, suiting the action to the word, he tied the horse to the wheel of one of my carts and went off.

The morning passed on and there the horse remained. What was to be done? "Do nothing. Let him remain tied there. It is none of your business," said my Mongol servant; but I could not well leave the beast tied up without food or drink simply because his master had a dispute with me. If, on the other hand, I let him loose, or if he took fright at anything, broke away and went off, I should be held responsible, and have to replace him if lost. I was unwilling to run the risk of being involved in farther complications with such a man as his owner had shown himself to be. To have quietly submitted and paid the hire would have been to make myself a proverb for incompetence, and would probably have rendered it extremely difficult for me afterwards to buy sheep, and hire men, oxen, or horses, at anything like reasonable figures.

The best thing I could do seemed to be to ask the advice of the local mandarin, whose abode was visible about a mile away. He was one of the sons of a wealthy family, the head of which was of high rank, and, at that time, held an important office. Arrived at his "*city*," as any cluster of tents belonging to two or three families is called in Mongolia, I found the dogs tied up to stakes driven into the ground, and was conducted into a small clean tent, spread with good cushions, but destitute of almost every other kind of furniture. This tent was evidently his office for the transaction of business, tea was set before me, and I was desired to wait till the mandarin should appear.

As I approached the place I had noticed several men busy among a large drove of horses, and among them the owner of the horse about whose disposal I had come to ask advice. When the mandarin appeared I recognised him as one of the group of men I had seen among the horses, and, after the ordinary forms of salutation had been gone through, I stated my difficulty, explained shortly how the trouble had arisen, and said that I had come to ask him what was the right thing for me to do in such circumstances. He was a young man, listened

MONGOL MANDARIN AND ATTENDANT.

quietly to what I had to say, and, before he had time to speak, an elderly lama, probably his uncle, who had been diligently counting his beads, suddenly broke out in a storm against the owner of the horse, who was present among the crowd that filled the part of the tent about the door.

"What kind of a sinful creature are you that would saddle and ride a horse with a sore back—are you a human being or a dog?" The mandarin joined in the invective, and between them the poor fellow got such a rating that I had to intercede for him. On asking what I was to do with the horse, which the owner still declined to promise to remove from my encampment, the mandarin said, "Turn it loose, and I'll be responsible for all consequences."

After some general friendly conversation the mandarin suggested that as the owner of the horse was poor, and was doubtless disappointed at not receiving the hire he hoped his horse would earn, perhaps it would be as well for me to make him a small present to soothe his feelings. I asked him to name what sum he considered proper, but this he utterly declined to do, saying that the man had no claim to anything, but had behaved badly, and that if I gave anything at all I gave more than he deserved. My business being now finished, I presented the mandarin with a small leather-bound note-book, was escorted a little distance beyond the "city," returned to my tent, handed a small present to the man who had caused all the trouble, and saw the steed led away.

My next appeal to a Mongol mandarin was made some years later, and was also connected with horse hiring. While encamped at the hamlet which was the home of my two Mongol servants, I had occasion to hire two horses, and somehow or other the natives laid their heads together to raise the price. I resented this by calling my servants into my tent, and saying that, however badly I might be treated elsewhere, I had hoped for fair play at their native place. This was in the evening after all visitors had left.

Next morning, as I was just finishing my toilet, I noticed five or six people coming towards my tent, and as I had one visitor already, an old man sitting with his young child in his arms, I was much pleased to find the day beginning so well, and hoped I should have a good time with them conversing on Christian topics. Just as I sat down in my place, several of the men entered, and one of them, without waiting to seat himself, addressed a few words to the old man already in the tent, and almost simultaneously dealt him such a blow on his bare and closely-shaven scalp (he was a lama) that the stick with which the blow was given broke short off, and the old man's head swelled up visibly till there was a lump almost as large as a hen's egg. It was the work of a few moments, and was all over before any one had time to interfere. A loud and angry altercation followed, which ended by the old lama slapping severely the face of his assailant, who was also a lama, but young. They flew at each other's throats, clutched the neck of each other's coats, and pushed and tugged violently; the spectators laid hold on the combatants and tried to pull them apart, the swaying and struggling mass of excited and shouting men reeled hither and thither in the narrow space of the tent, till a more violent lurch nearly carried away the pole, and narrowly missed bringing my abode down about their ears.

The noise and shouting attracted the other inhabitants of the hamlet, and by the time that we had separated the two wrathful and bleeding lamas the small population of the place had turned out in force, and the women of the community were running about talking, several of them simultaneously, and all of them with rapid utterance and in high-pitched tones. Excepting the first blow with the stick there was little damage done, the blood having come from some scratches of little consequence. The young lama was taken to my servants' tent, the women advised to stop talking and go home, and the old lama, placing again in his lap his young child, which he had disposed of in some way I had not noticed when the scuffle began, resumed his seat in my tent, and keeping all the while in his mouth a Chinese spherical brass button, which had been torn from his coat in the encounter, proceeded to call me to witness how that, while seated quietly in my tent with his child in his arms, he had been violently assaulted without offering any provocation.

After a little he rose to go, and a few minutes after there was an outcry among the tents of the community. It would seem that as soon as he reached his tent his senior wife (for though old and poor, and the owner of only one tent, not only was he married, but actually had two wives), really alarmed, or feigning to be alarmed at his swollen head, bruised face, and disordered garments, raised a great storm, invaded the quarters of the young lama who had been the assailant, said her husband was disabled, and gave warning that should he die within the year the young lama would be held responsible for his life.

At her instigation the old lama reappeared in my tent, said he was a poor man and had been hurt, and that "he would leave his coat with me." Suiting the action to the word, he pulled off his outer garment, left it on my box, and went away. Soon after he sent me a message to say that I must find a new servant, as one of my men, brother to the young lama, could not be permitted to leave the neighbourhood. A still later intimation warned me that I myself must not leave the place till this quarrel had been settled. The assault had taken place in my tent and I was an important witness in the case.

Now it happened that I wanted to make a journey on horseback with this very servant, who, according to the old lama, must not leave the place, and when the coat so ostentatiously deposited in my tent had lain some twenty-four hours unclaimed, I began to be curious as to what it all meant, and wished to know what truth was in the intimation that I was not at liberty to travel. So I made my way to the abode of the mandarin. Happily he lived in the hamlet beside which I was encamped, and he had actually been in my tent when the assault took place, so that he was well acquainted with all that had happened. As to the coat, he advised me to return it by the hands of my servant, and ask what was meant by leaving it with me, and then the old lama would doubtless say what his intentions were. As to travelling, both I and my servant might go anywhere we liked till we were forbidden to do so by orders from the government office of the tribe; and, he added, as a day and a half had elapsed since information of the case had been forwarded to the governor, and no reply had yet arrived, it was not at all likely that either I or my servant would be troubled by a summons.

Having thus delivered his official opinion he proceeded in a friendly informal way to tell me his private opinion of the whole affair. It was this. The old lama being greedy had reviled my servant for trying to hire me horses cheaply. My servant's lama brother had heard of this, and coming to my tent to resent it had, in a moment of passion, broken the old lama's head. who, mounting his horse, had ridden over the plain to where the young lama's horse was pasturing, had carried it off, and placed it for safe keeping in the hands of a third party. He said the old lama was making much ado about nothing, as a Mongol's head was not likely to suffer much from such a knock as he had received, and that it was evident that he had not suffered much, as he had ridden about for a great part of the day on which the attack had been made.

In Mongolia all tents, even those of mandarins, seem open to everybody, so that anything that is said is soon known to all. The old lama had evidently heard what had been said. He took his coat, said that if the mandarin approved of my going I was at liberty to travel, but persisted that my servant must on no account leave the place. Nevertheless, when the time for departure came, we mounted and rode off slowly, to give opportunity to any one who should pursue us to overtake us easily; but no one hindered our going, and on our return we were glad to learn that the attempts at reconciliation, which had been made in vain before we started, had proved successful in our absence, and that the two lamas were once more good friends. The young lama had broken the old lama's head, the old lama had seized and ridden the young lama's horse, and though two wrongs don't make a right, on the young man making an apology, the old man had been content to cry quits; peace was once more restored to the little community. The vexation and expense of a tedious lawsuit were thus avoided.

Such is the sum of my experience in appealing to Mongol mandarins. I have kept as clear of them as I could, and I find that for the most part they are not anxious to interfere. They avoid interference as much as possible, and their attitude towards missions seems to be much the same as that of the Japanese official, who is reported to have privately advised missionaries in that country to go on with mission work as much as they liked, " only don't bring yourselves and your work before our official notice

CHAPTER XI.

LAMA MIAO.

Situation. Meaning of name. Trading centre. Man being starved to death. The cage. Demeanour of the criminal. Tantalising the sufferer. The "*Mirth of Hell*." Jeering of the crowd. Death. Hardheartedness of the Chinese.

LAMA MIAO, as the Chinese call it, Dolon Nor, as the Mongols call it, is a great trading settlement in Mongolia, lying about a hundred and fifty English miles north-east of Kalgan. "Lama Miao" means "The Lama Temple," and this name it owes to the fact of there being two large Lama Temples about half a mile from it; "Dolon Nor" means "Seven Lakes," and this name it owes to the abundance of little pools or lakes in its neighbourhood. It has a large population of Chinese traders, and is famous as a market for oxen, and especially famous for horses. But it is not my purpose in the present chapter to speak of the lakes, the temples, the large Chinese population, or the flourishing barter trade that characterise the place. The name of Lama Miao is always associated in my recollection with a spectacle that I have witnessed nowhere else, namely, that of a man being slowly and deliberately put to death by being starved in a cage.

Near one end of the main street, and forming one of the boundaries of an open space used as a market, is a great wall forming the screen in front of the government office. As we passed with our caravan we noticed a crowd collected there, and after getting into an inn, on returning to the place we found that the object of interest to the spectators was a man, said to be a robber, who was fixed into a cage in such a way that only his head protruded. The frame fitted closely to his neck, and the cage being too low for him to stand up in, and too high for him to sit down in, he had to maintain a kind of half-crouching half-kneeling posture, which must have been very painful. We learned that being condemned to death he was fixed in that cage, and was to remain there until death terminated his sufferings. He had not the look of a man who had been kept without nourishment, and had endured the torture of a cramped position for two days, and his demeanour was as far as possible removed from that which might have been expected of a man undergoing sufferings which he knew must, in a day or two, culminate in his death.

As we came near we found him keeping up a brisk and bantering conversation with the crowd of Chinamen, who, in the slack of business and the cool of the evening, had come out to have their walk and a look at the doomed man. We made our way through the crowd, and he noticed us, spoke to us, made faces at us, and passed jeering remarks about us as being foreigners. Prominent among the loungers was a burly Chinaman, who, as he kept pouring cash from his one hand to the other, pointed to the tea-shops and eating-houses near at hand, and seemed to confine his conversation with the starving man to remarks about food and drink. The lively and careless appearance of the man, and the levity and mirth not only pervading the crowd, but which the caged man seemed to participate in as eagerly as any one of the bystanders, made it impossible to believe that the assembly gathered there was composed of men who had come to see a fellow being in the process of being starved to death before their eyes.

In China many things are not what they profess to be, and the most reasonable conclusion to be drawn from the man's appearance and the tone of the crowd, was that though nominally being starved to death he was being fed. We were assured, however, to the contrary, and while amazed at the apathy of the crowd could account for the boisterous conduct of the prisoner himself, only either by supposing that it was a striking instance of that hilarity of misery which some one has called the "mirth of hell," or by the more charitable supposition that the sufferings he had already endured had affected his brain, and that he was not responsible for his sayings and doings.

The following day I spent in my tent encamped at the Yellow or West Temple, and did not see the caged man myself, but as I returned with my camels in the evening I saw the cage being carried into the *yamen* amid the happy and jeering remarks of the crowd, and my companion, who had seen him during the day, reported a great change for the worse in the man's appearance since the previous evening.

The fourth day of his torture terminated the wretched man's sufferings, somewhat to the surprise of the inhabitants, who, probably from previous experience, expected that this horrible exhibition would have afforded them a rendezvous in their leisure and relaxation for a day or two longer. The man died, the cage was no longer exposed, and doubtless the whole circumstance soon passed away from the minds of the Chinese who had stood round the doomed man smoking their pipes and jesting with and at the poor wretch. But truly the tender mercies of the wicked are cruel.

China boasts, and with great right too, of her civilisation, but no particle of humanity can be claimed by that government, which, in exacting the forfeited life of a subject, condemns him to days of preliminary and entirely gratuitous agony, and, not content with simply starving him to death, exposes the famishing wretch in full view of the tea-shops, where he is tantalised by seeing thirsty men seated at tables leisurely drinking refreshing tea, and can smell the savoury viands with which hungry men satisfy their appetites. Government and people, too, are well matched. It was natural enough that Chinamen in such a place as Lama Miao should direct their walk in the leisure of an evening to such an exhibition as that in front of the *yamen;* and when it is remembered that the conducting of such a trade as that on which the Lama Miao depends, frequently necessitates the travelling of lone men with money through sparsely peopled regions, it is not to be wondered at that public indignation should burn strongly against such highway robbers as may fall into the hands of justice. Yet the amount of even dormant humanity must be but small in the breast of any man, whom even a justified and strong indignation could render perfectly callous to such sufferings as were endured by the miserable prisoner in the cage.

In a promiscuous crowd it would not have been strange had there been a proportion of heartless men, who, destitute of all proper feeling, could see nothing in the punishment of sin but subjects for jesting; but the remarkable feature of that Lama Miao crowd was the apparently entire absence of any trace of commiseration or compassion in every one, young or old. While it was impossible to look without horror on the condition of the poor dying wretch whose sufferings rendered him delirious, it was impossible to look on the multitude around him showing symptoms of being dead to all compassion, and not pity the hardness of their hearts.

Much has been said by scholars in favour of Confucianism. "By their fruits ye shall know them." Here we have a government which for centuries has professed to follow and to teach to its people the doctrines of Confucius, and a people who as far as they are anything are Confucian, and yet the government in carrying out the extreme penalty of its law, divesting itself of dignity and compassion, deliberately revels in ingenious cruelty, and the people, seemingly dead to all humanity, stand by pleased and applauding. If this is the fruit of Confucian teaching, it is high time that China had something better, and it will be a happy day for China and her people when Confucianism pales before the rising light of Christianity, and the government, ashamed of past cruelties, when compelled to exact the penalty of a forfeited life, shall be ingenious to mitigate the horrors of execution, and the people shall learn to have compassion and sympathy for misery even in the case of those whose sufferings are the just punishment of their sins.

CHAPTER XII.

URGA.

Religious capital of Mongolia. Situation. Mongol name. The "Green House." View from behind the Russian Consulate. Wind. The Chinese trading town. Chinese cash currency introduced. Chinese not allowed to take their wives to Urga. Temples in the Mongol settlement. Praying-wheels at street corners. Worship by prostration. Mongol reason for it. The open market. Audacious eagles. The priestly part of Urga. The trade of Urga. Tea agencies. Beggars in the market-place. Wickedness of Urga.

URGA is the great religious centre of North Mongolia, and a place of considerable trading importance. It is about six hundred miles from the north frontier of China at Kalgan, and about two hundred miles from the south frontier of Russia at Kiachta; it is situated on the north bank of the river Tola, and is called by the Mongols, Huræ, "Huræ" meaning "enclosure" or "encampment," the full Mongol name of the place being "Bogdt Lama en Huræ," the enclosure or encampment of the supreme lama. The Chinese call it "The Great Encampment," and the Russians call it "Urga," which is possibly a corruption of the Mongol Huræ.

On approaching it from the south, one of the most prominent objects is the "Green House," as the Russian consulate is called, which stands on elevated ground, and is visible from afar. Perhaps the finest view of the neighbourhood is to be had from a stony hill which rises behind the consulate. Standing on this hill, the consulate is immediately below in front. The Chinese trading town lies some distance to the left or east, the Mongolian settlement and temples to the right or west. The view is closed on all sides by mountains, some of which are high, and one, the large one right in front on the side of the valley, opposite to the consulate, is heavily wooded. The wood does not come to the base of the mountain, and seems darker at the top than lower down, owing probably to a different kind of tree preferring the greater altitude. This wood-clothed hill seems very beautiful, and its beauty is sometimes enhanced by great clouds which rest on it, hiding the top and coming some distance down its side, then clear away, leaving the submerged part of the forest white with the vapour frozen on the trees, the line marking the cloud limit being almost as level and distinct as the high-water mark on the sea-shore.

The sombre monotony of the valley is relieved by the gleaming waters of the Tola, which emerge from between mountains on the east, and flowing past disappears into a broad plain partly visible through a wide gap in the belt of hills which closes the view on the west.

Urga is a great place for wind, which during most of the months of the year is so cold as to make a spectator on the stony hill behind the consulate glad to descend to some less exposed position. The Chinese trading town on the east is well worthy of a visit. The population may be about five thousand, and there seem to be some wealthy firms doing a large business. Almost every courtyard is bounded by a high fence of the stems of young trees placed close together, and often plastered over with mud, and in nearly every establishment is visible from the street the brazen sheen of the brightly-polished Russian samovar. The streets are moderately busy, with Chinese going hither and thither, and with Mongols bent on shopping expeditions. It is said that recently Chinese brass cash has been introduced as the circulating medium for the retail trade but till within a few years ago buyers in the market used to be conspicuous from the clumsy bricks of tea which they carried in their arms or lashed to their saddles. The whole of the Chinese employed in trade at Urga live a life of self-imposed banishment, being prevented by law from bringing their wives and families, and for the most part revisit their native land at intervals of from five to ten years. Some of them return oftener, some of them stay away longer, but very few settle permanently, and thus the law forbidding the taking of their families is successful in its evident intention, namely, in keeping the traders attached to China and Chinese interests. The Mongol settlement is to the westward, and distant some two or three miles, the Russian consulate being situated between the two centres.

The most conspicuous objects in the Mongol town are the temples, which from afar look lofty and grand, but lose much of their imposing effect when approached and examined closely. In these temple premises, and at many street corners and busy places, are erected numerous praying-wheels, supposed to be filled inside, many of them decorated outside, and some of them almost literally covered all round, with prayers, the idea being that any devout believer who turns the wheel, by so doing acquires as much merit as if he or she had repeated all the prayers thus set in motion. These praying-cylinders seem to be seldom left long at rest. In the quiet deserted-looking precincts of the temple may be heard the creaking of the rusty spindle, as it is turned in its unoiled socket by worshippers, who most likely have come from the country to perform their devotion at this great religious centre. Many, both lamas and laymen, male and female, as they pass along the streets, lay hold of the inviting handle and give a turn to such praying-machines as they find standing in their path.

In front of temples may be seen sloping wooden platforms, at which men or women are busy making rapid prostrations towards these holy places; and all about the stony environs of this great stronghold of Buddhist faith may be met devotees painfully and slowly travelling round great circuits, measuring their way by "falling worship," that is, lying down flat on their faces and marking the place of their next prostration by their forehead or by a piece of wood held in their hand. This falling worship is very exhausting, and soon wears out the clothes and the hands; and those who perform long journeys in this way usually fit wooden sandals to the hands and sheepskins to the knees.

Ask the Mongols what is the supposed benefit of this bodily worship, and they have a very plausible answer at hand. They divide the sins which men commit into three classes, those of the body, the tongue, and the mind, and, say they, since the sins are committed by the body, the tongue, and the mind, it is only fair that these three should bear each their proper share in expiating the sins, so while they prostrate themselves they keep repeating prayers with their tongue and endeavour to fix their minds on sacred objects.

It is common in some quarters to bestow high praise on Buddhism, and there are not wanting men who, as far as they are anything, are Christians, and yet profess to doubt the necessity for attempting to supersede human religions by the Divine teachings of Christianity. But though full credit be allowed to all such doctrines of Buddhism as are good, the most indifferent and unenthusiastic Christian could not walk about the environs of Urga without wishing that these deluded people were taught a more excellent way of salvation.

The great Chinese trade is in the Chinese town, but there is a brisk retail trade in the Mongol town, in shops both Russian and Chinese, and in the market which is held daily in the great open square, where provisions and necessaries of all sorts are sold. Over the outskirts small eagles soar about, whistling and wheeling, watching for an opportunity to swoop down and seize the few ounces of mutton or beef carried in the one hand of a returning purchaser whose other hand is employed with the rosary, and whose gaze is for the moment directed to some passing object of interest.

These market eagles are adepts at their trade, and are great proofs of how the Mongols carry out the teachings of Buddhism with regard to the sacredness of life. In most countries these birds would soon have to give up their business, or shift their locality, but the Mongols take them as a matter of course, and, quickly recovering from the momentary fright caused by the rush of the wings, pick up the meat, which is more frequently merely knocked out of the hand than actually carried off, apply to the retreating bird the epithet "Patricide," and quickly go on their way counting their beads and looking about them as if nothing had happened.

On the extreme west of Urga, and on a higher level than the other parts, stands a town, consisting of a temple and a cluster of houses, which is regarded as peculiarly holy. It is said that no layman and no woman is allowed to live there, and this forms perhaps the most sacred part of Urga.

As to the population of Urga, one who has seen it for only a day or two is hardly in a position to hazard a guess, as temple buildings and lama residences are very misleading when relied on as affording indications as to the number of inhabitants. We may reckon the Chinese traders as numbering probably about five thousand, and the Mongols may exceed them by a thousand or two; but it should be remembered that Urga, being a sacerdotal town, the number of inhabitants fluctuates with circumstances. When I was there the residents of the place may have been fewer than usual, owing to the fact that the Supreme Lama had some time before died, and had not yet been recovered in his "transmigrated" form.

The main exports of Urga are hides from the wide districts of surrounding country and timber from its great hill forests. Its chief imports are tea and materials for clothing, which are distributed from here as a centre; but it depends for no small part of its importance on the fact that it is a great stage in the tea-carrying trade between China and Russia. It is true that some of the tea which goes north from Kalgan is contracted for by Mongols, who undertake to convey it right across the desert and deliver it in Kiachta, but the greater part is contracted for only as far as Urga, where new carriers have to be found to forward it over the remaining two hundred miles of desert. And it is not at all surprising that this should be so. In addition to the great distance from China, six hundred miles, which most carriers doubtless suppose a sufficiently long stage, the country north of Urga is so different from that to the south, it is not strange that one set of men should accustom themselves to the exigencies of travelling on the great plains of South Mongolia and Gobi, while another set of men should accustom themselves to the ascents and descents of the hills and valleys that lie between Urga and Kiachta. The Russian establishments at Urga seem to be mostly those of agents whose duty it is to receive consignments of tea from the south, examine into its condition, to see whether it has been allowed to get wet or been broken into during its transport, settle with the carriers, and arrange for its further transport to Kiachta. The presence of a consul is required to preside over this trade, and thus it comes that the Russians have a settlement at Urga. For the most part, the number of Russians at Urga is small, but when the unsettled state of the country demands it, armed force is sent sufficient to protect the consulate. In 1871 quite a formidable little detachment was moved from Kiachta and took up its position beside the "Green House." It would appear, however, that when the danger passed these troops were withdrawn, and Urga relapsed into its normal condition.

Urga is in many respects a remarkable place, and there are some grand and many strange sights to be seen in it, but in all probability the deepest impression will not be made by the grandly-wooded hill, the gleaming Tola, or the gilded temples; most likely the mind of the visitor will be haunted for years after by the sight of the beggars in the market-place. Urga swarms with beggars, both in the market-place and everywhere, but the ordinary beggar seen there is not much out of the usual run of mendicants, and does not elicit more than usual compassion.

There is a class of beggars to be seen in Urga, however, whom having once seen it is not easy to forget, and that is those who are too far gone and too helpless to beg more, and take up their abode out on the open, stony, cold market-place, live on what is offered them, and die when their time comes. It is a bleak, cold place, seemingly seldom free from wind, and though the able-bodied among the beggars manage to put up something behind which they lie down partly sheltered, the helpless ones lie exposed to all the blasts that blow. They are usually covered with an accumulation of pieces of old felt and skin-coat rags, and there they lie in all weathers, regarded with seemingly perfect indifference by those who pass, eating such things as charity may put into their cup, till some morning their lair is found empty, and any of the rags that are worth having become the property of such of the survivors as may be able to appropriate them. Considering the seemingly perfect indifference with which these dying creatures are regarded, it is a relief and almost a surprise to find that they are removed when dead. They are not carried far, however. A very short distance from the Russian consulate numerous skulls, many of them fresh, may be found lying about in the water-worn ravines, where they have been left after being picked as clean as canine teeth and perseverance can make them.

The visitor, on first walking about Urga, will be exceptionally indifferent if he has not his spirit stirred within him at the superstitious practices and devices that meet his eye. Should he happen to know the language and remain, especially in native lodgings, for a day or two, he will have his spirit much more deeply moved by the wickedness that comes under his notice. Urga is the head-quarters of the Buddhism of North Mongolia, it is also a stronghold of unblushing sin. Its wickedness does not spring from any one source, but the full tide of the stream of iniquity that rolls through it is fed by several tributaries, which uniting make up the dark flood of its evil. Thus it happens that the encampment of the Supreme Lama of Mongolia is reputed to be the most supremely wicked place in the whole of that wide country.

CHAPTER XIII.

WU T'AI SHAN.

The great sacred place of Mongol pilgrimage. Advantages secured by pilgrims. Surrounding scenery. "The hamlet in the bosom of the mountains." Temple on hill-top. Beauty of scenery. Temple above a gateway. Three hundred praying-wheels. Immense praying-wheel. P'u Sa T'ing. Pneumatic praying-wheel. "The ice that never melts." Shrines on hill-tops. Hardships of Mongol pilgrims. Worn-out pilgrims escorted home. Expeditions of lamas from Wu T'ai to Mongolia. System of granting annuities.

As Jerusalem to the Jews, as Mecca to the Mahometans, so is Wu T'ai Shan to the Mongols. All over Mongolia, and wherever Mongols are met with in North China, one is constantly reminded of this place. It is true that the mania which possesses the Mongols for making pilgrimages carries them to many other shrines, some of which are both celebrated and much frequented, but none of them can be compared to Wu T'ai. At all seasons of the year, in the dead of winter, in the heat of summer, pilgrims, priests, and laymen, male and female, old and young, rich and poor, solitary and in bands, on foot and mounted, from places far and near, may be seen going to and returning from this, the most sacred spot on earth to the Mongol Buddhist, the object of his devout aspirations during life, the place where he desires

PILGRIMS APPROACHING A TEMPLE. [*From a Native Sketch.*]
1. Cairn with praying flags flying.

nis bones to be thrown at death. The Mongols speak of it as one of the blessed spots of the earth, holy, purified, everlasting, indestructible, and destined to survive the otherwise universal ruin that is to ensue at the close of the present stage of the world's existence. They say that any beast which eats the grass and drinks the water of the place is sure to be born hereafter into a higher state. One visit made to it by a pilgrim is said to ensure him happiness for the period of one of his future lives, two visits for two lives, three visits for three lives, and so on. In this way every devout Mongol endeavours to make at least one pilgrimage to this mountain during his lifetime, a number of them go frequently, and there are some who endeavour to visit it every year.

In addition to this promise of happiness after death, a journey to Wu T'ai is frequently prescribed as a cure for disease, and the merit of making these journeys is supposed to be transferable, so that it is no uncommon thing to meet Mongols going to Wu T'ai, not on their own account, but for the benefit of others.

This mountain is situated, not in Mongolia, but in China, in the province of Shansi, and having heard a great deal about it, I, in company with two other missionaries, set out to visit it. On the afternoon of the eleventh day after leaving Peking, we found ourselves going up a valley, which became narrower and narrower as we went on. Temples began to be numerous, and just as the sun set we came upon an image cut out in the solid rock and painted with bright colours. On the same rock also were cut Tibetan characters, and from these and other signs we knew that we were coming near the famous Wu T'ai.

Darkness gradually settled down upon us, and the few people we met kept telling us that we were still a mile or two from the end of our journey. We would ask a man, "How far?" he would say, "A mile or two." We would go on, and still the next man would say as before, "A mile or two." At last we saw, a little ahead, the lights of the small Chinese village where we were to put up—"The hamlet in the bosom of the mountains."

Next morning we found that the name described the place very well. All round were hills, some of them so high that the morning light shone clear on their tops, while in the village below all was shade and gloom, and it was not till late in the forenoon that the sun was able to climb the east hill and look over the ridge down into the court of our inn.

Close to the village a hill rose steeply up, like a cone of loaf-sugar, and, seeing a temple on the top, we found it to be a shrine to which Chinese resort to pray for children. It seemed to be quite a famous temple, and was hung almost full of its own praises, written on red cloth and silk, the grateful offerings of votaries, who in this way returned thanks for having their prayers answered. In the temple we found only one priest, a Chinaman. He was old, deaf, could not read, and spoke a dialect so different from that of Peking that we could not talk much with him.

From the hill-top we counted about thirty temples. We could see almost no level land, but all up the hill-sides, nearly to the very summit, the Chinese had made terraces and sown them with oats.

The month was October, and the oats had been reaped, carried down, and piled up around the threshing-floors, where men were busy with flails threshing out the grain. There seemed scarcely enough level land to make threshing-floors, yet from the hill-sides good crops had been gathered, and there was abundance of food all along the valley.

While the brawling of the torrent rose mingled with the sound of the flail, it was a striking view to behold the encircling belt of mountains, the valleys with their streams, the forest on the south, the snow on the north, the temples flashing back the sunlight from their golden towers, the trains of camels winding slowly along, and the groups of worshipping pilgrims, sacred staff in hand, going the round of the temples.

One of the first temples we visited was a curious little upper chamber over the gate of the village. In the shrine, among the other images, was pointed out to us one, which, said the priests, had wonderful virtue. From a little mark on its brow could be drawn out a hair a thousand miles long, and from the body of the image a blaze of light shone out regularly three nights every month. So said the lamas. On the altars before the images were numerous little lamps trimmed and burning. The butter for the lights is supplied from the gifts of devout pilgrims. To give butter for the lamps is a common way of making an offering to the gods.

The priests lived in a little court below, and we had tea offered us in a very neat quiet room. The lamas of this temple were educated men, and we found them engaged in copying a large sacred book, in letters of gold, on blue cardboard. The Mongols believe that to write out a sacred book in black ink brings much merit, to write it in red ink brings more merit, but to write it in gold brings most merit.

Among the other temples which we visited was one

with a large tope or mound. At the base of the tope were mounted more than three hundred praying-wheels, which the worshippers set in motion one after the other as they passed round. Inside a building of the same temple, we came upon an immense praying-wheel, about sixty feet high, containing shrines, images, books, and prayers. To the devout Mongol, such a wheel is a most useful invention. It is filled with books and prayers which would take him a lifetime to read and repeat. Most likely he cannot read, or if he can read, he cannot find time to read so much, so he comes to the temple; two or three together go down to the cellar, lay hold on the hand-spokes, and with a long pull, a strong pull, and a pull all together, round goes the wheel, and each one of them believes he gains just as much merit as if he had read the books, repeated the prayers, and knocked his head to all the gods that grin from the shelves and shrines of the wheel. No wonder that the Mongols travel hundreds of miles to reach so quick a method of making merit!

But the temple of all the temples at Wu T'ai is P'u Sa T'ing. It stands central among the others, and in it lives the Zassak lama, who rules all the other lamas. The P'u Sa T'ing is built along the ridge of a hill, and is reached by a very steep path, at the top of which rises a flight of over one hundred steps. We climbed up and entered. We found a street lined on both sides with houses built in the Tibetan style, and evidently crowded with lamas and pilgrims. The houses and the people did not look clean, and the street looked worse than either, being partly blocked up with piles of wood and argol, to be used as fuel. We were taken to the room of the attendant of the great lama, and a snug room it was, being clean, comfortable, and kept warm by a charcoal fire in a well-polished brass brasier. Near the ceiling, just above the charcoal fire, hung a paper cylinder, like an inverted wheel of life, which kept constantly turning. This also was a praying-wheel, and was kept in motion by the hot air ascending from the fire. In this way, whether the lama slept or ate, was at home or abroad, entertained his friends or attended to his superior, the wheel kept continually turning, and merit was always coming to his abode. Such was his idea.

We sent in a present of a New Testament and some tracts in Mongolian to the Zassak lama, and said we would call on him if he wished to see us. He sent back a polite message, asking for our welfare and comfort on the journey, begging us to accept a small present in return, and saying he was sorry he could not see us, as he was engaged in preparing for a great festival called the Ch'am Haren, or Sacred Dance.

Our last day at the T'ai I spent on the mountains. On one mountain—the central terrace—there is what the Chinese call, "The ten thousand years' ice," what the Mongols call, "The ice that never melts." This ice is held in high esteem by the simple-minded pilgrims, and when at Wu T'ai some of them go up the hill and carry off a piece to work cures on their sick friends at home. The place was not difficult to find. It is at the foot of a precipice high up on the north side of a steep hill. A spring issues from the rock, the water freezes up in winter, and part of the ice, untouched by the sun's rays, lasts all the summer through. It is quite easy to see why the ice does not melt: but the Mongols are taught that it is a miracle, and also believe that the ice can work miracles. One lama assured us that the ice was a cure for all disorders and a preserver of general health. If what he said had been true, I could not have been in danger of any sickness for some time to come, because my lunch for that day consisted of Chinese biscuit and a lump of the ice that never melts.

Leaving the ice I climbed the north terrace, perhaps the highest of the five hills. The crest of the hill was speckled with snow, and the view from the top was grand. On every side, as far as the eye could reach, was one vast sea of mighty mountains, some of which, it is said, rise ten thousand feet above the level of the sea. Only one thing was out of keeping—the temples in the valley below, and the gods in the shrines on the hill-tops. Wherever there is a pretty spot in China or Mongolia, there the Buddhists build their temples and bow themselves to their idols. The shrines on the hill-tops were very rude affairs, enclosures formed by rough stone walls, and containing ragamuffin gods—stocks of weather-beaten wood, blocks of battered stone, and lumps of rusty old iron. The carved wooden gods were so much the worse for the weather, that their features, if they ever had any, were altogether defaced. One, not made of a single piece, like the rest, but built together by joiner work, had fared worse than its more humble neighbours. His arms were gone, and his breast, heart, and stomach had all fallen out, strange to say, his head remained; and it was laughable to see such a hollow mockery stare at you with a solemn face. The stone images were sadly battered by tumbling about among the rubbish, and the cast-metal gods mostly had their heads broken off and set carefully on again, to stand there till the next storm would send them rolling. Thus God is not only robbed in the valley, but men climb up as near to heaven as they can, and insult Him to His face. They put up their wretched images and say, "These are the gods of the hills." It is to these and such-like gods that the Mongols come from far to pay their vows and offer their donations; and all along the road, going and returning, the Mongols asked us if we were going to Wu T'ai to worship; the Chinese, if we went to burn incense. This always gave us an opportunity to tell them about the true God and the true worship. By selling books and distributing them, by preaching and conversation at the T'ai, and on the way, we sought to teach Mongols and Chinese to know and love the God who is not to be represented by images, and who is to be worshipped neither on Mount Wu T'ai, nor in Peking, but in spirit and in truth.

We returned by a route different from that by which we went, but along both roads we found evidences of Mongol pilgrimage in Mongol notices printed on the front of the inn, saying that—" The men of this inn are honest and mild, everything is ready and cheap, therefore, O ye Mongols, our brothers, you could not do better than rest here." We put up at one of these inns, and the men may have been honest and mild, but certainly things were neither ready nor cheap, we had to wait a long time for a poor dinner, and pay a long bill for it when it came.

Though the Mongols seem to take naturally to pilgrimages, and travel long distances in their own country without much inconvenience, the travelling through the Chinese territory that separates Wu T'ai from Mongolia is a great hardship to them. In Mongolia they feed their cattle on the plain and pay nothing for lodging, in China they have to pay for lodging, cooking, fodder, and, in many cases, even for the watering of their animals. In some cases a large company of pilgrims travel with carts and cattle along the plain till they reach the point nearest to Wu T'ai. Arrived there they leave their carts and most of their cattle in the keeping of Mongols, and thus, in light marching order as it were, make the best of their way to Wu T'ai, avoiding in this way the heavy demands that would be made upon their slender stock of money if accompanied by many beasts of burden. On returning once more to Mongolia, they heave a sigh of relief, pay a small fee for the keeping of their cattle, and journey homeward joyously through their own inexpensive country. There is no more severe test of the earnestness of the religious devotion of the Mongols than their being willing thus to journey for days through the country of unsympathetic Chinamen, whose language they do not understand, and who lie in wait for their money, ready to fleece them at every turn, charging them even for the water that their horses drink, which, though fair and just according to Chinese custom, the Mongols regard as the height of extortion.

The lamas of Wu T'ai seize every opportunity of strengthening and extending their connection with the Mongols of the plain. Sometimes a party of pilgrims reach Wu T'ai on foot, but are so worn out by the journey that they feel unable to return home. The temple they lodge at sends them home under the care of one or two of its lamas, who receive gifts for their temple not only from the families of the pilgrims they have thus assisted, but also from the devout inhabitants

LAMA DEPUTATIONS.

of the neighbouring country, to whom the assisted pilgrims introduce them as their benefactors. In many cases the succouring of a company of distressed pilgrims proves a paying speculation.

Not content with this, the temples at Wu T'ai are in the habit of fitting out annual collecting expeditions, which, consisting of several lamas, start in spring, travel about with carts and tents in summer, and return before winter, carrying with them sometimes large sums of money and driving before them flocks and herds, the offerings of the faithful. These expeditions are numerous and indefatigable, and perhaps there is no tent, rich or poor, throughout the whole length and breadth of the eastern half of Mongolia, which is not visited by such deputations every year. These collectors penetrate even beyond the bounds of the Chinese empire, and carry off rich offerings from the Buriats, who, compared with Mongols, are wealthy. Food, tea, skins, cattle, money, all are eagerly received, and one of the considerations that induce men to make these offerings is, that the names of donors are entered on the subscription list; they thus become in some sense patrons of the temple, and they are pleased to think that they have connections with Wu T'ai, and that the next time they visit that sacred place, they will not be going among strangers, but will be received as old acquaintances by those who experienced their hospitality in the desert, and were the recipients of their pious gifts.

The lamas of Wu T'ai also seek to increase their influence by a practice which resembles the granting of annuities. When a Mongol has been rich in his younger days, but in his old age is somewhat reduced in circumstances, and has no son on whom he can devolve the management of his affairs, he sometimes seeks to escape from the losing battle of life by transferring all his property to some temple at Wu T'ai, on condition that the temple will feed, lodge, and clothe him and his for the term of their natural lives. This arrangement has a great fascination for some; it relieves them from anxiety about their temporal affairs, frees them from the necessity of labour in their declining years, and permits them to devote the close of their life, without distraction, to the duties of religion. It is not uncommon for Mongols, suffering from some disease that is considered mortal, to leave their homes, and await death in the temple belonging to their native place; but happy above all others is he considered, who, before sickness has laid its hand upon him, can leave the turmoil of the world, and withdraw himself to the longed-for sanctity and peace, which he hopes to find in the holy temples among the sacred valleys of the blessed Wu T'ai Shan.

Knowing the intense worldliness, the unblushing wickedness, the thievish dishonesty, and the envy and strife that characterise, with but few exceptions, almost the whole tribe of lamas, one cannot but pity decent, quiet old men, who, for the peace of their souls, retire to such dens of iniquity. But they do it with their eyes open, after life-long experience of lamas and temples, with all their faults and wickednesses, and, to tell the truth, the abominations do not seem to disturb them.

Mongol Buddhism and holiness have long ago parted company, and it seems possible for men and women living among and partaking in scenes of unblushing evil, to be at the same time experiencing in their souls the effectual consolations of their religion. This seems at first sight almost incredible, but I am convinced it is true, and perhaps no more serious charge could be brought against any religion than this, which holds true of Buddhism, that notwithstanding many excellent doctrines that characterise it as a theory, its practical effect is to delude its votaries as to moral guilt, to sear their consciences as with a hot iron, to call the wicked righteous, and send men down to the grave with a lie in their right hand.

CHAPTER XIV.

KALGAN.

Meaning of the name. A table-land eaten away by water. Picking the bones of the skeleton. Picturesque rocks. "Heavenly fish." Houses perched on the hill-side. Difficult entrance. Custom of dismounting at the gate. Upper Kalgan. Lower town. Building land scarce. Falling stones. Thunderstorm at dark. Kalgan a great market for Mongol wants. The Chinese trade. The tea trade. Tea villages on the plain. Transport of tea to Siberia. Imports. Soldiers' quarters. Government offices. American missionaries.

MANY Mongols live and die without seeing any Chinese town but Kalgan. The Chinese call this place Chang Chia K'ou—or the pass of the Chang family, but as it is entered from the north by a gate through which Mongols pass the Great Wall and thus enter China, they habitually speak of it as "THE GATE" or "Halga," and the term Kalgan has been introduced to the foreign world generally by the Russians, who adopted it as shorter and more easy to pronounce and write than the corresponding Chinese term.

Travellers from the plain before reaching this Chinese mart have to cross a mountain range, the highest part of which is said to reach an elevation of 5,400 feet above the level of the sea. The view from this part of the road is grand, and embraces a vast panorama of mountains and dry torrent beds, with one permanently flowing river, gleaming away far off in the west and looking narrow, as the actual stream at any one time occupies only a small portion of the broad belt of desolate gravel which marks the area within which the wanderings of the stream are confined.

Standing on the pass above Kalgan, the nearer landscape presents only one feature—the long-extended edge of a high table-land in process of being eaten away by the action of water. Grand and striking as the view at first appears, closer examination soon makes it manifest that there is little but uniformity in the whole landscape, and that the vast bed of the distant river and the great valley close below are nothing more than magnified exhibitions of the little stream close at hand, and the little ditch worn in the ridge by the last rain. This process of eating away has gone on till its progress was suddenly arrested by the great rocky barrier which forms the edge of the plateau.

Standing on the top of the pass, it is not difficult, even for an unimaginative spectator, to conceive that the great low-lying plain visible before him was formerly a table-land, and that the untired energy of the floods of successive summers kept washing away the gravel and loess composing it, leaving as mountains anything hard enough to resist the action of water.

From the plain great valleys run up into the present edge of the remaining table-land, their course being determined by rocks which defied the streams. These great valleys have running off from them many smaller valleys, these again have their numerous smaller branches, which again ramify into numerous subdivisions, the whole system resembling much the trunk, limbs, branches, and twigs of a tree. The great period of rapid and unimpeded disintegration has long since passed, and though the wearing away still goes on, it is on a scale small as compared with what it must have been ages ago. The waters are now for the most part working out the soil and gravel from rock-bound situations—picking the bones of the skeleton, as it were.

Mongols, however, bound from their homes to Kalgan, do not lose time viewing the landscape or indulging in geological theories as to changes on the earth's surface. Dismounting and leading their horses, they scramble down the steep as best they can, re-adjust their saddles on reaching the bottom, have a smoke, and, sticking their pipes into their boots, remount and hold on their way down the stony torrent-bed which leads to Kalgan. The valley varies in width, and is, along most of its course, hemmed in by steep hills, some of them many hundreds of feet in height. Clinging to the hill-sides in two or three places, where the valley widens out a little, are villages, and many of the houses are simply excavations in the cliff, with doors and windows fitted in to form a front. The washing away of the soil has in places brought out curious-looking rocks into bold relief, to one of which, shaped something like the handle of a cup, the Mongols say that one of their legendary heroes tied his horse, from which this avenue to Kalgan is named the "Handle Pass."

Except during floods at the rainy season there is little water in this valley. About half of its course is dry, the permanent stream being so small that it disappears among the stones and comes to the surface again a long way farther down. When a flood does come, which is but seldom, perhaps once or twice a

MONGOL PIPE AND POUCH.

year, it fills the broad bed of the torrent from shore to shore, sweeping everything before it, carrying down with it in its headlong course thousands of tons of gravel and stones, which strike against the rocks with such force as to leave them marked with fresh bruises to a height of several feet.

A curious phenomenon which follows floods in this valley, is the presence of little fish, which are found in the stream when it has become clear and quieted down to its ordinary limits. The Chinese come out with bowls and catch them, taking them home to their shops as a curiosity, and calling them "Heavenly Fish." They are tiny little creatures, and the question is, where do they come from? It is not to be supposed that they are in the stream while the flood lasts—the violence of the torrent and the gravel would dash them and grind them to pieces. They must emerge then afterwards. But whence? And why do they come only after a flood? Can their home be in some subterranean cavern, from which they can escape only when its waters overflow from the replenishment of a flood?

The traveller coming from the north by the zigzag course of the torrent-bed leading down from the "Handle Pass," travels ten or twelve miles without seeing anything of Kalgan, till, turning a corner, he comes upon houses so crowded upon insufficient standing-ground in a recess of the valley, that some of them are perched high up on natural or artificial terraces on the hill-side. This may be called the north-west suburb of Kalgan, and here it is that the Russians engaged in the tea trade are located. From this point down to Kalgan proper, the traveller passes between two almost continuous lines of Chinese shops, defended from the river by substantial masonry, and pressed back close to the steep hill, looking like spectators forced up against the walls when the street is cleared to allow a procession to pass along a narrow road-way. The great highway from the river-bed into Kalgan goes straight up a breakwater, rising so high and so abruptly, that it is only with great difficulty that loaded carts can ascend or descend. Attempts are made from time to time to make the ascent more gradual by heaping up gravel, but it seems to be no one's duty to keep this part of the road in permanent repair; the continual traffic, or a flood in the river, wears down, or carries away, this temporary embankment, and the struggling of horses and oxen to drag their loads up this breakwater are painful to witness. Most likely, when this point is reached, the traveller finds the way blocked by some disabled team, which makes repeated and ineffectual efforts to scramble up the steep, the obstruction thus offered to the traffic not only causing a crowd of carts to collect in the river, but packing up the narrow street leading to the gate in such a way as to make it difficult even for a horseman to pass. At the gate itself, it seems to be the custom for riders to dismount, probably as a means of showing respect to, and thus in a manner propitiating, the officials and underlings who watch the traffic in the interest of the inland revenue.

Upper Kalgan, for it is divided into two parts, upper and lower, is a busy, crowded place, with streets not much too wide for carts to pass, and paved with great blocks of stone. When first laid, these stones were doubtless smooth and made a good road, but long wear has made havoc of them. In some places they are worn into deep ruts, in some places large parts seem to have disappeared, and there could be no greater proof of the excellence of the Chinese wheelwright, than the fact that there are carts, day after day all the year round, plying for hire, carrying passengers and conveying merchandise along these terrible streets, and yet the wheels do not seem to suffer much.

Should the weather be at all wet, great parts of this causeway swim with deep black mud, which the horses and carts as they struggle along splash up plentifully upon the foot passengers on the high sidewalks. Peculiarly fatal is this rough road to the wooden axles of the soda carts, which come in from Mongolia in long trains, and a very common sight in Kalgan is that of a man sitting watching such a cart, which has been wrecked by the shock of plunging into a hole deeper than ordinary.

The mountains come close down to Kalgan, and by climbing one of the lower heights the traveller will realise that the Mongol was not far from the mark who, sitting on a bank and watching a swarm of men building a river-wall, exclaimed, "Kalgan is badly situated, right in the middle of the waters."

A mile or two down the main river is situated the lower town, and between the upper and lower towns are situated the Government offices and the rectangular encampments of the Manchu garrisons. About midway between the upper and lower towns, and in perilous proximity to the abodes of the soldiers, is another great torrent-bed, the dread of whose floods is sufficiently attested by the immense breakwaters erected to restrain their fury and guide their course. Great as these breakwaters are, they are not more than sufficient.

The dangers of the surrounding waters make land suitable for building hard to obtain in Kalgan; but in the upper city at least there is another danger to be

MULE LITTER FOR MOUNTAIN TRAVELLING.

guarded against, that of the mountains. Bounded on one side by the river, the houses are built so closely into the foot of the steep hill that forms the limit of the town on the other side, that some considerable danger is to be apprehended lest masses of rock, disintegrated by frost and rain from the precipices that frown above, should rush down the hill-side and crush the houses beneath. One night in summer people in bed heard the rush as of an avalanche on the side of the hill, and the light of next morning revealed a mass of stones that had descended from a position high up the cliff. Many of the stones were large, but one larger than the rest, and of a shape somewhat resembling that of a block from which a millstone nine feet thick and twelve feet in diameter could be conveniently hewn, had bounded away far beyond them all, and had been brought up only by having happened to leap down into a water-cut gully, where it stuck fast. Had this boulder not been stopped here, it would have leaped crashing down through the roofs of the outhouses of a Chinese merchant's store. The story goes that some time before a missionary had made some attempt at buying or renting the premises in question, but unsuccessfully. The sight of the stone, however, and the narrowness of the escape, were not without effect on the Chinaman's mind, and it is said that a few days afterwards word was sent to the foreigner that he might have the place if he wished it.

In some places the houses come so closely into the foot of the mountain that in climbing it is needful to be careful lest the foot should dislodge a stone that might fall down, endangering life and property. The houses so situated, however, are for the most part those of the poorest class, but the shops and establishments of many wealthy firms, though situated on the main street, do not consider themselves safe from the dangers of the floods, and the observing stranger on his first arrival may be puzzled by noticing grooved stones or timbers standing on either side of the front entrances of places of business. A set of planks are kept in readiness somewhere inside, and when a dangerous inundation seems imminent, these planks are brought out, let into the grooves, and driven home, thus forming a barrier to the flood, should it come surging down.

One of my most weird recollections of Kalgan, is that of making my way to an inn along the great length of its streets one summer evening, fording or being carried across the yellow streams that flowed from a thunderstorm in which I had been caught when out on a visit. The light of day was prematurely extinguished by the great clouds that were fast gathering, black and thick among the mountain-tops, belated travellers hurrying homewards clambered eagerly on the backs of bare-legged men that stood on the edges of the streams ready to transport passengers for a few cash, and from end to end the street resounded with the din of the shopmen hammering in their water-boards, afraid of a flood in the night. The weirdness of the situation was heightened by the recollection of the flood which a year or two before had broken its bounds, and, amid the horrors of storm and darkness, had swept to destruction some scores of panic-stricken people.

To many of the Mongols, Kalgan is important only from its being a great mart where all the wants arising from what civilisation they have can be supplied. All kinds of farinaceous food; cotton fabrics, both native and foreign, Chinese silks and Russian woollens; saddles, bridles, and all kinds of riding gear; crockery, iron, and copper-ware; and the numerous odds and ends of every-day needs, such as needles, buttons, fiddle-strings, and lucifer matches—all these and many more, the Mongols resort to Kalgan to purchase, and find them both superior and cheap. Some come to Kalgan with carts on which to carry back their goods, but the majority pack their purchases in leather bags, throw these across the saddle, perch themselves on the top, and thus return home, the rider being only part of the load which the horse has to carry.

But the Chinese do not simply wait to supply such customers as come to their shops, they send out trading expeditions which travel about Mongolia, and a great number of small traders make a living by buying an ox-cart load of goods in Kalgan, dragging it over the pass as best they can, and disposing of their merchandise by going round from tent to tent, taking most of their payment in articles of barter. This supplying of the domestic wants of the Mongols who live within reach is no inconsiderable trade, but after all it is only a small part of the business done in Kalgan.

The trade of Kalgan is the tea trade. Tea in Mongolia ranks, not as a luxury, but as a necessary of life; the quantity consumed is immense, and the whole of this article used in vast districts of Mongolia finds its way into the country through Kalgan, coming from the south to Tientsin by sea, from Tientsin to T'ung Chao by Chinese river boats, and from T'ung Chao to Kalgan on the pack-saddles of donkeys, mules, and camels. From Kalgan it is distributed over Mongolia, being conveyed to such trading centres as Urga by camel-caravans or trains of ox-carts. This business of carrying tea attracts Mongols, with their travelling cattle, from all parts of Mongolia.

In addition to what is used in Mongolia, there also passes through Kalgan the whole of the tea which finds its way into Siberia and Russia through Kiachta. A part of this trade is in the hands of the Russians themselves, who always maintain agents at Kalgan to receive the tea as it comes from the south, and forward it to the north. These agents live in Kalgan outside the gate, but space is so scarce in the mountain gorges where their abodes are, that a great part of the tea has to be sent up over the pass and stored out on the open plain. Poles are laid under to keep it clear of the ground and free from damp, the chests are piled up in long broad ridges, which are carefully covered in with reed mats, two or three thicknesses of which are practically waterproof, and the quantity sometimes stored up thus waiting for transport is so immense, that at a distance it looks like a village, with streets and lanes. Should the quantity of tea be unusually large, or should it need to be sent off quickly, a higher price is offered for transporting it; and one season not long ago, the number of chests waiting for conveyance was so great, and the price offered for carrying it so high, that for a few months oxen and ox-carts were bought and sold at nearly double their ordinary value. The tea thus forwarded by ox-cart is for the most part the coarse brick tea used in North Mongolia and Siberia, the finer sorts of overland tea used in Russia being usually transported across the desert on camel-back.

The main imports received in Kalgan from Mongolia

are salt; soda, for the refining of which Kalgan possesses many wealthy-looking establishments, which seem to vie with each other as to the size of the coal-hill, faced with a neatly built wall of great blocks, which they display in some part of their yard, visible to any one who passes their great gate; hides and skins, for the preparation of which Kalgan possesses exceptional facilities in her streams; and timber, which for the most part comes across the desert from Urga, forming the return cargo of a large proportion of the carts that go north with tea.

Kalgan owes part of its 75,000 of population to its garrison of Manchu soldiers, who, with their wives and children, occupy several permanent encampments of built houses, each encampment being surrounded by a wall, and distinguishable from a village mainly by the too great regularity and uniformity of the buildings. Its dignity is considerably enhanced by the presence of the government offices, where the official business of a great part of Southern Mongolia is conducted; and no small number of the better class of Mongols seen about the streets, will be found on inquiry to have come to Kalgan on matters connected with their government duty, or for the purpose of prosecuting before the higher courts law pleas in which they may be engaged with their neighbours.

Since 1865 Kalgan has formed one of the stations of the American Board of Foreign Missions, whose agents have not confined their attention to the city alone, but have endeavoured to propagate the gospel in the regions lying around, including in the sphere of their operations the nearer districts of the plain of Mongolia.

CHAPTER XV.

DOCTORING THE MONGOLS.

Mongol doctors numerous. Mostly priests. They live in their patients house. Mongols make good patients. Belief in water cure. Almost all Mongols suffer from disease. The missionary swamped in the doctor. Mongol admiration for the missionary doctor. The successful eye operation. Mongol suspicious of morning walk. About an evening ride. About writing. Missionary must not be a sportsman. Diseases prevalent in Mongolia. Religious element in medicine. Feeling the pulse. Swallowing medicine for external application. Patients duped by Chinese traders. Curious cases. Dying Chinaman. Mongol views on the galvanic battery. Divination. The doctor taking his own medicine for example's sake. Medical knowledge helps to gain the good-will of the people.

NATIVE doctors swarm in Mongolia, if swarm is a proper term to be applied to any class of men in so sparsely peopled a country. They are mostly lamas. There are a few laymen who add medical practice to their other occupations, but the great majority of doctors are priests. That this should be so is not strange. In the first place, the lama life is an idle kind of existence, affording opportunities of acquiring what medical knowledge is to be had. In the second place, a lama in riper years, being free from family cares and government duty, has his time more at his own disposal than in the case of the layman, and so can make more opportunities of using his medical skill. In the third place, Mongol, seldom separate medicine and prayers, and a clerical doctor has the advantage over a layman in that he can attend personally to both departments, administering drugs on the one hand and performing religious ceremonies on the other.

How much real knowledge these men possess would be difficult to decide. They seem to have a rather elaborate medical system, but part of it at least has no better foundation than ignorance or superstition. One curious practice is, that when they have a man under treatment, they go and live at the house of the patient, remaining there till the cure is accomplished, or the doctor confesses he can do no more.

Mongols make, on the whole, good patients. They are credulous, have great faith in medicine, are ready to swallow great quantities of drugs, and the more nauseous the drugs are, the more faith have they in them. On one point Mongol doctors are sound, and Mongol patients are sensible. They believe greatly in the water cure. They often advise their patients to try the effect of such and such a hot or cold spring, and the celebrated springs in North China and in Mongolia count, among the sufferers that resort to them, many natives of the plain. Some patients, of course, receive no benefit from these rude hydropathic establishments, but the majority go away feeling benefited—a fact not to be wondered at, when it is remembered that a great proportion of Mongol suffering arises from skin diseases, contracted or aggravated by want of cleanliness.

The inhabitants of Mongolia are few and far between, and in this sense Mongolia is not a favourable field for a foreign medical missionary. But it must not be forgotten that when at length you do meet an inhabitant, he or she is almost sure to be suffering from some disease or other, and it is almost true to say that the number of possible patients to be found in any one place is equal to the total number of the inhabitants.

When a foreign missionary, speaking Mongolian and carrying a medicine chest, appears on any part of the

GOING FOR THE DOCTOR.   [*From a Native Sketch.*

plain, the news spreads far and wide. The story too gathers as it rolls, and in a few days he is credited with the most extraordinary powers of healing, the exaggerated stories about his abilities being equalled only by the exaggerated stories of the virtues of the medicines and appliances. It is in vain that the missionary insists he has come not merely to heal, but to teach Christianity. Christianity they can do without. They don't feel the need of it. They are eager to get rid of their pains and aches. They apply to the missionary in his capacity of doctor, they talk of him as a doctor, and the real truth of the matter is, that they want him only in so far as he is a doctor. In the case of some places where Mongols are numerous, such as at populous temples, government gatherings, and religious festivals, the number of patients that present themselves in one day is so great, that while attending them very little religious instruction can be imparted. Some of them have come a long way and can ill spare time, and are in a hurry to get home again; some of them have run out in the interval between services and must be back in time; some of them have waited long and patiently, or impatiently as the case may be, while earlier comers were being treated, and are eager to be attended to when their turn comes; and in these cases the *missionary* is in danger of being swamped in the *doctor*.

But the reception accorded to the missionary is not the same in all places. In most cases when a locality is visited for the first time there is a great crowd of people eager to be patients; but as a great proportion of them have diseases which are incurable, they soon learn that the report that the foreigner can cure everything is not true, and, finding he can do little or nothing for them, they gradually drop off. The second time the place is visited matters mend a little, and by the third visit the people's ideas have become pretty correct, and, for the most part, only such cases as can be helped are pressed upon his attention.

For a man who carries medicines and can cure a few diseases, and who lays himself out patiently and attentively to benefit his patients, for one especially who cleans and attends to neglected, loathsome sores on dirty unwashed persons, showing the same attention to the poor as to the rich, for such an one the Mongol admiration is unbounded. It is long before they can convince themselves that money or recompense is not wanted, and if they could only believe that these things were done, as they profess to be, for nothing else but for Christ's sake, those who saw them would be doubtless inclined to think highly of a religion which produced such fruits But, in the opinion of the Mongols, it is too good to be true. They cannot believe it. That men should be sent out from distant lands, fitted out with travelling appliances and furnished with medicines, and go about ready and willing to cure and heal, and want no money for it, no reward of any kind —a Mongol's faith staggers at that. Explain to him the religious sanction and motive for it all, the theory of such a thing he could understand, but in practice it staggers him. If he read it in his sacred books as a thing related of old Buddhist saints, who lived in distant countries and in old times, he would accept it, but to see it with his own eyes, in this his own time, and in his own country—that is too much for his faith. So he sets himself to invent a reason. If he is near China, or if himself or friends have had much intercourse with China, he perhaps has heard the stories of foreigners digging out people's eyes to make photographic chemicals, or perhaps he has heard of the operation of couching for cataract, perhaps he has seen it performed, and though he himself may know and believe that it is all right, the friends and neighbours, who did not see the operation but only heard his report, find in it plenty to confirm their suspicions. Very great care is needed if a Mongol missionary wishes to avoid giving rise to rumours among the Mongols which will prove prejudicial to his influence and work.

On one occasion I was living some weeks in a Mongol's tent. It was late in the year. Lights were put out soon after dark. The nights were long in reality, and, in such unsatisfactory surroundings as the discomforts of a poor tent and doubtful companions, the nights seemed longer than they were. At sunrise I was only too glad to escape from smoke and everything else to the retirement of the crest of a low ridge of hills near the tent. This, perhaps the most natural thing in the world for a foreigner, was utterly inexplicable to the Mongols. The idea that any man should get out of his bed at sunrise and climb a hill for nothing! He must be up to mischief! He must be secretly taking away the luck of the land! This went on for some time, the Mongols all alive with suspicion, and the unsuspecting foreigner retiring regularly morning after morning, till at length a drunken man blurted out the whole thing and openly stated the conviction that the inhabitants had arrived at, namely, that this extraordinary morning walk of the foreigner on the hill-crest boded no good to the country. To remain among the people, I had to give up my morning retirement.

On another occasion, a missionary, who had a turn for geology, was in the habit of strolling about on summer evenings after sunset and picking up a few specimens of stones. This gave rise to the most wonderful stories that spread far and wide over the plain. Among other things he was actually supposed to have discovered and dug out of the earth immense masses of silver of almost untold value, and these stories obtained such credence among the people, affording as they did a very plausible explanation of how men could travel about healing and asking no fees, that in one neighbourhood to which I and my medicine had been specially invited, no one would have anything whatever to do with us, simply because these prejudicial stories had arrived a few hours before us.

On one occasion my wife and I, while encamped at a large temple, after having our tent crowded with visitors and patients all the hours of the long summer day, used to have our horses saddled up, and go for a short ride at sunset, returning at dusk. This, it afterwards appeared, produced a great ferment among the lamas, who, voluminous with lies as usual, concocted and circulated all manner of absurd reports about our searching for treasure in the night; so much so, that after a few days a messenger appeared and in the name of the government authorities and ruling lamas ordered us to leave the place.

At first sight it might be supposed that a traveller would be so free nowhere as in the thinly peopled, far-reaching plains of Mongolia. And, as far as a mere traveller is concerned, this is the case. But with the missionary it is different. To have any prospect of success among the Mongols, the missionary must avoid raising suspicions, and, if he is to avoid raising suspicions, he must climb no hill, pick up no pebble, never go for a walk, and never manifest any interest or pleasure in the scenery. If he does any of these things, stories and rumours are at once circulated, which effectually close the minds of the inhabitants against his teaching.

Another thing that must be refrained from is writing. The Mongols are very suspicious of seeing a foreigner writing. What *can* he be up to? they say among themselves. Is he taking notes of the capabilities of the country? Is he marking out a road map so that he can return guiding an army? Is he a wizard carrying off the good luck of the country in his note-book? These, and a great many others, are the questions that they ask among themselves and put to the foreigner when they see him writing, and if he desires to conciliate the good-will of the people, and to win their confidence, the missionary must abstain from walking and writing while he is among them. In both of these respects the minute the border is crossed and China entered, a delicious sense of freedom is experienced, and a man feels that his legs and his pen are once more of some use to him again.

On another point, too, care must be exercised. Shooting has to be avoided. Killing beasts or birds the Mongols regard as peculiarly sinful, and any one who wished to teach them religious truth would make the attempt under great disadvantage, if he carried and used a gun. This, however, is a prejudice that it is not so difficult to refrain from offending. It is true that a gun would, on many occasions, add a pleasant variety in the shape of ducks, geese, and hares to the pot, but for the most part mutton can be obtained without much difficulty, and as the wild deer are very difficult to stalk on the open plain, the temptation to carry a gun is not so great as might at first be supposed.

One of the most prevalent diseases in Mongolia is *itch*. The Mongols very seldom change their clothes, and practise the least possible amount of washing, either of their persons or their garments, having a superstitious belief that if they use too much water, after death they will become fishes. In their tents they live so closely huddled up that when one gets itch, all soon have it. Travellers and visitors, who pass the night in an infected family, are pretty sure to catch the disease too, as they have to borrow a garment to serve as a blanket. Everything is in its favour, and it flourishes. Many of the Mongols go on religious pilgrimages, and many of them roam about merely for the pleasure of the thing. These catch the disease and spread it; and as the Mongols know of no effectual cure, the wonder is not that it is so prevalent, but rather that it is not universal.

Other skin diseases are also prevalent, and from pretty much the same causes as mentioned above. A scratch or something makes a small beginning, dirt and hair from their sheepskins irritate and increase it, and it goes on from bad to worse.

Rheumatism is perhaps the most prevalent disease. It is induced by the climate of the country and the manner of life. Some fine morning a man debates with himself whether he will wear his summer coat or his sheepskin. If he thinks it will be a warm day he puts on his summer coat and rides off. Suddenly a cold wind blows, and he must endure the cold till he reaches home again in the evening. Or, perhaps, he is the night watcher of a drove of horses, and tired out, lies down on the damp ground and soon feels it cold, even through his sheepskin.

Even at home in a well-to-do tent it is not much better. In winter there is a fire in the centre; all sit round it and are warm enough in front, but cold at the back; and there is always a current of air coming from the sides of the tent towards the fire. In summer it is even worse. The cow-dung basement round the tent, which was intended to keep out the cold, is now removed, and a clear space of from four to six inches left, through which the four winds blow at their sweet pleasure. During the day it is not so bad, but at night, even in summer, the air is not warm, and the tent is never without a cold draught. Add to this the fact that the Mongol's blanket is his coat, which, being rather short to cover all his person, is apt to leave the shoulder exposed, or, at least, not well protected, and it is not difficult to understand why almost every man and woman in Mongolia suffers from rheumatism. Not only men and women, but youths even, suffer from it, and this is partly to be accounted for by a notion the Mongols have, that it is good for a youth to sleep with insufficient covering. Thus rheumatism runs riot among them, and will do so till they change their mode of life and can be taught to take some care of themselves.

Their own faculty have no remedy for this disease. Kneading, as a baker kneads dough, gives a little relief at the time, and the boys and girls are in pretty constant requisition to perform this operation on the backbones and shoulders of the elder members of the family. Old people who have no young folks in their tents manage to *knead* themselves by means of a stick with a great V-shaped crook. This stick they call the "*Rheumatism curer.*" Holding it in front, they can knead their own shoulders almost as effectually as by the knuckles of the youngsters.

Eye diseases are very common. The glare of the sun on the snowy expanse in winter, and on the plains in spring and autumn, is very trying. Summer is more agreeable, as the eye can then rest with pleasure on the soft green of the grass and herbs. In spring and autumn the grass is withered and brown — often bleached till it becomes of a whitish hue, which can be comfortably looked at only when the eyes are furnished with protectors. Riding through Gobi, I had the misfortune to lose my tinted spectacles. The consequence was an affection of the eye, which did not quite leave me for a twelvemonth afterwards.

In addition to the sun out of doors, there is the smoke indoors. The argol smoke has no offensive smell, as some suppose, but it is bad enough and bitter enough, and has much the same effect on the eyes as is produced by the smoke of wood.

To an inflamed or bad eye, a Mongol doctor can do next to nothing; and some of the simplest and commonest remedies known to western science work cures which to them seem wonderful.

On one occasion I was taken to see a lama of rank who was suffering from an eye disease which rendered him almost entirely blind. I found he was troubled with the lashes of the lower eyelid growing into the eye. I removed them, taught a man how to do it again, if it should become necessary, and when next I heard of the lama, he was collating the Ganjore. When I passed that way the following year, he came and acknowledged that he owed his eyesight to me, and was profuse in his thanks.

Spring diseases is, perhaps, not a proper term, but it indicates a feature in Mongolian life. Many people tell you they are well all the year round except in spring. When winter leaves, and the year begins to open, they are ill. Others again who are slightly indisposed always, are much worse in spring. Cattle suffer in the same way. Many sheep and horses that weather out the winter succumb to the bleak cold winds of spring. Perhaps the damp of the thaw has something to do with it.

Ague is not common, but not altogether unknown. It greatly alarmed a part of a tribe once by spreading itself among them. The lamas did not know what to make of it, and at last concluded that it was a contagious disease, introduced into the country by the Mongol soldiers who had gone on government duty into China. The popular account of the visitation proceeds to say, that, when Mongols got so ill under it as to be delirious, *they raved in Chinese.*

Narry is the Mongol name for the disease which is brought on by drinking whisky. The stomach is burnt to such an extent that almost nothing will enter it, or entering it, cannot remain. It is soon returned, and the patient gets thinner and weaker day by day, till he dies of starvation. I have no means of getting statistics, but, from subjects I have seen, and from the many eager inquiries I have heard made about the possibility of curing it, it would seem that a good number die of this disease.

The women of Mongolia are hardy and capable. They look ruddy and strong-limbed. They work hard, and are badly treated. Woman's place in the tent is next the door; the felt she sleeps on is the thinnest and poorest. She does the milking and drudgery generally, and when she sits in the tent, usually has nothing better than a worn cow-hide to protect her from the damp and cold of the ground. She jumps into the saddle and rides over the plain as recklessly as a man. She takes little care of herself, and has little care bestowed upon her. An old woman spoke some truth, at least, when she said to me, "The women are treated like the dogs which are fed outside the tent."

The result is as might have been expected:—strong, hardy, and healthy as the women look, almost every one who has passed the stage of girlhood has some chronic malady or suffering. There are many exceptions, especially among the richer class, but, as a rule, women suffer more, age sooner, and die younger than the men; and there is little prospect of a change for the better, in this respect, till women are treated more considerately, and have accorded to them a fair share of the meagre comforts of tent life.

Mongol patients and Mongol doctors believe in the efficacy of prayer as a curative agency. When a man puts himself under medical treatment, he usually starts temple or lama services, giving gifts according to his means, and knowing that the nature and extent of the services will depend on the value of the offering presented. There are numbers of people who believe that their recovery from sickness was through the power of the services performed; and it is worthy of note that they do not consider the prayer and medicine as two *rival* methods of cure, but rather the two sides of the same thing. Medicine is the human means, the praying is the appeal to the superhuman.

People who cannot afford temple services, or patients suffering from a minor affliction, usually have a lama come to their tent and recite the necessary prayers. Throwing about small pinches of millet seed is a usual part of such a service. A man who had called a lama to say prayer to reduce the inflammation of his eye, had his purpose frustrated in a singular manner. The lama threw the millet towards the patient, one of the seeds struck the eye and produced an ulcer, or cloud, as the Mongols call it, which dimmed his vision ever after. The precise nature of the service appropriate to the occasion is usually determined by some lama of high standing. Some of the living Buddhas have a great reputation, from the responses they give when consulted as to whether a patient will recover, and what means he should use. A very common response is, "Not alarming; drink medicine, and have prayers said." Pilgrimages are often prescribed, and have the reputation of being effectual. I once heard it seriously proposed to send a man who had lost the use of his legs on a pilgrimage of some hundreds of miles. His advisers seemed seriously to think that if he could crawl there and back, he would stand a good chance of being cured!

On another occasion I met a man just reaching his home after accomplishing a long pilgrimage for the cure of tooth-ache. He was no better; and a few seconds with a pair of forceps did more to relieve him than all the hundreds of miles he had walked.

Mongols don't believe much in prophylactics. When they come and say a certain kind of food disagrees with them, they think you are making fun of them when you tell them to avoid that article of diet. Cure a man of his rheumatism, and he will think you are admitting the feebleness of your remedy, when you instruct him to avoid damp and cold in future. If inaction or sedentary occupation has made him ill, he thinks you are a poor doctor if, in addition to your medicine, you prescribe exercise. Their habitual contempt and disregard of precautions makes it a thankless task to attempt to relieve them from some kinds of suffering.

In a short time their carelessness makes them as bad as ever again.

In many cases when a Mongol applies to his doctor, he simply extends his hand and expects that the doctor, by simply feeling his pulse, will be able to tell not only the disease, but what will cure it. As soon as the doctor has felt the pulse of one hand the patient at once extends the other hand, that the pulse may be felt there also, and great surprise is manifested when a foreigner begins his diagnosis of a case by declining the proffered wrist and asking questions. No less surprise is manifested when, in cases where it is necessary to feel the pulse, the foreigner contents himself with feeling the pulse at one wrist.

The question of "How did you get this disease?" often elicits some curiously superstitious replies. One man lays the blame on the stars and constellations. Another confesses that when he was a lad he was mischievous and dug holes in the ground, or cut shrubs on the hill, and it is not difficult to see how he regards disease as a punishment for digging, since by digging worms are killed, but what cutting wood on a hill can have to do with sin it is harder to see, except it be regarded as stealing the possessions of the spiritual lord of the locality. In consulting a doctor, too, a Mongol seems to lay a deal of stress on the belief that it may be his *fate* to be cured by the medical man in question, and if he finds relief, often says that his meeting this particular doctor, and being cured, is the result of prayers made at some previous time.

One difficulty in curing Mongols is, that they frequently, when supplied with medicines, depart entirely from the doctor's instructions when they apply them; and a not unfrequent case is that of the patient who, after applying to the foreigner for medicine and getting it, is frightened by his success, or scared by some lying report of his neighbours, or, staggered at the fact that the foreigner would not feel his pulse or feel it at one wrist only, lays aside the medicine carefully and does not use it at all.

As the inhabitants of Mongolia are few and far between, it is seldom possible to make long halts at any one place, and, in consequence, it is often necessary to leave behind medicine for the cure of diseases that require continuous treatment.

One evening, when sitting in my tent door, looking towards an encampment where I had given some medicine to be used after my departure, I noticed some children rush out and come straight towards me at full speed. Long before they reached me I guessed that what I had often feared had happened at last. I was not mistaken. The children came first, and after them a woman, all out of breath, to say that the younger children had got hold of the medicine bottle, and, thinking it whisky, had drunk it! Finding what they had done, the anxious mother had also tasted it, to see what it really was that they had taken, and now they wished to know if they as a family had poisoned themselves, and what was to be done! Happily the medicine was not deadly, and the quantity drunk small, and no harm followed, but this incident shows a danger which has to be constantly guarded against; and it is often difficult to heal diseases simple enough in themselves, because it would be unsafe to leave, in careless hands, medicine in sufficient quantity to complete the cure.

A foreigner is often asked to perform absurd, laughable, or impossible cures. One man wants to be made clever, another to be made fat, another to be cured of insanity, another of tobacco, another of whisky, another of hunger, another of tea, another wants to be made strong so as to conquer in gymnastic exercises, most men want medicine to make their beards grow, while almost every man, woman, and child wants to have his or her skin made as white as that of the foreigner.

The fee of the Mongol doctor is an important matter. Sometimes it is a stipulated sum of money, more frequently a sheep, or so many head of cattle—in almost all cases payment depending to a certain extent on cure. Comparatively speaking, medical attention is very expensive, and well-to-do families are often greatly reduced in circumstances by some visitation of sickness, which entails heavy doctors' bills. Though it is known that I take no fee, I am usually offered the "*hatug*," a kind of silk handkerchief worth about three farthings, an offering which seems to be the preliminary to nearly every request preferred by one Mongol to another. This I at first accept, then return, saying that they by giving it have conformed to their custom, and I by restoring it have conformed to mine.

Occasionally a rich man offers me a large sum of money to induce me to effect a cure, and even the poorest seldom fail to offer something in addition to the inevitable "*hatug*."

The most common offering is a small rectangular cheese about an inch thick—an article of diet much appreciated by Mongols, but in reality a very poor affair, dirty, tasteless, and, to a foreigner, indigestible.

A degree less objectionable than the cheese is a lump of salt "for my tea," an offering frequently made, but which I can decline without hurting the donor's feelings, seeing that I can truthfully say that I drink my tea without salt.

At temples, during the festive season, a young lama will sometimes produce from his bosom a "scone," a hard solid-looking, glistening disc of flour, which it is impossible to look at without thinking of indigestion. One man, judging, probably, from his experience of Mongol doctors, thought he was offering me a great inducement to undertake a case, when he assured me that at his place and under his care I should want for nothing, but might pass my time in drinking, feasting, and gambling!

When a Mongol is convinced that his case is hopeless he takes it very calmly, and bows to his fate, whether it be death or chronic disease; and both doctors and patients, after a succession of failures, regard the affliction as a thing fated, to overcome which implies no lack of medical ability on the doctor's part.

Mongol patients are very credulous, and fall an easy prey to designing Chinese traders and doctors, who go about the districts nearer China, vending plaisters many and various, of which they do not scruple to tell round lies, warranting one plaister to preserve all a man's teeth from decay for the whole period of his natural life, and affirming of another that it needs only to be placed on the body of the patient anywhere, when it would of itself find out and move away to the affected part and heal the disease. These plaisters cost a little money, but are harmless.

A more serious case was that of a lama, who, disappointed at a foreigner's refusal to perform in Peking an impossible operation on the eye, went back indignant to his home in Mongolia, and fell into the hands of a plausible Chinese doctor, who took the lama's money, performed the desired operation, and completely destroyed the eye. This lama's misadventure with the Chinese doctor raised his opinion considerably of the skilful foreigner, who pronounced the proposed operation impossible.

A few curious cases are met with now and again. A woman afflicted with disease of the jaw-bone, had allowed it to heal up in such a position that the teeth were tightly closed. She could not open her mouth at all, and for years she had subsisted upon liquid food sucked into the mouth by way of the interstices between the teeth. She wished one or two teeth removed, so as to allow of a free avenue for food entering the mouth. All the teeth were well set and in beautiful condition, and the mouth was so tightly closed that it was a work of some difficulty to get sufficient hold of any one tooth, but the old woman's courage was good, and a road was eventually opened for the passage of solid food, for which she had before longed in vain.

An old man, who was a very long distance from home, was conspicuous as he rode about the country, by a curious stick hanging from his saddle-bow. It turned out that this baton was used lever-wise, to reduce a rupture, and, by long habit, he had become so accustomed to its use that he could operate quite deftly as he sat in the saddle.

One old lama, who had been severely bitten by a dog, had stopped the wounds with fur from the animal's hide, evidently believing in the healing efficacy of "a hair from the dog that bit him."

I met once a deaf and dumb man. He was uneducated, but of great quickness and intelligence. He could converse easily and readily with his fellow Mongols by signs, and I could ask many simple questions and understand his answers without trouble. His perception was remarkable. While sitting in the dusk outside my tent, a messenger came from his father's tent to tell him that some of the sheep were missing. A single turn of the hand followed by a puzzled glance around as if searching for something, was all that was required. He had been sitting quietly in the circle looking at us talking, but the moment the communication was made he uttered an inarticulate sound betraying great excitement, knocked the ashes out of his pipe, stuck it into his boot, threw himself into the saddle, and rode off into the gathering darkness to search for the lost sheep. All agreed that he had an extra share of intelligence, and he was rightly regarded as a capable and useful member of the community.

At another place I was astonished to see a man, looking about fifty years old and four feet high, walk into my tent and sit down. He walked on his knees. He had lost both his feet by the ankle when about nineteen, and by long practice could now get on very well without them. He could walk quite cleverly; but I was curious to see how he mounted his horse. It was a quiet animal. Going up to it he tightened the saddle-girth, put up one knee into the stirrup, and in another second was in the saddle all right. His footless stumps terminated in boots stuffed with camels' hair, so that when he rode with his boots in the stirrups, his deformity was not noticed.

At one place I met a man with two thumbs on his left hand. One was of the proper size and in its normal position. The joint was a little stiff. The smaller thumb shot off like a branch from the side of the larger one, and, though seemingly perfect, had no movable joint. A few days later a boy came to my tent with the same monstrosity. His mother, who came with him, was anxious to have the superfluous finger amputated. In both cases the peculiarity was confined to one hand, the other hand and the feet were quite normal.

One of the *sad sights* seen was that of a sick Chinaman near his end. He was one of a company of four, who went about dressing skins of which the Mongols make garments. He had been an opium taker, and an incurable diarrhœa had seized him. At the time he was lodging with the Mongol for whom the party had come to dress skins, but the Mongol, seeing he would die, and fearing trouble and expense over his death, ordered him off the premises. Borrowing an ox-cart, his companion had him conveyed away some five or ten miles, jolted in the rude vehicle and suffering from the blazing sun, to a place where some Chinese acquaintances were digging a well. They had a tent of their own, most likely a poor ragged white cloth affair, open to the winds and pervious to the rain, and in this the poor man hoped he might be permitted to die. It was the dark side of the picture. The glorious summer, the green and flowery plains, the fattening flocks, the herds exulting in the deep pastures, the gay Mongols riding about, the white tents bathed in the sunlight and gleaming from afar In the midst of all this, a feeble man far from home and kin, sick unto death, cast forth from his poor lodging, and seeking for a place to lie down and die in. The Mongols are a hospitable race, but pray ye that ye may not get sick on their hands.

Of all the healing appliances in the hands of a foreigner, none strikes the fancy of a Mongol so much as the galvanic battery, and it is rather curious that almost every Mongol who sees it and tries its effect exclaims, what a capital thing it would be for examining accused persons. It would far surpass whipping, beating, or suspending. Under its torture a guilty man could not but "confess." Some one in England has advocated the use of the galvanic battery in place of the cat in punishing criminals, and it is curious to note the coincidence of the English and Mongol mind.

The Mongol doctors are not, it would seem, quite unacquainted with the properties of galvanism. It is said that they are in the habit of prescribing the loadstone ore, reduced to a powder, as efficacious when applied to sores; and one man hard of hearing had been recommended by a lama to put a piece of loadstone into each ear and chew a piece of iron in his mouth!

Divination is a point on which Mongols are troublesome. It never for a moment enters their head that a man so intelligent and well-fitted out with appliances as a foreigner seems to them to be cannot divine. Accordingly they come to him to divine for them where they should camp to be lucky and get rich, when a man who has gone on a journey will return, why no news has been received from a son or husband who is serving in the army, where they should dig a well so as to get plenty of good water near the surface, whether it would be fortunate for them to venture on some trading speculation, whether they should go on some projected journey, in what direction they should search for lost cattle, or, more frequently than any of the above, they come, men and women, old and young, to have the general luck of their lives examined into. Great is their amazement when the foreigner confesses his ignorance of such art, and greater still is their incredulity. They simply disbelieve him when he says he cannot divine, and think that he is merely lazy or disobliging, and return again and again to the charge, begging and entreating, hoping thus to overcome his unwillingness. One foreigner, not a missionary, tells the story of himself, that, yielding to the Mongol importunity, he consented to divine for lost camels, and, judging that the beasts must have retreated before a gale of wind the previous day, sent the Mongols to look for them in that direction. The camels were actually found there, and the foreigner's reputation established for divination.

On the whole I have been very well received everywhere, and have been treated with great confidence. I have sometimes wondered at the readiness with which they take medicines which they know nothing about, from the hand of an utter stranger, though this confidence is not universal. Once or twice, when anxious to effect a cure on a timid patient, I have found no means of inspiring courage but by taking a dose of the medicine myself, by way of example, and as proof that it was not deadly. One reason why they are ready to trust me, doubtless, is that going among them, they can go round my tent and see that there is nothing secret and terrible behind it; they enter it and see all that is in it. They know and see that I am utterly in their power, and, perhaps, reason that I am there with no intent to harm, because if I made trouble I could not move another step without their consent. There are, of course, slight disadvantages and annoyances, such as people coming to get medicine to make them intelligent and clever, to have spots and marks on their bodies removed, to have imaginary diseases cured, and to have divinations performed to assist them in the recovery of lost cattle. Drunken Mongols too, who come and *won't* be reasonable in their conduct and demands, and who *won't* go away, are a trouble. The perpetual restraint, too, imposed on one's actions and movements by the superstitious fears of the natives, proves irksome in the long run, but in a missionary point of view these are as nothing compared with the great advantage of gaining the confidence and good-will of a people.

I have as yet seen no converts from among the Mongols, but it has been my privilege to tell many of them of the way of salvation, and the seeming interest and apparent friendliness with which many of them have listened to the Gospel message, has, under God, been mainly owing to the fact that I tried to heal their diseases while I said that the kingdom of God had come nigh unto them.

CHAPTER XVI.

THE GOSPEL IN MONGOLIA.

Halt at tents. Scripture pictures. Books. Utility of tracts as compared with Gospels. Difficulty experienced by a heathen in understanding Scripture. Bibles and tracts should be sold together. Mongols despise our Scriptures as small in extent. Buddhism not to be successfully attacked through its deficient astronomy and geography. The hope for Christianity among the Mongols.

WHEN a missionary travelling in Mongolia reaches a cluster of tents, a halt is called, the tents are set up, the goods unloaded, a fire of the quick argol is started, and soon master and men abandon themselves to tea-drinking. Meantime natives of the place have gathered round. Sometimes they are very friendly and assist in setting up the tents, sometimes they stand by counting their beads and looking on, but almost always they are ready and willing to join in the tea-drinking. Some o. them are attracted by the medicine, which they have heard by report going before is dispensed gratis, some are drawn merely by idle curiosity, some few come in the hope of getting a Mongol book. For the most part they are a little distant at first. Tea even fails to thaw completely their reserve, and it is not till a case of Scripture pictures, gaudy with colours, is produced, that old and young find their tongues, and crowd around, all eye and ear. A selection of the pictures gives a good opportunity for stating the main doctrines of Christianity, and in the case of the picture, the eye assisting the ear, even people of small intellectual ability often apprehend clearly the teaching, and remember it distinctly.

The pictures exhausted, then come the books. These comprise three or four tracts, some of which have illustrations, a catechism, and the Gospel by Matthew. The tracts, being written in an easy style and free from proper names, present no difficulty to a moderately good scholar; the catechism does not run so smoothly, but when he comes to the Gospel, any but a very exceptionally good reader stumbles badly, and frequently lays down the book, saying it is too much for him. Indeed, long experience of many different Mongol scholars attempting to read the Gospel in the tent, leads to the belief that the portions of Matthew's Gospel of which an unassisted Mongol can make sense at all are comparatively few. In justice to the translators it is only fair to state that the fault does not seem to lie with the translation. The difficulty seems to arise from the want of acquaintance, on the part of the reader, with Gospel truths and doctrines, from a slight indefiniteness inherent to Mongol writing, and, perhaps mainly, from proper names, Old Testament references, and Jewish customs occurring or referred to in this Gospel.

From the combination of all these causes it happens that a Mongol, although a good scholar, seldom, even after a good deal of trying, succeeds in extracting much meaning from Matthew's Gospel, and one is forced, rather unwillingly it must be confessed, to the opinion, that in propagating Christianity among the heathen tracts and other books of elementary Christian teaching are, in the initial stages at least, a necessary introduction to the Bible itself. Of course, after a man has been taught somewhat of the doctrines and facts of Christianity, the most useful book that can be put into his hands is the Bible, but it seems very doubtful, if, in many cases, much good is accomplished by placing the Bible in the hands of a heathen as a first step towards his enlightenment. This refers first and mainly to Mongolia, and if tracts and treatises are understood more easily than the Bible in Mongolia, may not the same thing hold true in China? Granting that the Chinese language is free from the indefiniteness inherent to the Mongol, do not heathen Chinese in reading the New Testament stumble at proper names, references to the Old Testament prophets, and allusions to Jewish manners and customs? In selling Bibles in China, for the most part, the reader takes his purchase and disappears, and the colporteur or missionary hopes the best from the transaction; but if, as in Mongolia, the missionary or colporteur had the opportunity of sitting with the purchaser for half an hour or a whole hour and helping him to read his book, it is just possible that by-and-by the earnest Christian evangelist would hope more for the spiritual enlightenment of the man who bought a *Peep of Day*, for example, than of the man who bought a Gospel or even a New Testament. The great Bible Societies sell their Bibles far and wide over China. They do well. But it is scarcely possible to escape the conviction that they would do much better if they allowed their colporteurs to sell tracts along with the Bibles. If the nature and constitution of the Bible

Societies make this impossible, could not it be arranged that a Bible man and a tract man should go together? It is known and admitted that there are instances of men converted from heathenism to Christianity, men who never met a Christian, and who never handled a Christian book except the Bible, but these men are very rare, and in the general circulation of the Bible it would very much increase the number of those who get to understand the Sacred Word if it were accompanied by treatises and explanatory tracts.

After a Mongol has received some idea of Christianity, he for the most part expresses himself entirely satisfied. He says it is good. It is like his own religion. It is the same. And he says this, though what he has read, or what he has had told him, includes prominent and pointed statements of Christian doctrines diametrically opposed to the fundamental beliefs of his own Buddhism. It is then necessary to go back with him and point out the differences, and if he at last understands that a man cannot be a good Buddhist and a good Christian at the same time, his next thought is that it is quite superfluous to bring any other or any new religion to him who is supplied with what he regards as such an excellent one already.

When a Mongol understands that Christianity is intended to supersede Buddhism, his first thought seems to be a tendency to despise the smallness of our Scriptures as compared with his own. Their Scriptures form a library of large volumes which it takes a good string of camels to carry. The idea of such Scriptures being superseded by a small book which a child can carry in one hand! When, too, it comes to a comparison of the doctrines contained in the two Scriptures, the Buddhist can, if he is well up, produce no mean list of excellent doctrines; and when it comes to miracles, the Buddhist thinks that those he can quote are not a whit behind those of our Scriptures. It is true that there is a vast difference in the tone of the teaching, and the spirit, aim, and circumstances of the miracles of the two Scriptures. It is also true that a Christian man, of fair intelligence, can see the difference of aim and bent and tone of the inspirèd writing and the Buddhistic compositions, as plainly and readily as an ordinary man of common intelligence can tell a wall raised by the hands of a competent builder from the attempted imitation of a bungling amateur. This is all true. And in the case of a man educated in Christianity and intelligent as to Buddhism, this palpable difference would carry overwhelming weight with it in favour of Christianity. But blindly and enthusiastically bigoted for Buddhism as they are, the Mongols are hardly in a position to feel the force of arguments drawn from this source.

It might be thought that the erroneous astronomy and geography mixed up in, and forming an integral part of the Buddhistic Scriptures, would lay these Scriptures open to successful attack. But the truth seems to be that a devout Buddhist is no more disturbed as to the reliability of his Scriptures, when their false geography and astronomy are attacked, than a devout Christian is alarmed for the stability of his Bible when he hears a geologist lecturing on the first chapters of Genesis.

Superadded to these intellectual difficulties, which are met with in attempting to propagate Christianity in Mongolia, is another difficulty, grosser in its nature, and only less powerful in its operation than those mentioned above. This is the almost all-powerful sway that

Buddhism has over its Mongol votaries, and the intensity of the bigoted enthusiasm with which the Mongols cling to their religion. Considerable acquaintance with Mongolia, with Mongols, and with Mongolian habits and arrangements of life, lead to the conviction that any one Mongol coming out of Buddhism and entering Christianity would lead a very precarious existence on the plain, if in fact he could exist there at all. It is perfectly true that were a Mongol really impressed with the truth of Christianity he, like many other martyrs, would not confer with flesh and blood, but still the hardship that would follow a confession of Christianity must not be forgotten in stating the difficulties that lie in the way of Mongols becoming Christians.

But there is one point where the superiority of Christianity can be made manifest to the Mongols, that is, by its fruits. Buddhism is an elaborate and in many respects a grand system, but in one thing it fails signally, that is, in producing holiness. A Mongol when attacked on this point, for the most part, does not make much of a defence. He knows and admits that his religion does not purify the heart and produce the fruits of holy living; on the contrary, the commercial view taken of the relation of sin and merit militates against morality, and if he be not one of the ignorant devout, but a man of good information, he will admit that the temples are often little more than cages of unclean birds. Here then is the hope for Christianity. If it can be made manifest to the Mongols that Jesus can cleanse a man's heart and reform his conduct, can make the vile man pure and the thief honest, that would be an argument which they would find it difficult to answer Their own lamas make plenty of fuss and mystery over their medical system, but there are things that with all their fuss and mystery they cannot cure. And when a little foreign medicine is applied and a cure follows, no carefully reasoned-out argument, no erudite chemical lecture is required to convince them of the efficacy of the remedy. In the same way it is to be hoped that a closer acquaintance with the effects of Christianity, will, when they see its purifying power, convince the Mongols of its superiority, in a way that arguments and discussions on its internal, external, and historical evidences never could do. In this seems to lie the only hope for the success of Christianity in Mongolia.

CHAPTER XVII.

MONGOLS' DIFFICULTIES ABOUT CHRISTIANITY.

Christianity regarded as superfluous. The grandeur of Buddhism. If Christianity is true, Buddhism is false. The various forms of Christianity. Paucity of Christian Scriptures. No liturgy in our Bible. The Trinity. Resurrection. Suffering. How do we know our Bible to be true? Mongols as a rule admit that they are sinners. Counting beads. Buddhism says a man can save himself. Thinks Christianity too easy. Finds Christianity too difficult. Answers to prayer. Some of the objections are earnest, some are frivolous. Answer to many objections. Material difficulties in the way of Mongols willing to accept Christianity.

THE first and one of the greatest difficulties that a Mongol feels about Christianity is, that it seems to him to be superfluous. He has his Buddhism, and what else does he want? In what is it defective that he should want another religion? It seems to satisfy all the wants of his soul, and his reverence for it is unbounded. Buddhism as referred to here is not that religion pure and simple in the abstract, but the version of it now extant in Mongolia, which seems, in some things, to have adapted itself to meet human wants more fully than is possible if the rigid letter of the theory be adhered to.

Buddhism, as the Mongol knows it, is a magnificent system in its abstract doctrines, in the size of its

Scriptures, in the grandeur and number of its temples, in the imposing nature of its ceremonials, in the antiquity of its history, in the extent of its empire in the world, in the number and reputed power of its living Buddhas, and in the prominent part it plays in his native country. It strikes his senses with an overwhelming power; almost no one disbelieves its creed, almost no one is remiss in the practice of the duties it enjoins. Christianity is, in his opinion, quite superfluous.

But to any one who gets over this preliminary difficulty, and listens to the doctrines of Christianity, there soon arises a much more serious consideration, namely, If Christianity is true, Buddhism is false! This staggers him. Buddhism false! with its cart-loads of Scriptures, with its hosts of miracles in the olden times, with its hosts of miracles in the present times, and its crowds of constantly reincarnating living Buddhas! False! Is it possible, he asks, that a religion *can* be false which has lived so long, spread so far, flourished so greatly, and struck its roots so deeply into human nature, that millions live in it enthusiastically and die in it happily? Can falsehood be so prosperous? Can falsehood be so powerful?

If too, he says, of all the religions, Christianity alone is true, how is it that it has been so long in coming to us? It has been established eighteen hundred years, and we are only now for the first time hearing of it! If it alone is true, and if its doctrines are so important, how comes it that we have been left in ignorance of it so long? Would it not have spread itself more rapidly, and, in virtue of its being true, have long ago conquered every other false system?

Then again when a Mongol is pressed to accept

Christianity, he professes himself bewildered by the various forms of it with which he comes into contact. Of old he has known the Russian Christianity of the Greek Church. Most probably he has heard or seen something of the Roman Catholic religion, which has large colonies of Chinese adherents inhabiting localities either in, or bordering on, Mongolia, and now he is presented with a third form of Christianity. The Russian says his is the best form, the Roman Catholic advances as stout a claim for his system, and the Protestant not only makes a similar claim, but offers to prove that his is the best of the three.

In addition to Christianity, the Mongols come into contact with Mohammedanism, in the persons of many Chinese traders, who, of course, stand up for their particular religion; and thus, among "Black Lamas" (as the Russian clergy are called in Mongolia), Romish priests, Protestant missionaries, and "White Hats" (Mohammedans), the Mongol pretends that his head is turned, and he knows not whom to believe. It is fair to add that this last difficulty is not a common one, but is urged only by the few men of inquiring minds who have put themselves in the way of learning something of these four systems.

A difficulty that seems to be *generally* felt is the paucity of the Christian Scriptures as compared with the voluminous Buddhistic writings. Very few, even among the learned Mongols, have I found able to tell exactly to how many volumes their sacred books extend. The explanation perhaps, is, that in different places and editions they are put up differently, but the Ganjore, one of their sacred collections, is usually stated to contain a little over a hundred volumes, and the Danjore, represented to be a kind of commentary on the former, a little over two hundred volumes.

Visitors to Buddhist temples usually have these collections pointed out to them, standing ranged up frequently one on each side of the great service hall. The volumes are about two feet long, seven or eight inches broad, and four or five inches deep, and carefully swathed up in their yellow wrappings. They present a most imposing appearance, and when a rich man or a community has occasion to borrow them, a string of camels or a small train of carts is necessary for their transport. Remembering this, it is not difficult to understand the amazement of the Mongol when he hears that the Christian Scriptures are contained and complete in the one moderately sized volume, which the missionary lifts from his side, and hands across the tent to the visitor for inspection.

By nothing is the Mongol more surprised than to find that our Bible and our religious system has no set form of liturgy to be got off by heart and repeated, as in his services and prayers. His idea of Scriptures seems to be something to be learned off and repeated by rote, and he is much astonished to find that we have nothing resembling even in a distant way his "Nom," except the Lord's Prayer.

The idea of the Trinity is apt at first to prove a difficulty, and many questions are asked about the various persons, and their relations to each other, and how Father and Son can be of the same age. Some part of the difficulty is removed by explaining that human nomenclature can only inadequately represent Divinity; and in his own religion he is accustomed to find things hard to understand, and thus, when he meets with anything in Christianity which he cannot fathom, a Mongol can lay it aside with the remark that the "doctrine is deep."

A question frequently asked is, "How about those who lived and died before the coming of Jesus? If it is only Jesus who can save men, are all those lost who died before Jesus came?"

Vicarious suffering too seems strange to them, their own system teaching that for his sin a man must suffer, and there is no escape; but when explained to them, this doctrine presents no difficulty.

The Christian doctrine of a future state involves an utter denial of the Buddhist theory of transmigration, which is interwoven with almost every other doctrine of that religion, and is perhaps the tenet of all his theological system which is most firmly believed by a Mongol, and which seems ever most vividly present to his mind. To deny this doctrine dissipates at once any idea that the two religions may be one and the same, and gives rise to a whole host of difficulties.

If souls do not transmigrate, where do they come from at birth, whither do they go at death? If they did not exist before this life, does their existence cease at death? The idea of an eternal heaven seems to be easily enough received, but a Buddhist, though familiar, through his own religion, with inconceivably long periods of punishment for sin, seems to stagger at the idea of a hell, to the duration of which no period is assigned, and from the sufferings of which no efforts of the sinner or his surviving friends avail to open a way of escape.

Admitting, for argument's sake, the Christian doctrine

that we can recognise and expect to meet such of our friends as go to heaven, he asks, How about those whom we do not meet there, and who are gone to the place of torment? Knowing that they are suffering, can we be happy? And how does God regard them and their sufferings? Can He see them and be happy? And if God knows everything, and knows before He has created them, that such and such men will be sinners and not be saved, but go to hell, why, knowing all this, does He, who is goodness and love, make such men at all? And why did God, who made the world and rules it, and knows all and can do all, why did not He prevent the serpent from deceiving our first parents, and keep sin from entering the world at all?

Then again, asks the Mongol, How can a man's body live again? It is taken out to the plain, and thrown down on the ground; the dogs, wolves, and birds devour it and where is it, or how can it be again gathered together?

But this is not all. How, he asks, if souls do not transmigrate, is the presence of suffering animals in the world to be accounted for? That dog, starving, diseased, miserable, enduring, in short, a living death, what about it? If souls do not transmigrate, and if this suffering now be not the punishment of sin committed in a former life, what then is it?

A Mongol sometimes asks how we know all that our Bible tells us of a future state to be true? Has any one among us died, gone to the world to come, seen these things, and come back to life to report on them? Not only does he ask this question, but seeks to establish the truth of his own tenets, by affirming that the doctrines of Buddhism have been corroborated by the testimony of men who have risen from the dead.

Some difficulty too is occasionally made on the doctrine that all are sinners, by men who maintain that in Mongolia there are individuals, admittedly very few, who are not sinners. The speakers do not, openly at least, claim this saintship for themselves, but usually for some other man known or reported to exist, whose place of abode, when minutely asked for, is commonly stated in a very indefinite sort of way, as for example, "north-west," and at a very great distance, and whose existence is evidently, even in the mind of him who brings up the case, theoretical.

As a rule, Mongols do not need to have the doctrine that men are sinners pressed upon them. That they admit. They also admit the necessity for cancelling guilt. It is the peculiar method of cancelling it advanced by Christianity that they hesitate to receive, and one of the greatest objections they have to this method is, that, in their opinion, a sufficient value is not attached to good works in wiping away sin. Buddhism does not fail to inculcate good works and virtuous actions, and, as an incentive to the performance of them, teaches a doctrine of sin and forgiveness, which, stated in simple language, amounts to this, that at death all a man's good actions are balanced against his bad actions, and if his good actions preponderate he is entitled to reward, and if his bad actions preponderate he has to suffer punishment. A man who has been thus taught to think and act does not like to be told that all his good works and virtuous actions are no more than his simple duty, and that no amount of such works and actions can wipe away sin.

Then again Buddhism puts into his hand a rosary, and tells him that each prayer repeated has a certain value in cleansing away sin, and sends him on long pilgrimages to famous temples, assuring him that all such journeys are added as large items to the account of merit by which he hopes after death to do away with the accumulated sins of his life. Christianity tells him that counting beads and making pilgrimages can do nothing towards taking away his sin, and he is greatly shocked to find that if he admits Christianity as true, he must be content to learn that he has wasted a great accumulation of attention and persevering energy on what is useless; but when he is told that he can do absolutely nothing to wipe away his sin, he is more shocked still, and many a man who might be content to let the labour he has spent on his beads and pilgrimages go for nothing, if some other better way of making merit were shown him, is not only staggered but entirely offended, when he has pressed upon him the doctrine of human helplessness.

It frequently appears to a Mongol that salvation, according to Christianity, is altogether too easy. He is surprised to find that a Christian, a teacher of Christianity even, may kill vermin, eat flesh, nay even marry a wife without infringing any of the doctrines of his religion; his surprise is much increased when he learns that Christianity is free from the almost endless prohibitions, restrictions, vows, and rites with which Buddhism abounds; and when the freedom of Christianity dawns upon him he sometimes expresses himself in terms which are an unconscious echo of the words of Christ, "My yoke is easy and My burden is light."

A little more knowledge, however, is sufficient to change his opinion. When he learns that salvation, according to the Christian idea, is not merely the cancelling of a long score of old sins, and of the current sins of the present, but purification from sin itself, and the renewal of the heart, he thinks the aim an impossibility, and regards the purification as a process which he is not willing to be put through. To enter upon a contest with evil, and strive to eradicate it from the heart, this is a task from which he shrinks. He is discouraged by the thought on the one hand, that as far as he succeeds, he can claim no merit; and on the other hand, by supposing that he has to maintain the unequal strife in his own strength, an error into which it is quite natural for him to fall, seeing that in working out his own salvation, according to the Buddhistic method, he is not accustomed to rely on any power higher than his own.

One great difficulty in explaining Christianity to a Mongol is that all his life, having looked upon salvation as a thing to be accomplished by him, he is very slow to take up the idea that it is something that has been done *for* him, and is to be done *in* him, by an omnipotent Saviour, and that the part he himself has to play in the process is the very subordinate one of yielding a willing submission to the power of God which operates upon him, and of humbly following the footsteps of One who treads the path before him, shelters him in all dangers, supplies all needed strength, and guarantees that every true-hearted follower shall, in good time, arrive at the desired goal of that heavenly joy which springs from the consciousness of forgiveness, and the felt freedom of purity from sin.

Answer to prayer is now and then brought up as a difficulty by men who profess to think that a man might pursue a premeditated course of deliberate sinning, and by means of prayer obtain forgiveness, and so go on in iniquity with impunity—a difficulty to be traced directly to the demoralisation produced by the theory of a man's future state depending simply on the preponderance of his good or bad actions.

Sometimes a man wants to know how far satisfactory would be the state of one who, disregarding Christ, confined his worship to reverencing a supreme God in an indefinite sort of way; and nearly every man who converses much about Christianity wishes to know what has become of all the heathen who have died without hearing of Christ.

Did Buddha live at all? it is sometimes asked, and if the Buddhist writings are not received as true, how can the authenticity of the Christian Scriptures be established?

Such are the intellectual and spiritual difficulties raised in the minds of Mongols by the doctrines of Christianity. Of these some are brought forward by men who seem to be earnest enough, and who may perhaps be really in perplexity, but it is to be feared that the greater part of them are advanced merely for the sake of argument, and are welcomed rather as subjects of debate than felt to be barriers to the acceptance of Christianity.

Many of these questions admit of answers and explanations which seem to recommend themselves as satisfactory to the Mongol mind, and as to subjects not treated of in the Bible, and doctrines difficult to fathom, perhaps the most successful method of dealing with an objector is to explain that the Bible does not claim to be a complete set of treatises explaining everything, but a guide book pointing out clearly the way to heaven.

informing the traveller of everything which it is needful or helpful to him to know, but leaving a multitude of things to be seen and learned by him when he arrives at his destination. Many Mongols go to Peking, and every one can understand that a handbook for the road might be perfect, although of thousands of things in the capital it made no mention at all, and only made vague allusions to others.

There is another set of difficulties which meantime form the real barrier to the acceptance of Christianity, and these are material. For a Mongol to profess Christianity would be to face ruin. It is very doubtful if a consistent native Christian could subsist on the plain among his Buddhist countrymen. So great is the power of the lamas, and so intense seems to be the spirit of bigotry that pervades the whole community, that any one who refused to conform to the requirements of Buddhism would perhaps find it impossible to remain in his native country; and men who knew something of Christianity, when pressed to accept it, have offered to do so if the missionary would undertake to support them, adopting and protecting them as part of his own establishment. Parents, too, offer their children on the same condition, namely, that the missionary feeds and clothes them for the present, and makes himself responsible for their future career.

A man thoroughly convinced of the truth of Christianity, and powerfully moved by the Holy Spirit, would not be deterred by considerations of hardship from professing Christ, and a simultaneous profession by even a small number would lessen the difficulty immensely. There are not wanting in Mongolia men who, not endowed with any official authority, but possessing great natural force of character, exert a powerful influence on the communities in which they live. Should such a man be among the first to declare for Christ, he might greatly lessen the difficulty in the way of others. But it is useless thus to speculate. If only the truth can be made to reach their understanding, it is not to be doubted that God will in His own time and way, even among the Mongols, and notwithstanding all difficulties, apply it with living power to the hearts of men, and call out from among them those who will confess Him before their countrymen, and smooth the way for those who afterwards shall follow their example.

CHAPTER XVIII.

MONGOLIAN BUDDHISM.

Buddhism as it exists now in Mongolia. Power of Buddhism over its votaries. Noble ideas it has given the Mongols. Immortality of the soul. Ten black sins. Five *Zabsar ugwei* sins. Rewards and punishments. Humanity. Heaven and Hell. Power of prayer. Adaptation to the capacity of its votaries. Motives are recognised. Resemblances between Buddhism and Christianity. Buddhism hinders material prosperity; by the number of lamas; by its arrogant self-sufficiency. Hinders learning. Oppression exercised by the lamas. Deceit practised by them. The living Buddha system. The lama system a curse; to the lamas themselves; to the people generally. Buddhism has no intelligent worship. Buddhistic worship is debasing. Buddhistic good works often do harm. Buddhism makes men sin in actions which are indifferent. Buddhism fails to produce holiness. Buddhism is a usurper.

THIS chapter does not profess to give a systematic account of Buddism. On that subject numerous and learned treatises have been written, with which most people are more or less familiar. What I propose here to do, is to consider the superficial aspects of Buddhism —the practical part of it, as embodied in the life and habits of the Mongols at the present day.

One of the first things the missionary notices in coming into contact with the Mongols, is the completeness of the sway exercised over them by their religion. Meet a Mongol on the road, and the probability is, that he is saying his prayers and counting his beads as he rides along. Ask him where he is going and on what errand, as the custom is, and likely he will tell you he is going to some shrine to worship. Follow him to the temple, and there you will find him one of a company with dust-marked forehead, moving lips, and the never-absent beads, going the rounds of the sacred place, prostrating himself at every shrine, bowing before every idol, and striking pious attitudes at every new object of reverence that meets his eye. Go to the quarters where Mongols congregate in towns, and you will find that quite a number of the shops and a large part of the trade there are dependent upon images, pictures, and other articles used in worship. Go to Mongolia itself, and probably one of the first great sights that meets your eye will be a temple of imposing grandeur, resplendent from afar in colours and gold. Approach tents, and the prominent object is a flag-staff with prayer-flags fluttering at the top. Enter a tent, and there right opposite you as you put your head in at the door, is the family altar with its gods, its hangings, its offerings, and its brass cups. Let them make tea for you, and before you are asked to drink it a portion is thrown out by the hole in the roof of the tent, by way of offering. Have them make dinner for you, and you will see a portion of it offered to the god of the fire, and after that perhaps you may be asked to eat. Wait till evening, and then you will see the little butter lamp lighted, and set upon the altar as a pure offering. When bed-time comes, you will notice as they disrobe, that each and all wear at their breast charms sewn up in cloth, or pictures of gods in metal cases with glass fronts. In the act of disrobing, prayers are said most industriously, and not till all are stretched on their felts does the sound of devotion cease. Among the first things in the morning you will hear them at their prayers again, and when your host comes out with

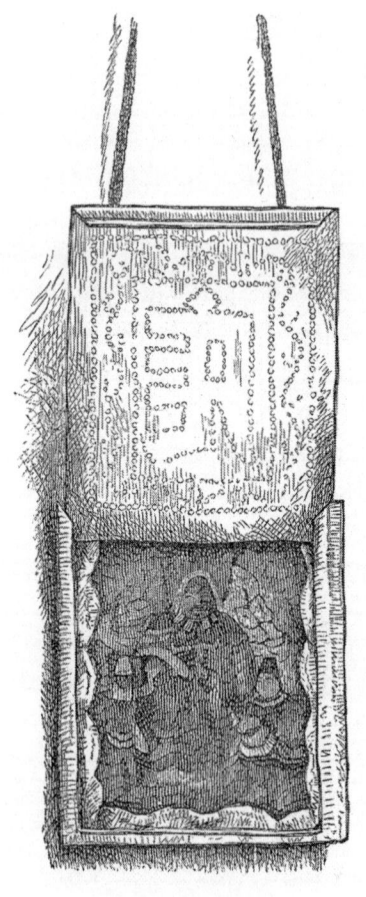

MONGOL CHARM.

you to set you on your way, he will most likely give you as your landmark some cairn, sacred for the threefold reason that its every stone was gathered and laid with prayer, that prayer-flags flutter over the sacred pile, and that it is the supposed residence of the deity that presides over the neighbourhood.

Nor is this all. The Mongol's religion marks out for him certain seemingly indifferent actions as good or bad, meritorious or sinful; he has days on which he will not give, days on which he may bargain but may not sell, places to be avoided and places to be frequented, times to perform certain works, and times to refrain from works. There is scarcely one single step in life, however insignificant, which he can take without first consulting his religion through his priest; and the result of the consultation is probably an answer which will cause him great trouble and annoyance. But he submits to it. Not only does his religion insist on moulding his soul and colouring his whole spiritual existence, but it determines for him the colour and cut of his coat. Perhaps no other religion on the face of the earth holds its votaries clutched in such a paralysing grip. It would be difficult to find another instance, in which any religion has grasped a country so universally and completely as Buddhism has Mongolia. The Mongols themselves say that some of them have more piety, some have less, but that throughout the length and breadth of the country there is not a single infidel. I partly believe it, and it is this universality of dominion which enables the religion to build such rich and costly temples, in such a poor and thinly-peopled country.

The Mongols themselves are in the habit of saying, that before Buddhism came to them, they were in ignorance and darkness, given up to deeds of superstition and cruelty, and addicted to such practices as putting their mother to death when she reached the age of fifty. Now, they say, see what we are and how we act—all this has been brought about by the sacred books.

The most prominent doctrine in their religion is *the immortality of the soul*. This their mind grasps firmly and clearly. I never yet met a man who for a moment doubted it, or hesitated in the least when asked to tell what he knew about it. They scorn the thought that the soul began its life with the body, and scorn the idea that its life should end with the death of the body. For countless thousands of ages the soul has been living on, sometimes taking one birth, sometimes another; for countless thousands of ages it shall live on, taking higher or lower births, according to its merits or sin; but still the same individual soul, the same unchanged spiritual being. There never was a time when the soul was not alive, and there never shall be a time when it shall not be alive. And this is not a doctrine that is held simply as an article in their creed, and referred to by the learned only in their discussions; it is an ever-present feeling with young and old, learned and illiterate, with man, woman, and child. The body is merely the case or shell in which the soul lives; it is not the man, any more than the house is the inhabitant; and nowhere is their faith in their soul's distinctness and independence more apparent, than in the manner in which they take the dead body which has been vacated by the soul, and cast it out on the waste, to feed the wolves and the birds.

Moreover, they acknowledge souls not in men merely, but also in every living thing. The beast, the bird, the insect, the reptile, are animated by souls as everlasting, and as capable of great things as their own. The bodies of these beings are, in fact, only soul-cases; and at a former period their own souls, as they suppose, may have taken such births, and may take such births again. Mongolia is thinly peopled, and Mongols have much solitary travelling and herding, but they are not alone, as we should be. Everywhere around them, in the flocks they herd, in the beasts they ride, and in the birds that flit past them, and in the insects that annoy them, they recognise spiritual existences.

The Mongol's religion has its *Decalogue;* not that of Moses, but a list of ten black sins, divided into three classes, according as they are committed by the Body the Tongue, or the Mind. Those of the Body are three in number, viz. :—killing; uncleanness; theft. Those of the Tongue are four in number, viz. :—the false word; the harsh word; the slanderous word; the idle word. Those of the Mind are three in number, viz. :—covetousness; malevolence; heresy. Killing includes not only the taking of human life, but also the taking of the life of any animal, even to the insect or reptile.

But the list is not yet complete. In addition to the ten black sins there are five *Zabsar ugwei* sins. *Zabsar* is a split, crack, little opening—an interval of space or time. The black sins are bad enough, and are to be followed by terrible punishments in purgatory, which, however, may alternate with periods of comparative comfort. The *Zabsar ugwei* sins are worse, and to be followed by a hell of intense suffering, and that without cessation.

The five *Zabsar ugwei* sins are patricide; matricide; killing a Doctor of Divinity; bleeding Buddha; sowing hatred among priests. By a Doctor of Divinity is meant, a lama of exalted learning, and who is under more and stricter vows than the common priests.

Drawing blood from the body of Buddha is a figurative expression, after the manner of Hebrews vi. 6; which speaks of backsliders "crucifying the Son of God afresh, and putting Him to an open shame."

No religion could promise more in the way of rewards, and scarcely any religion could threaten more in the way of punishments. The Mongol believes that his future state depends on his actions in his life. At death his good and bad actions are balanced against each other. If the good are more, he rises in the scale of existence, if the bad are more, he sinks. Hence it is that his religion has such a practical effect on him. He goes on long, difficult, painful, and expensive pilgrimages, because he is taught that this is meritorious. He makes costly offerings to temples and to the lama class, because he believes this has its reward. He feeds the hungry, he clothes the naked, gives tea to the thirsty, and relieves the oppressed, because these things have their reward, and go into the scale that decides his fate. He endeavours to eschew evil and follow righteousness, because these things have their reward. Evil in all its forms he tries to avoid, because he believes that every sin will weigh against him, and drag him down in the scale of being. As surely as plants grow according to their kind from their seeds, so surely shall joy grow from good, and pain from evil. Making merit occupies a large part of a Mongol's thought, and all animated existence that comes within his reach is the better treated, because his religion teaches him that kindness shown to the meanest creature receives the same reward as if the recipient had been the most exalted in the universe.

Thus it comes that his religion teaches the Mongol

the noble lesson of *humanity*. Perhaps nowhere will you find less cruelty than in Mongolia. Not only do their cattle and flocks receive expressions of sympathy in suffering, and such alleviation of pain as their owner knows how to give; but even the meanest creatures, insects and reptiles included, are treated with consideration. One of the best proofs of the habitual kindness of the Mongol, is the tameness of the birds on the plateau. Crows perch themselves on the top of loaded camels, and deliberately steal Chinamen's rusks and Mongol's mutton, before the very eyes of the vociferating owners; hawks sweep down in the market-place at Urga, and snatch eatables from the hands of the unwary, who simply accuse the thief of patricide and pass on; and swallows, year after year, build their nests and rear their young inside the very tents of the Mongols. A Mongolian's pity seems to flow out freely towards the suffering of all creatures, even the meanest and most vexatious. My bald-headed camel-driver was nearly driven to distraction one evening by a cloud of mosquitoes, which kept hovering over and alighting on his shining pate. During the night there came a touch of frost, and when we rose in the morning not an insect was on the wing. Looking at them as they clung benumbed to the sides of the tent, he remarked, " The mosquitoes are frozen;" and then added, in a tone of sincere sympathy, the Mongol phrase expressive of pity, "*Hoarhe Hoarhe.*" There was no sarcasm or hypocrisy about it.

The *popular idea of heaven* is, that it is a place where hunger and thirst are felt no more, where there is no more sickness or weariness, no more suffering or pain, no scorching heat, no biting cold; a place where the holy in perfect bliss rejoice in the shade of trees green with perpetual spring, and pluck fruits mellow with perpetual autumn; a place where old friends meet and pass their existence for ever, within sound of ceaseless prayers, which are said for the benefit of all animated beings. The tortures of hell, or purgatory, whichever you may prefer to call it, are described with a minuteness and detail too horrible for us to dwell on; but there is one thing worth remarking, that is, the fitness of the punishment to the sin. Just take one example. A man has lived and died a glutton. The consequence is, that he is punished by hunger. He is born with perhaps a body as large as a mountain, and a stomach capacious as a cavern; food is within his reach, and he is as hungry as all the wolves in Siberia; he would eat, but his mouth is as small as a needle's eye, and his throat is as narrow as a hair. Gluttony was his sin, and hunger is his punishment. It is the same all through; a man's punishment springs directly from his sin.

Another of the good things of Mongol Buddhism is *the power it ascribes to prayer.* On one occasion a lama came to my tent, and asked me to divine for him. I said I could not divine, and asked him what the matter was. He said that the other day his temple had been robbed, and he wanted me to discover in what direction the thief had gone. Next morning I pitched my tent at the temple, when, hearing the sound of long-continued services, I asked what it meant, and was told that they were holding services, in the hope that their god would have the thief apprehended. That very day the thief was brought in, and still the sound of service went on. Asking again, I was told that they were now holding a thanksgiving service.

WORKS OF MERIT.

Every Mongol believes most devoutly in the value of prayer. Many of his prayers are mere charms, perhaps, or simple repetitions; but no concurrence of circumstances can arise in which he does not believe it advantageous to say them. As to the decision of the nature of his future state, he believes not only that he must pray, but also that he must work. Many instances of works could be quoted. I heard of a man who kept silver beside him bound up in little parcels of three mace, and gave one of these packets to every lama, good, bad and indifferent, who came and asked for it. I have seen miles of stony road cleared and smoothed, and the stones piled up in pyramids by the pious hands of one man.

Mongol Buddhism affords *doctrines and speculations* whose depth and magnitude surpass the grasp of the greatest minds. For the understanding of the weak, it veils its glory, comprehends itself in the smallest possible compass, and gives the ignorant six syllables, *Om mani padmi hum,* to pronounce, as the sum and substance of all. If a man's spirit is of a wandering nature, or disinclined to devotion, it puts into his hand a wheel filled with prayers, and tells him to turn that, and it will count as if he had repeated the whole of the printed formulæ contained in it; and if even this is too much for him, he can depute the duty to the flutter of a flag or the crank of a windmill.

It is scarcely possible to believe that the present Mongols are the descendants of those who rode behind Genghis Khan in his wild career of bloodshed and slaughter. Their bravery seems completely gone. Not long since a perfect stampede was created in Central

Mongolia, by the report that robbers had been seen travelling together in a body. Everybody fled; flocks and herds were driven off, heavy goods abandoned, and a large district left without inhabitant. The panic overtook a caravan in which were some travellers in

PRAYING-MILLS DRIVEN BY WIND.

camel-carts. The camel-carts were left in the desert, and the whole company fled to the hill country. For some weeks the Russian post was interrupted, and things looked serious. It was afterwards discovered that it was all a mistake. The supposed robbers were a few people going to Urga to pray; so few that even had they been robbers of the bravest, a tithe of the men who fled might have driven them off; and the whole flight might have been prevented, had there been found one man with bravery enough to reconnoitre the supposed enemy. More than the half of the male population now are lamas, who of course from their vows could never be warriors.

Mongol priests recognise the power of motive in estimating actions. One night a hungry dog entered my tent, and stole nearly my whole stock of mutton. A day or two afterwards, in talking of the event to a lama, I asked him, in joke, if he would consider that I had any merit in thus feeding the starved animal. "No," said he keenly, "you did not mean to do it, and you were sorry for it when it was done. If you had voluntarily taken the mutton and fed the dog, your act would have been meritorious; but as you did not mean to do it, you get no merit by the event." And so throughout all their actions. The attitude of the mind decides the nature of the act. He that offers a cup of cold water only, in a proper spirit, has presented a gift quite as acceptable as the most magnificent of donations. The theory of the religion, and even the popular notion of it, lays stress on the attitude of the spirit in prayer also; but the practice so notoriously disregards the spirit and exalts the letter, that on this point it is impossible to say a friendly word.

Many of the teachings of Buddhism resemble those of our own Christianity. To enumerate them all would take up too much time and space. It will suffice to speak of a few. The flood. The teaching of this narrative—the destruction of the wicked, and the escape of men and animals for the sake of one righteous man—agrees quite with Mongol doctrine. Abraham, a man the result of whose faith and piety is felt to the latest ages; Joseph and David, men whose faith carried them through the mightiest adversities, up to the highest rank of honour; these three the Mongols hail almost as heroes of their own religion, while the story of Elisha multiplying the widow's oil (2 Kings iv.), they say is exactly like their own legends. The parable of the prodigal—sin followed by suffering, and repentance by forgiveness—and of the Pharisee and publican, they also welcome as orthodox; but that which delights their hearts most of all, is the picture of the Good Samaritan beside his kneeling camel, pouring medicine on the wounds of the sufferer. When they see how he has bound up the wounded parts, and hear how he conveyed the wounded man to the inn, paid his reckoning, and gave him something to go on with, their enthusiasm rises, because they recognise in the Samaritan the ideal of their own religion—self-denying help to the distressed. Though the listeners are frequently lamas, they never fail to express their hearty disapprobation of the red-coated priest who passed by on the other side. "The religions are one. The dress is different. The meaning is the same. Exactly alike." These and similar phrases are constantly on the lips of Mongols who listen to such parts of our Bible as are mentioned above. These phrases are often uttered unthinkingly, and sometimes by men who wish to draw the conversation to a close, that they may ask what your coat is made of, or if you have a telescope; but such expressions are not always the result of indifference. Even the Christian student of their literature is often struck with points of resemblance, and finds cause to be glad that Mongol Buddhism has such noble teachings.

The great points of contrast are—the Christian doctrine of one life of probation, the resurrection of the body, salvation by faith on Christ, as opposed to their doctrine of escape by works, creation by a pre-existent Creator, and government of the world by the same all-powerful Creator. On these points, the two—Christianity and Buddhism—are diametrically opposed; but, with the exception of these and a few others, the teachings of the two religions bear a striking resemblance.

This then is what is to be said in favour of Buddhism as now existent in Mongolia. It is a religion of mighty power, of noble teachings, adapting its precepts and exactions to the meanest capacities and the most comprehensive intellects; searching behind the actions of men, and trying their motives; quenching the thirst for blood in fierce tribes, and moderating them into kindness and hospitality; a religion some of whose teachings rise nearly to the level of inspiration itself; a religion which has perhaps more redeeming qualities than any other false system of worship which the world has yet seen.

Having thus spoken as far as I could, justly and impartially, in *favour* of the religion, it is only fair that its *faults and defects* should now be discussed.

Buddhism hinders the material prosperity of the country by the lamas swarming in Mongolia. Young and old, rich and poor, outwardly devout and openly wicked, you meet them wherever you meet human beings at all. Diligent and lazy, intelligent and stupid, men of prayer and men of trade, they are continually coming across your path From personal observation, I am inclined to think that sixty per cent. of the male population of the country is quite a moderate estimate. The ambition of these men is to live by their religion. Most of them try, many succeed, and thus the energy of the country is clogged and crushed by the incubus of just as many men as can manage to find standing-room on the superstition and piety of the people. As for the lamas who cannot get a footing to support themselves on the religious needs of the people, they have to betake themselves to trade, work, herding cattle or performing the most menial offices. Even by them the country is little benefited, because, having no families to support, they have no great stimulus to exert themselves much in any line, and, as a matter of fact, do just as little as they can—nothing more than hunger and cold compels them.

Buddhism hinders the material prosperity of the country *by its arrogant self-sufficiency.* Said a lama to me once: "You foreigners are very clever in your way. Your telegraphs, steam-boats, railways, postal system, newspapers, manufactures, trade and medical and scientific knowledge, are very well in their way; but you lack one thing—the knowledge of our religion and sacred books. Notwithstanding all you know, your mind is but like the mouth of this flour-bag, bound up and drawn together, and so contracted that nothing can enter. Read our books, and then"—shaking out the untied mouth of the flour-bag—"your minds will become enlarged in breadth and grasp, and you will have intellectual capacity enough to take in all the wonders of heaven and earth. You send letters and telegrams, and run to and fro to know things distant. The student of our books sits in his tent, and by the power of his attainments in learning, knows all things in all parts of the universe."

This kind of assumption, which is perhaps more generally felt than expressed, has something to do with the repression of the spirit which prompts men to visit unknown countries, establish new lines of commerce, seek out unexplored knowledge, and generally improve the mental and material prosperity of a people. They have everything already; what more do they want? Let the English make, and the Russians and Chinese sell, their every article of dress and household furniture. These benighted peoples, whose only thought is wealth and pleasure, who in fact live like the beasts; let them busy themselves with these earthly trifles. A Mongol knows something better. He should occupy himself with his religion. This is the kind of feeling with which they regard us outsiders. To insinuate that their religion lacked anything that was really worth a man's while to search after, would be heresy. On the same level of authority with which it speaks of the soul, sin and merit, reward and punishment, their Buddhism also settles, distinctly and definitely, all points of medicine, geography, and astronomy. If any man wants to study any one of these subjects—to the sacred books—what should he want outside of them? If a man has money to spend, let him spend it in acquiring merit; and not seek to increase it by trade, like a worldly-minded Chinaman. If a man has time, money, and inclination to travel, let him go the round of the Buddhist sacred places and temples, and not ramble aimlessly over the world, like a demented Englishman. In this way, their religion always, tacitly at least, and often outspokenly, frowns upon any attempt at adding to knowledge, or advancing in any way from their present state. If a man prepares to venture on new fields of study or enterprise, he will find himself beaten back, or at least formidably opposed, by the united power of the piety, learning, and superstition of his country. The consequence is just what might have been expected. The Mongols can do nothing. They are dependent on others for everything. It might be supposed that Mongols would know at least how to fatten cattle; perhaps they do, but one thing is certain, that the fat carcases displayed in butchers' shops in North China, though originally Mongol sheep, were not fattened by Mongolians. Chinamen go to Mongolia in spring, buy up likely animals, lead them till autumn in green pastures, tend them well night and day, and after that, the original Mongol would not know his own sheep. Even in the very thing which is a Mongol's born profession, he is outdone by the superior intelligence and enterprise of the Chinaman. Ask a Mongol why this comes about, and he will tell you it is because his countrymen are deficient in ability. Examine and investigate the cause of this lack of ability, and you will find that much, if not all the blame, is to be laid at the door of his religion, which systematically and persistently frowns upon and opposes every attempt at increasing knowledge and enterprise, without which increase of prosperity is an impossibility.

Mongol Buddhism hinders learning. About three-fourths of the Mongol children go to school, but not more than about one-tenth of them ever learn to read. Those who can write decently are fewer still. The reason of this is, that their Buddhism insists on their learning Tibetan; that is, learning the pronunciation of words, so that they may be able to read, that is pronounce, the words of the sacred books. Arrived at this state of perfection, they think they know enough, and rest

MONGOL LAMA OF HIGH RANK.
From a photograph.

content. Priests, lamas, seldom can read a word of their own language. Most of the few laymen who can read Mongolian have studied it in the hope of government employment. A few lamas do read, say three or four per cent. Of the laymen more can read, say thirteen or fourteen per cent. This is a lamentable state of matters. It is much worse than if only the same percentage of Chinamen could read; for while the Chinese character is difficult, the Mongolian, having an alphabet like our own, is very easy, and it is much easier to learn to read Mongolian than English, because the words are spelt much nearer their pronunciation than in our own language. That so few people can read is therefore a heavy charge against Buddhism; because the whole effect of its influence is to deter men from learning.

The oppression of the lamas is another charge I have to make against Mongolian Buddhism. The lamas oppress the people by their exactions. Suppose a man gets sick. He sends for a doctor. He is a lama. He must have his fee. Be the patient rich or be he poor, the money, or the sheep, or the ox, or the horse must be forthcoming, else the medicine is not forthcoming. The only oppression about this is in the case of the poor, from whom medical help is withheld, if they cannot make some return. But this is not all. Work without prayer is of no avail. The patient has medicine, he must also have lama services, or perhaps temple services even. What then? Does the temple—do the lamas exact fees for praying? No, they don't *exact* them; but they *expect* them, and the people are trained to believe that they need expect no good from their prayers, except they make handsome donations to the lamas or the temples employed. If he is rich, he spends sheep, camels, horses, oxen, money. If he is poor, he must still find something. If he gets better, all right, the lamas have the gifts and the credit of the recovery. If he dies, so much the worse for him, and so much the better for the lamas. They merely say, "Oh, his true time to die had come, and when that comes there is no escape." But they are not yet finished. Prayers must be said, and services held for the benefit of the departed soul. More gifts must be made, more money must be spent. When sickness and death enter a Mongol's tent, they come not alone; they often come with poverty and ruin in their train. I know a man who was once rich in cattle and herds. He had flocks of sheep, herds of cattle, droves of horses, and strings of camels. Now he has not a sheep to bleat at his door. It is the old story, too common in Mongolia. Sickness came, then death; first of one child, then of another; till of a large family only one son and one daughter remain. The stricken parents spared no expense on doctors and prayers to save their children; then, after death took their sons and daughters, lavished out their means on prayers and services on behalf of the departed souls. Now they are old, poor, head-and-ears in debt, and he who once was famous, and rich, and regarded the countenance of no man, is fain to eke out his unhappy existence on the proceeds of begging, borrowing, teaching, and a government office worth twelve taels a year. No language is too strong to use in the condemnation of these merciless robbers, who "devour widows' houses, and for a pretence make long prayers"; and no terms are too severe for the reprobation of a system which fattens and gorges itself by torturing the feelings of natural affection, when laid bare and bleeding from sorrow and bereavement.

Many lamas are, I doubt not, quite sincere. They are not so much deceivers as deceived. But the whole system is founded on deception, and the wires are pulled by lamas fully conscious of the frauds. Take three instances.

At Wu T'ai, there is an image in a little temple over the gateway of the village. From this idol, we were told quite seriously, light streams far and near on certain days of the month. This of course raises the fame of the temple, and brings revenue; and most lamas perhaps believe it, but those who carry on the deception know all about it. This is merely one case of a class, and it is on devices like this that the lamas rely, to keep up the reputation of themselves and their temples.

When famous lamas die and their bodies are burnt, little white pills are reported as found among the ashes, and sold for large sums to the devout, as being the concentrated virtue of the man, and possessing the power of insuring a happy future for him who swallows one near death. This is quite common. I heard of one man who improved on this, by giving out that these pills were in the habit of coming out through the skin of various parts of the body. These pills called *sharil*, met with a ready sale, and then the man himself reaped the reward of his virtue, and did not allow all the profit of it to go to his heir.

The living Buddha system—living Buddhas, Gegens, as they are called, abound in Mongolia. Peking boasts two inside the walls, and another outside, at the Yellow Temple. The current belief is, that these men when they die take another birth, remember their former state, and prove their identity by using phrases characteristic of the former Buddha, selecting things that belonged to him from among a heap of things that were not his, describing the temple, lamas, etc. Great parade is made of the testing of the child. The truth of the matter is, that the head lamas arrange everything, and "coach" up the child; but the common people, perhaps the majority of the lamas even, believe the hoax most implicitly. Those who manage the business are as conscious of the fraud as they are of their own existence, and it is even whispered that the Gegen is not only their dupe, but their victim, ruled with a rod of iron, honoured and made much of as long as he is yielding to the board of lamas, but quietly poisoned or otherwise murdered when he begins to be refractory, or, discovering his power, tries to exercise his own will. The living Buddhas are the pillars of the present Mongol religious system—a system that owes its support to deliberate fraud and falsehood, and that on the part of its highest lamas.

The great sinners in Mongolia are the lamas, the great centres of wickedness are the temples. It is the system which makes the lamas, and places them in hot-beds of vice. Few lamas have any hand in their assuming the sacred garb. When children of six or ten years of age, their parents or guardians decide that they shall be lamas. The little fellows are pleased enough to put on a red coat, have their heads shaven, carry about the leaf of a Tibetan book between two boards, and be saluted as lama. It is all very fine at first. As mere children they do not know how much the full extent of their vows means. After some years they do know, but then it is too late to turn back. They cannot get free from their vows—they cannot keep them; so they break them repeatedly and systematically; their conscience is seared, and now that they are started they do not stop with merely violating vows they cannot keep, but, having cast aside restraint, and acquired a momentum in sin, they go on to the most unthought-of wickedness. Thus it comes that the great lama religious centres are the great centres of sin. The head-quarters of Mongol Buddhism is Urga, where Satan's seat is. If you go there you will be

LAMA'S CAP WHEN OFFICIATING.

warned never to go out after dusk, except you are well armed; and a foreigner who knew something of the place once remarked that he believed that the lamas there lived in the daily practice of all the sins known among men, murder alone excepted. Most of these men, had they not as children become the victims of this cursed system, might have lived useful lives, free from at least the grosser forms of iniquity, which as lamas they drink up like water.

The lama system is a curse to the people generally. Like priest, like people. The influence of the wickedness of the lamas is most hurtful. It is well-known. The lamas sin not only among themselves, but sow their evil among the people. The people look upon the lamas as sacred, and of course think that they may do what lamas do. Thus the corrupting influence spreads, and the state of Mongolia to-day, as regards uprightness and morality, is such as makes the heart more sick the more one knows of it. I suppose there are good lamas here and there, and I do not forget that the guilt of sin lies upon the sinner himself, not upon a system; but, nevertheless, the guilt of the tempter is as great as that of the sinner; and *this* guilt must be laid at the door of the system of lamaism, which Mongol Buddhism regards as one of her brightest ornaments.

Mongol Buddhism has hardly any intelligent worship. Most of the prayers are Tibetan; but there are a few Mongol prayers in use also, which the users seem to understand more or less. Make allowance for this—say one per cent., to be very liberal—and then it is safe to say, that Mongol Buddhism has no intelligent worship. The reason the Mongols themselves give for using Tibetan in preference to Mongolian is, that as water when poured from one cup into another becomes less in quantity and loses its purity, so the prayers suffer in translation from one language to another. So they keep to the Tibetan, and maintain that the merit lies in saying the prayer, not in understanding it. They carry this out to its legitimate results.

I once saw a huge pile of a ten-volume work in a

Mongol's tent, and asked what use was made of it. I was told it was read through once a year. As this would have been a good task for the owner, who was fonder of whisky than piety, I asked a little more about it, and was told there was no difficulty in the matter. Ten lamas were sent for to the temple, entered a tent prepared for their use, took each man his volume, and the whole ten rattled away simultaneously till the task was completed. This is no exaggeration. Ask almost any lama the meaning of his prayer, and he will think you a queer fellow, even to ask such a thing. Remember the windmills and the prayer-wheels, and there you have proof that the worship is neither intelligent nor spiritual. It is simply mechanical, whether performed by the mouth, the hand, or the windmill. The worship is simply a hollow form—nothing more.

There is an improvement on mechanical worship even. In the cupboard under the altar in a Mongol's tent, I once came upon a bundle nicely done up. I was curious to see what was in it; but the very mention of opening it threw the Mongol into a state of excitement and he hastily explained to me that it had been put up by a celebrated lama, and that its very existence there was sufficient to bring luck to the tent and merit to the inhabitants.

The Buddhistic worship is debasing. The lamas make much of the attitude of the mind in devotion, they say, indeed, that in offerings and worship the state of the mind is everything. They also maintain that in bowing before idols, the worship is not directed to the image, but to that which the image represents. This is all very well in theory, but as we are now dealing with the practical aspects of Buddhism, it is impossible to overlook the fact, that the great mass of the people worship the lumps of brass, wood, or mud before which they bow. A devout Mongol has to worship not only images, but must also pay his devotion to books, father and mother, and above all his Bakshi or teacher. His teacher he esteems more than father and mother; to the latter he owes his body; to his teacher he owes the

MONGOL WOODEN IMAGE OF BUDDHA.

enlightenment of his soul. Nay, he ranks his teacher as high as Buddha himself. Buddha's revelations are great and good, he says, but except through his teacher he would never have known them; and thus it is that he ranks his teacher on a level with Buddha. Some even speak more boldly, and hold that the teacher does more for them than Buddha, and therefore deserves more honour. In this way it comes about that Buddhism takes a man, sinful, vile, passionate, full of lies and duplicity, a man whose imperfections and sins you are perfectly acquainted with, and sets him up as your highest object of reverence.

Buddhistic good works often do more harm than good. To relieve distressed animals is meritorious, say the Buddhist books. Country Mongols sometimes, on going out at the gate of the great lama temple in the city of Peking, find a Chinaman sitting with sparrows cooped up in cages. The sparrows are for sale cheap— a cash or two each. He appeals to the Mongol, and not in vain. It is a chance to make merit cheaply, so the latter buys one or two birds, sets them at liberty, and goes away with the comforting feeling that he has done a meritorious action. He has let two sparrows free, and by that very act causes other three to be trapped. Indeed, it was simply to meet the Mongol demand that these sparrows were caught; and thus from want of a little reflection, he causes birds to be distressed by the very act of relieving them. This is a small matter, and the thing is so apparent that most of the town Mongols are not to be caught thus. A more serious matter is the giving of alms. Almsgiving is a splendid virtue in itself, blessing him that gives and him that takes, when carried on with discretion. When carried on without discretion, it becomes, as in Mongolia, a blast and a curse to the land and the people.

Indiscriminate charity has flooded the country with beggars. Not only do you find sturdy fellows begging round the country, under the shallow pretence of praying for the good of the land, but mounted beggars are quite common. Beggars ride in Mongolia, and sometimes ride good horses too. They come and live on the best the tent affords, and, not contented with this, expect a gift in money or kind when they leave. No one likes to refuse admittance or withhold the gift, lest the lama should blast them with his curse. The clover in which beggars revel induces many to adopt the profession who have not the excuse of helpless poverty; and not only do these fellows ride about on horseback, but some of them band together in companies, and travel about with camels and a tent. However, there is another side to this picture. One of the saddest pictures to be seen anywhere is in the market-place of Urga, where human beings lie night and day on the stony ground, covered with a few scraps of filthy skins and cast-off felts. Most of them have no fire, and there they lie exposed to the intense frost that prevails five or six months of the year, and to the piercing night winds which blow all the year round. Said a Buriat once to me, as we stood looking at them: "These are worn-out creatures; the half of them die." The truth of his words was manifest, when morning after morning one lair after another was found empty. Such is the end of the Mongol beggar when he becomes too weak to beg more.

The inducement to go to the Urga market-place is the fact that people of the place, and pilgrims, with an eye to merit, prepare food by the pailful, and have it distributed to the famishing. The manner of distribution is unique. One man takes the pail and a ladle; the instant he is seen approaching, men, women, and children, producing from the breast of their garments the ever-present cup, rush at him, and he would never reach the helpless creatures at all, did not his companion, a stalwart lama, lay about him with a pole about eight feet long, and keep back the eager crowd. Skirmishes and fights ensue over the spoil, and the whole crowd behave more like a pack of savage dogs than human beings. This is one of the deplorable fruits of that charity without discretion which has some attractive things about it, but which in reality causes more suffering and misery than it relieves.

Mongol Buddhism makes men sin in actions that are really indifferent. To kill sheep, for instance, as food, is right enough in itself. Buddhism says, "Thou shalt not kill." But a Mongol must have mutton, so he invents all manner of excuses. If he is within reach of a market, he goes there and buys, persuading himself that he has no hand in the killing of the animal. He pretends not to see that by purchasing the flesh he makes himself partaker in the sin of killing. The lamentable thing is, that the Buddhist finds himself hampered with so many impossible commands, which he finds he cannot keep, that by a constant practice of juggling with his conscience, he at last comes to have very vague ideas as to what he is responsible for, and what he is not responsible for. When religion has succeeded in blinding a man, so that he cannot tell right from wrong, it has well-nigh prepared him for any sin, even the most atrocious.

There are, however, right-minded men in Mongolia, who do not stoop to such juggling at all. They say it is a sin, but mutton they must have; they cannot help it, so they go in for the sin, hoping to wipe out the stain by extra diligence in making merit. I once met such a man, and was the occasion of his being a good deal grieved. He was a lama, and sold me a sheep, engaging as part of his bargain to find me a layman to kill it. The sun set, and no layman turned up. If the animal had only been killed, there were plenty of lamas about who would have been only too glad to assist in skinning it and cutting it up; but no one would strike the blow. He had to take his sheep away again, and, in addition to being sorry at the loss of the money, he seemed much exercised in his mind because he by selling the animal for slaughter felt himself guilty of killing it; and as the transaction had fallen through, foresaw that he would have to sell it to some one else, and thus be twice guilty of killing the same sheep! It is impossible not to have sympathy with such straightforward men, in the superfluous dilemmas in which they are placed by the unreasonable demands of an over-exacting religion.

One day we pitched our tent near the abode of a family, which I found to consist of one old man and two old women. I asked for milk, and, as they were poor, offered to give them some rice in return. We had been living on rice and millet for days, and were eager to taste milk. They had run out of grain, and for days had been living mainly on preparations of milk. They had plenty of milk and no rice; we had plenty of rice and no milk. Exchange was for the good of both parties. The old women seemed to jump at the idea, but referred the question to the man, put the end of a fragment of a gun-barrel into her toothless mouth, and set about blowing the fire. The old man made short work of the question. He would like the exchange, but there was a religious prohibition for the day. It could not be done; so they must drink their milk, and we must boil our rice in water. So it seemed, at least; yet in a few minutes we had a basinful of good milk in our tent. The old women were pious, but not destitute of common sense; so sending off the old man to look after the goats, they quickly brought us milk, and carried off the rice; and I hope did not shock the old man's piety by offering him a share of the spoil. This is only a sample of one among many vexatious prohibitions and requirements, and of the manner in which common sense often disregards them. These ordinances, which the Mongols feel binding upon them, cannot be thus disregarded, without doing violence to the conscience, but, after all, the blame of disregarding such meaningless commandments rests, not so much with the offenders, as with the system which appoints the ordinances.

Buddhism fails to produce holiness. It holds out the greatest inducements to virtue, and shakes the direst terrors over vice; but it succeeds neither in destroying vice nor producing virtue. Religious Mongols steal, seemingly without the least sense of shame, and do not hesitate to tell lies even when saying their prayers. A Doctor of Divinity of my own acquaintance, on one occasion deliberately and predeterminately lied, that he might retain possession of a few inches of wood, which he knew belonged to a Chinaman close by; and the fact may perhaps not be generally known that the disciples of one of our Peking living Buddhas have quite a widespread reputation for being notorious thieves! It is unnecessary to multiply examples. Perhaps discouraged by long failure, Buddhism seems to have given up trying to make men good and pure, and seems to have no hesitation in extending her consolations and countenance, even to those who professionally live by the wages of iniquity. The great aim of religion is to make men good and holy, and when a religion fails in this so utterly that it gives up the attempt altogether where, I would ask, can it find an excuse for its existence? "It is henceforth good for nothing, but to be cast out and trodden under foot of men."

Buddhism is a usurper. Apart from this, there is a superabundance of charges against this religion, sufficient to condemn it utterly again and again. But even though there were *no* other charges, *this* one would be sufficient to condemn it. It usurps haughtily and with a high hand the worship and honour due to Jesus Christ alone. By teaching that men can, unaided, free themselves from sin, and pass to the life beyond, from the regions of sorrow and suffering, it makes the Cross of none effect, and says that the death of Christ was superfluous. It not only usurps His rightful dominion, but actually vaunts itself as greater and mightier than He; and this too, when it knows itself to be an utter failure, quite incapable of performing the smallest of its many boasts; and is conscious, in the person of its highest officers, that, foundation and superstructure, it is a fabric of lies, warp and woof it is a tissue of falsehood. Lamas are either deceivers or deceived, or partly both; temples are gilded cages of unclean birds; the whole system is an utter abomination, an offence to God, and a curse to man. Let us pray for the speedy destruction of this religion, which haughtily robs God, and remorselessly pollutes and crushes man. May it soon fall, and its oppressions be replaced by the mild sway of that Master whose yoke is easy and whose burden is light; and may we at length see the Mongol leave off his pilgrimages and his vain repetitions, being taught that " pure religion and undefiled before God and the Father is this, to visit the fatherless and widows in their affliction, and to keep himself unspotted from the world."

CHAPTER XIX.

THE FIRST OF THE WHITE MONTH.

Preparations. Mongol mode of eating. Amazement at the size of foreigners' noses. Seven dinners on the last day of the year. Reflections suitable to the season. Embracing. Salutation. "Lucky airt" for the year. Duration of the feast and time of ceremonies.

THIS is what the Mongols call New Year's Day. Having an invitation from a friendly lama to spend the day with him, I took care to arrive at his tent, which was not far from the Russian frontier, on the afternoon of the last day of the old year. This afternoon is always a busy time with the Mongols. Enter a tent at this time, and, as soon as your eyes recover from the blinding glare of the sun on the white expanse of snow outside, and the bitterness of the smoke-cloud inside, through which you must pass before sitting down, you see all hands at work. They are preparing for next day's feast. In the tent of my host they were making *banch*. This is made by mincing mutton very small, mixing it with salt and chopped vegetables, and doing it up in small nuts covered with a casing of dough.

The amount of manipulation necessary before the nut is complete, and the unusual cleanness of the Mongols' hands *after* making it, always made me shudder when I saw them about to honour me with this delicacy; but the knowledge that they would feel much hurt if I seemed not to appreciate their hospitality, always made me swallow a little of it. They themselves consider it a luxury to be indulged in only on great occasions, and on this occasion prepared a large quantity. As soon as a nut was finished, it was placed on a board near the wall of the tent, where, notwithstanding the great fire blazing in the centre, it froze through in a few minutes. When frozen, the nuts were put away in a bag ready for to-morrow.

While the rest of the company were making the *banch*, my host, the lama himself, was making repeated attacks on a basinful of boiled meat which stood before him. As soon as the *banch* was finished, every man pulled out his knife and set to work on the meat. It is a little alarming to see a Mongol eat. He takes a piece of meat in his left hand, seizes it with his teeth, then cuts it off close to his lips. The knife flashes past so quickly and so close to the face, that a spectator seeing it for the first time, has his doubts about the safety of the operator's nose. Practice makes them expert, and their hand sure, and I never heard of any one, even when drunk, meeting with an accident in this way. The configuration, too, of the Mongolian face makes this method of eating much safer for them than for us. A Mongol's nose is not at all prominent, sometimes hardly projecting beyond the level of the cheeks, and the greater prominence of a foreigner's nose lays him under a considerable disadvantage in dining after the Mongol fashion. Next to the colour of the hair, the size of the nose is the first thing that strikes a Mongol as peculiar in a foreigner; and not unfrequently a group of Mongols, after standing round and staring at some newly-come foreigner, may be heard remarking among themselves, as they disperse, "What a tremendous nose!" The alarm felt by a foreigner at seeing a

MONGOL LAMA.
From a photograph.

group of Mongols eating meat is somewhat akin to that experienced by a Chinaman when for the first time he sees a party of foreigners at table, flourishing sharp glittering knives and putting food into their mouths by means of forks. He is astonished that the eaters do not cut themselves, and thinks his own harmless chopsticks much the safer way of eating.

While we were at dinner, I expressed my surprise at finding them taking their meal so early in the afternoon, and not after dark, as usual. The reason they gave was that the Mongol fashion was to eat seven dinners on the last day of the year. I rather liked this idea at first, as the custom in the north of Mongolia, of only one meal per day, and that after dark, with nothing but tea, tea, tea, the whole day long, does not seem to suit a European so well as a Mongol. My satisfaction, however, was short-lived, for I soon discovered that they had made up their minds that I should do justice to the whole seven, and that a sly old yellow-coated lama on my left had installed himself as tally-keeper to the guests. As the day wore on, matters began to look a little serious. The solemn voice of the man in yellow had only pronounced *three!* What was to become of the remaining four? As I was wondering how I could best get out of the difficulty, deliverance came in an unlooked-for way. Some one sitting in a tent about a dozen yards off shouted, "Ocher, come and drink wine;" and Ocher, though as a lama he had vowed to abstain from wine, and just then was employed in counting my dinners, at the summons disregarded his vow, threw up his office of tally-keeper, and the next time we saw him was in too genial a frame of mind to find fault with any one for their shortcoming in the past.

During the course of the afternoon two large pails were filled with tea and set aside. When all the preparations were finished we had a pleasant time round the blazing fire, talking of the customs of our respective countries, etc., etc. Among other things we talked of the speedy course of time, and, in return for some of our Christian metaphors, my lama gave me some wise Buddhistic sayings, such as:

"From the moment of acquiring wealth, parting with it is our doom.
From the moment of union, separation is our doom.
From the moment of birth, death is our doom.
Moment by moment we approach death."

Next morning, New Year's Day, all were astir early, and the every-day routine gone through as usual. The customary question, "Have you slept well?" was asked, but no reference made to the new year. The only manifest difference was, that the whole household seemed to have got new caps. After a time, a neighbour came in and asked, "Have you not embraced yet?" This seemed to stir up our host; glancing at the crescent of sunshine, which, streaming in through the smoke-hole above, indicates the time of day as it traces its way round the circumference of the tent, he remarked, "It is time now." But he was not quite ready. He unlocked a spacious box, and after bringing out a pile of things, new and old, at last succeeded in fishing out a new red coat and a fine fur cap, trimmed with yellow silk. The cap cost perhaps as much as the coat, and with the two our host looked quite imposing. When all was ready, all stood up in the cloud of smoke, and each embraced each, saying, "Sain O?" (Are you well?) Their embrace is a very simple affair. When two persons perform this ceremony they stretch out their arms towards each other, and the one puts the ends of his coat-sleeves under the ends of the coat-sleeves of the other. When we had all embraced we sat down again, and after wiping away the tears, which the bitter smoke, as we stood performing our ceremonies in it, had forced from our eyes, each one ate a small portion from a plate containing bread, fruits, roasted millet, and a preparation of milk. This done, we hastened to the next tent, in which a petty officer lived. By the time we all got in, the tent was crowded; each one of us embraced the host, putting our sleeves under his, in token of respect, asked, " Sain O ? " found a seat where we could, drank his tea, tasted his fare, were offered Chinese wine in small Chinese cups, conversed a few minutes, and returned to our tent to receive visitors. They were not long in coming. Some were near neighbours. These merely drank tea and tasted bread, but when visitors came from a distance the bag of *banch* was produced, a quantity of it boiled and handed to the strangers. The ease and rapidity with which this can be cooked makes it a very desirable kind of fare to have on hand on a day when numerous visitors are expected at different times.

As we had a gilling lama—a kind of doctor of medicine and divinity all in one—for our guest, we soon had a number of people in our tent anxious to know their "lucky airt" for the year. The gilling was nothing loath to be consulted, produced his books, and soon satisfied the inquirers. The process of determining this lucky airt is simple. The visitor tells his age, the gilling consults a table, and the point of the compass is found at once. I tried for mine among the rest, and found that I had a double airt, north-west and north-east, as far as I remember.

During the course of the day we had many visitors. Our tent possessed unusual attractions. My host was a man of influence; his guest, the gilling, had a great reputation for learning; the yellow-coated lama, Ocher, presided over the wine, and made a very good master of the ceremonies; and then there was "the man from the far country."

After we had for a time entertained the numerous visitors whom these attractions drew to our tent, we dispersed in various directions to make the round of our several acquaintances. A young lama who had spent the night keeping a vigil in a temple took me in tow, and conducted me to all the tents within a reasonable distance. In almost every instance we found the altar decked out with a great display of offerings. These consisted for the most part of bread and mutton, the broad piece of fat which forms the tail of the Mongolian sheep often being the centre-piece. One of the great injunctions of their religion is abstinence from flesh, and on expressing my surprise at finding the forbidden thing presented as a religious offering, an intelligent Mongol replied, "It all happens through stupidity. Stupid men among us Mongols are many." It was noteworthy that on the altar of the man who made this remark the offerings consisted of grain, fruit, and bread only. In all the tents which we entered not only were the altars furnished with a profusion of offerings, but the altar-lamps—little brass cups filled with butter—were lighted, and in some of the more pretentious tents the altar was inclosed above and around with silken hangings. The altar stands almost exactly opposite the door, and a New Year's Day visitor, on entering, turns first to the altar and worships; that done, he may address himself to the human occupants of the tent. I noticed only one departure from this rule throughout the entire day. When we were in an old woman's tent a dashing young Mongol entered, and, dispensing with the worship, proceeded at once to salute the old lady. The occasion for the manifestation of his irreligion was unfortunate—the old lady was just recovering from the effects of a broken limb, and her beads and hand praying-mill were her constant companions. In such circumstances it was not wonderful that she should be incensed at such levity. She rejected his proffered civilities with scorn, and with Puritanical sternness ordered him to worship God. The young spark did not relish his rebuke much, but did not dare to disobey.

In addition to bread and tea, visitors are in most cases offered wine; and as every man is expected to visit the tents of all his friends, and as very few refuse wine when it is offered, there is some danger of a man drinking more than is good for him. Two things tend to keep the Mongol sober—the small size of the cups, and the distance from tent to tent. But sometimes the Mongol gets tired of the minute Chinese wine-cup, throws it aside, and pours a good dram into a large wooden tea-cup. This, frequently repeated, produces its effect, and then follows horsemanship extraordinary! A Mongol, long after he is too drunk to stand, can keep his saddle very well, if he can be hoisted into it, and one of the sights to be seen on the afternoon of a New Year's Day, is that of half-a-dozen madcaps careering in company over the snow, performing all manner of antics, and apparently in momentary danger of breaking their necks. Many of our visitors were a good deal more than half-seas over, but throughout the whole day we saw only two who could not take care of themselves.

The northern Mongols usually restrict the festivity to

one day, but their neighbours, the Buriats, keep up the celebration for a week or more, perhaps—as the Mongols say, with some scorn—in imitation of the Russians. Should friends be beyond reach on the first day of the year, the sacred duty of salutation is performed on the first occasion of their meeting. Far into the year it is quite common for Mongols meeting in the desert to remark, " We have not embraced yet, have we ? " and then duly perform the ceremony that would have been appropriate months before. Southern Mongols, on the other hand, say they cease embracing at the end of the White Month.

CHAPTER XX.

NORBO'S MARRIAGE.

Making a mistake. All hands at work. The silversmith. Broken-legged brother of the bride. Cart-load of ladies. Bridegroom and party arrives. Fight. Adorning the bride. Ceremony at starting. A true weeper. Bridegroom's tent barricaded. Homœopathic remedy.

"You've just come in good time for the wedding," was the greeting with which I was received in a small cluster of Mongol tents, where I went to pass a few weeks one autumn. I had heard nothing about it, but was well pleased at the prospect of seeing so grand a marriage as that of the daughter of a high Mongol mandarin. The evening conversation in the tent was all about the forthcoming match, the various things that were to be made, the presents that would be given, and the feasting that would take place.

Next morning, before I had gone out, a tall young girl came to our tent with a present for me from the mandarin, and, as I was told she was his daughter, I thought I was doing the polite thing when I referred to her coming marriage. She looked confused, and soon left the tent, when I was informed that I had been guilty of great rudeness, as no bride in Mongolia is supposed to know anything about her marriage till she is carried off to be delivered over to her husband. The bride herself, of course, *does* know all about it, and even assists in making the garments; but still she is *supposed* not to know, and my mistake lay in taking it for granted that she did know. I did all I could to repair my error by sending her two silver roubles to make buttons.

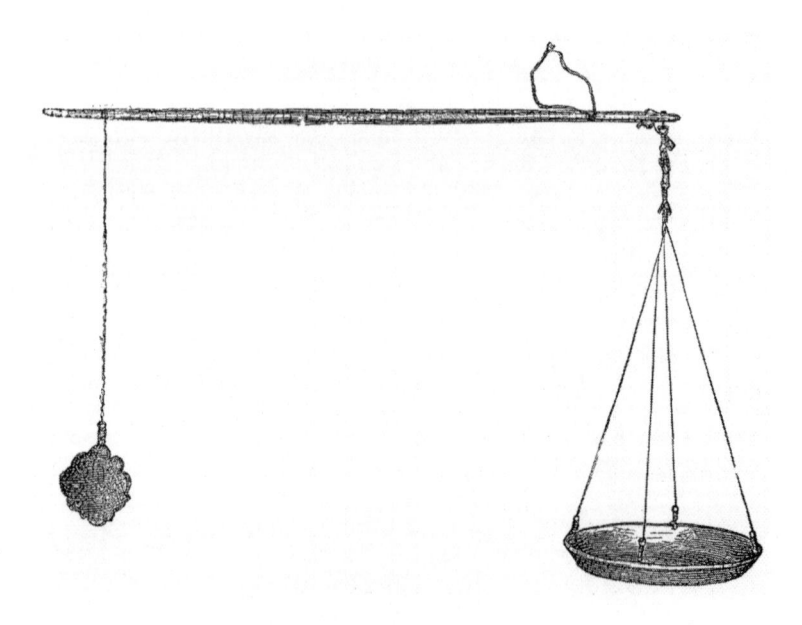

SCALES FOR WEIGHING SILVER.

When I got out about among the tents I found that all hands were busy. Extra tents were being set up, carpets, felts, boots, garments, cushions, were being sewed, and, in short, everybody was so busy that, as the brother of the bride said, they had not time to eat or drink. Attracted by the "click, click" of a light hammer, I entered a tent, and found a silversmith busy making the silver head ornaments. He was a lama, and explained to me that he had been accommodated in another tent till the lama son of the mandarin was brought home with a broken leg. The smith had then to give place to the doctor, and shifted himself, his scales, his clothful of tools, his blow-pipe, and his pieces of silver, to a humbler tent, where he was the guest of a married lama. I called on the broken-legged son, and found him an intelligent and pleasing young lama who, without the least reserve, was describing how he had come by the broken limb. He had been intoxicated, fallen from his horse, and actually made two attempts to remount before he discovered what was the matter. The eldest son, a layman, and married, lived in a cluster of tents about a mile away. His dependants also were busy at the same wedding outfit. In the course of conversation I was repeatedly asked how we managed such affairs, and the usual remark made when I described our weddings was, "How easy!" In Mongolia it is a formidable business, lasting about a week, more or less.

The first thing that arrived was a cart-load of provisions from the nearest Chinese town, prominent among the *provisions* being two piculs[1] of strong Chinese whisky. On expressing my surprise at the largeness of the quantity, I was told that it was rather small, and that the amount of spirit provided at the *other end*—that is, at the bridegroom's house—would be much greater. The slaughter of an ox and several sheep followed, and elicited grumbling rather than admiration from the neighbours, who thought the quantity of meat thus provided by no means sufficient. However, they made the excuse that though the

[1] A picul is 133 lbs.

mandarin was high in rank he was poor in purse, and could not well afford more. The bridegroom's father, on the other hand, was only a commoner, but very rich, so they hoped to make up for the deficiency at home by the extra abundance at the *other end*.

One afternoon a cart-load of ladies arrived. The cart was of the Peking model, drawn by two spirited horses, and guided by a driver on horseback. The ladies were grandly dressed in embroidered robes, flaming with all manner of figures, in almost all the colours of the rainbow. These first arrivals were near relations of the family, and had come early to assist and superintend. Some few days passed, the activity and excitement getting greater. The mandarin drank whisky, took snuff, and wrote requisitions borrowing horses, carpets, and felts from his neighbours all round, while the women of his family rushed about with sewing that had been forgotten, half commanding, half entreating the neighbouring females to help them to be ready in time.

Preparations were at length completed, and feasting began. I have now only an indistinct idea of how many days the feast lasted, and as great part of the fun consisted in drinking whisky, I did not join the revellers often. I was once taken to see a tent full of ladies in full dress. They were fully dressed indeed! The most striking thing was the gown, glaring with colours and fierce with embroidered dragons, whose eyes seemed ready to start from their heads. Though inside a tent, they all wore great fur caps exactly like those worn by men. At their side they each had a hanging of silk, silver, and gilt ornaments, but the most curious part of the adornment was the head-dress of beads, which seemed to hang down all round, and made it a matter of some difficulty for the fair dames to convey the cups to their mouths. I watched the process of drinking tea under difficulties for some time, then withdrew, trying to calculate how many oxen each of these women carried about on her person. The silver ornaments were of native workmanship, the dresses, the caps, and beads, were purchases from Peking, and, with Chinese interpreters, squeezes, merchants' profits, and allowance for the time that the bill would lie unpaid, must have cost a great sum.

One morning I was informed that the young bridegroom would come that day. Soon after, when out walking, I saw a troop of horses tied at some tents on a rising ground about a mile off. Presently the riders issued from the tents, mounted their steeds, and made directly for our cluster of tents. They came on in beautiful style, till brought to a halt by a steep-sided ravine cut out in the plain by the water of the summer rains. For a moment they halted, confused, on the farther edge, till some one discovered the pass; they then converged on one point, and one after another disappeared below the level of the plain. A few moments more, and bonnets, then heads, then horses, rose up into view again. The troop widened out once more, and the twenty horsemen, picturesque with their bright costumes, and mounted on their best steeds, swept past at full gallop. The bridegroom, conspicuous by the bow-and-arrow case he carried slung from his shoulder, seemed a mere boy, fourteen or fifteen years old, but he was mounted on perhaps the finest animal in the troop, and rode well, keeping side by side with his father.

The company dismounted at the poles a little way in

front of the tents, where horses are generally tied, put themselves in order, and advanced formally towards the principal tent. Every one seemed to carry something in his hand, and I noticed that several, who carried little open casks of whisky, asked eagerly what they were to do with it. I suppose they brought it in bladders on horseback, then filled it into the casks when they dismounted. As they stood before the tent, each man holding his present with both his hands, the bride's big brother, a tall, broad man, with a good-natured face, came out and planted himself right in front of the door, demanding of the strangers what brought them there. "We want to enter your tent," they replied. "Then you'll have to fight for it!" answered the giant, and, suiting the action to the word, the strangers and the mandarin's followers instantly began a scuffle, pulling each other about a good deal, but, as I could not help remarking, taking good care not to spill the whisky.

The sham fight lasted a few seconds, when the defenders gave in and invited the assailants to enter the tent. But now another struggle began. No one would enter first. The two head men stood bowing each other in, neither entering, till at last the stranger allowed himself to be pushed in, and his host followed The second pair had the same struggle, settled in the same way, and finally after a great ado the whole crowd entered, and business began.

I did not enter, but was told that the marriage contract was there and then made, the bridegroom—or his father rather—promising to treat the bride well and make such and such provision for her. Consuming whisky seems to form an important part of the ceremony, as it was remarked that though all were able to mount and ride off when the bargain was concluded, several of them rode only a mile to the nearest tents, and were unable to go on till next morning.

That afternoon a great cry arose among our tents, and, running out to see what had happened, there were half-a-dozen women leading the bride, newly adorned with her matron's ornaments, from the silversmith's tent to her father's abode. Just at this stage she was supposed to have discovered what all the preparations meant. She howled most vigorously, very much after the fashion of a distressed calf, but the Mongols said it was all right, it was a part of the ceremony! Still crying and reluctant, she was dragged into the tent, and there set aside in state.

Next morning all were astir early. The proper hour for a bride to start depends on the year in which she was born, and men skilled in such lore said that this girl should have left her home at two o'clock in the morning. When the proper time falls at such an inconvenient hour, the difficulty is got over by starting her, going a few yards, and alighting in another tent, the journey being commenced in earnest—*resumed*, they would say—at a more suitable time of day. In this case the ceremony of starting was not performed at the proper hour, but deferred till daylight. When all were mustered and ready, the old mandarin stumped about impatiently, saying repeatedly, "Why don't you start?" The truth was, that, to have everything proper, all the women of the place had to assemble in the tent and weep over the poor girl, who was now crying away most energetically.

The proper amount of weeping having been at length accomplished by the tearful dames, a young man obeyed the command of the father, pushed aside the women, drew back the curtain, took up the bride and carried her along under his arm as a man would carry a bundle of grass, taking care not to bump her head ornaments on the lintel of the low door, and, by the help of two others, hoisted her into the saddle of a remarkably quiet horse, which stood ready to receive her. In the hands of the men, the girl seemed a lifeless form, and, but for her crying, and the fact that she covered her veiled face with her hands, no one would have supposed that she possessed the least command of her limbs. She took no care to balance herself or keep her seat, all that she left to the attendants; her part in the performance was to cry, and cry she did in the same calf-like howl of yesterday.

The horse was led a step or two in the direction determined also by the year of her birth, and then the starting was an accomplished fact. She was taken down from the saddle and stowed away in a Peking cart, her mother got in beside her, the mounted driver called on his two lively horses, and the whole party fell into the line of march, while the crying of the disconsolate girl became fainter and fainter in the distance.

As we turned to our own tent we saw one truly sorry for the separation. The elder sister of the bride stood weeping at the door of her father's tent, following with tearful eyes the cart and the riders till they disappeared over the hill. Her grief was not mere affectation or compliance with custom, but the natural expression of a sisterly affection.

The bridal procession, as we afterwards heard, had a long ride over hill and dale, and finally drew up late in the day before some tents, within sight of which were feeding flocks of sheep, herds of oxen, and droves of horses, indicating the wealth of the possessor, and all judiciously displayed for the sake of effect.

The door of the bridegroom's tent was barricaded, and quite a war of words ensued, the strangers reproachfully asking, "What sort of people are you, to live with doors inhospitably barricaded?" The besieged reproachfully asked, "What sort of brigands are you, to come riding up to any man's tent in that threatening manner?" The comers replied, "We have brought So-and-so's daughter to be So-and-so's bride." "Oh, that alters the case!" answered the bridegroom's friends, and after some more ado the door was opened and the bride delivered over.

Feasting, drinking, singing, mirth, and quarrelling followed, and late next day the friends of the bride arrived home, reporting all well, with the exception of the slight indisposition of the bride. The wonder would have been if she had not been indisposed, after the excitement, rough travelling, and vigorous crying through which she had gone, but the Mongols accounted for it by saying that she started at six o'clock in place of two, and to cure her set a lama to read through the almanack—quite a homœopathic remedy.

The wedding was now over, but the interchange of friendly visits and hospitalities lasted a long time. The unintermittent feasting lasts about a week, but there are feasts, rejoicings, ceremonies, or visits at intervals for several months.

CHAPTER XXI.

FRIENDLY MONGOLS.

Mongol dogs. Snuff-bottles. Running the gauntlet. Furniture and appearance of tent. Swallows' nest in tent. Common sense *versus* Buddhism. White food. Home-made fiddle. Mongol song. Pleasant recollections. A suffering inhabitant.

WHEN we got within two or three hundred yards of the tent, the dogs set up the usual barking and began to make for us. The noise soon brought out some one, who gave the alarm that the Russians, as all foreigners are called in Mongolia, were coming, and the whole family defiled out for our protection. A little girl, swift of foot, gave chase to the biggest dog of the community, and overtook it just in time to head it off from us. He was a huge brute with hanging jaws, and when prevented from devouring us, walked slowly and sulkily away, seeming never once to look towards us again. This was rather dignified conduct, for Mongol dogs usually make frantic endeavours to seize strangers, increasing in outcry and vehemence as the object of their wrath approaches the tent. Even after a guest has been safely convoyed into a tent, it is no uncommon thing to see a dog put his head into a door and growl as if he felt he had been unjustly robbed of his due,

This great fellow, though, had better manners, and, when driven off by the little girl, busied himself most actively smelling at herbs and grasses, as if he had been a born botanist. At various distances from the tent we encountered various members of the family restraining various individuals of the dog community. As we passed them, they fell into rank behind, as forming a kind of rear guard, so that when we got to the tent door we were inclosed in a semicircular wall of men, women, and children, outside of which barked, in baffled rage, the sum total of the dogs belonging to the encampment. Etiquette demanded that we should make a show of desiring the master of the house to enter first; etiquette also demanded that he should insist on *our* entering first, but the fury of the dogs, increasing every moment, made it safer to cut this ceremony short, and after only a momentary and feeble resistance, we dropped our sticks, ducked our heads, and hurried into the tent followed by the whole tribe of the family and neighbours. The disappointed pack of yelling dogs slowly dispersed, and peace and quietness ensued.

Snuff-bottles were produced, and kind and pointed inquiries were made as to the condition of the various Mongols, the state of their cattle as to fatness, and our peace and well-being as to travelling. All these formalities had been gone through the day before in our tent, but custom seemed to require that they should be gone through again, with as much apparent attention and earnestness as if we had been in total ignorance of each others' states.

We had just finished these salutation ceremonies, when the barking and uproar of the dogs outside indicated the approach of another visitor. A girl was being sent out to see who the comer was, when, to the intense astonishment of the Mongols and our own great amusement, in leaped our little white dog, and the doorway was instantly blocked by the great heads and open mouths of the dogs of the place, through which the little adventurer had successfully run the gauntlet. We

NARROW ESCAPE OF THE LITTLE DOG

had left him tied up in our tent, but somehow he had slipped his tether, run the blockade, and escaped by a few inches only. The Mongols were so amazed at his pluck in venturing among their pack of dogs, that they were inclined to think him *uncanny*, a suspicion which was manifestly increased when they learned that such adventures and escapes of our little companion were of frequent occurrence.

In a pause of the conversation we had time to look about us. The tent was large, and well floored with clean white felts. In the centre stood the grate, innocent of a fire. This tent being the "*best room*," was not commonly used, the roof felts and rafters were guiltless of the usual smoke varnish, and, except at New Year's time and other great occasions, a fire was never lit in it. Round and round were ranged large red-painted boxes, indicating the affluent circumstances of the family, and making good back-rests to lean against. Suspended close to the roof and near to the door was a tiny piece of board, on which a pair of swallows had built their nest and reared their young. In a minute or two both parent birds appeared at the hole in the top of the roof with their mouths full of flies. Though the nest is quite low down, within reach, the birds take no notice of the Mongols, but go and come at their own sweet will, and after eying us suspiciously for a little, they ventured down to their clamouring young. Swallows' nests in tents are quite common. The Mongols like the birds, and the birds like the Mongols. Building places are scarce, and when a little board is hung up a pair of swallows are likely to come. Those that fail to get "house accommodation" usually build in sand-banks. As we were looking at the parents we asked what they fed their young with. "*Flies*," replied the Mongols. "They take life then, are they not sinful, why do you harbour them?" Said a lama: "They have no udders, they have nothing but flies to feed their young on, and what can they do? *Hoarhe*, dear little creatures.

This is one of the many instances in which the Mongol's common sense and natural feelings get the better of his religious tenets. To take life is sinful, says Buddhism. A swallow employs most of its time taking life, and though, perhaps, theoretically, the Mongols regard the swallow as very sinful, practically they make a favourite of it and welcome it to their homes.

Meanwhile the women of the tent had been busy. A little table was placed before each of us, and, as we had protested against drinking tea, white food, in various shapes and dishes, was handed over with due and friendly formality. Most of the varieties of white food, as preparations made from milk are called, are not palatable, but here we found some extra good sour cream, thick and clean, in glass cups, and served up with the uncommon addition of brass spoons. This we did ample justice to, but of course had to break off and taste a crumb from the corner of one piece of a trencherful of hard sour masses of material for which there is no appropriate name in English. This rite accomplished, we were at liberty to clear the tables by handing back, with due formality, the various dishes, etc., that had been set before us.

Then followed conversation about the texture and make of foreign clothes, about foreign customs, and about the distance from Peking to foreign countries. When these subjects were exhausted, a curious-looking instrument lying on the top of one of the boxes attracted notice, and one of the lamas volunteered to extract music from it. It was a fiddle, but *such* a fiddle! The main parts of it were a hollow box about a foot square and two or three inches deep, covered with sheep skin, and a stick about three feet long stuck through the sides of the box. It had only two strings, and these consisted of a few hairs pulled from a horse's tail and lengthened at both ends by pieces of common string. The fiddle itself was uncouth enough, but the bow beat it hollow. This last was a bent and whittled branch of some shrub fitted with a few horse-hairs tied on quite loosely. The necessary tension was produced by the hand of the performer as he grasped it to play.

Fiddles are not uncommon in Mongolia, but this one seemed so rude and primitive, that, even though we were the guests of the maker and owner, it was utterly impossible to refrain from laughter on beholding it. The lama to whom it belonged was not in the least annoyed or disconcerted at our mirth, but, smiling quietly, took his bow, set the box on his knee, went through the preliminaries of tuning with all the gravity of an accomplished musician, produced from his purse a small paper of resin, applied the minutest quantity to the hairs of the bow, and, subsiding into a permanent attitude, proceeded to entertain his guests with the Mongol air of "Pinglang yeh." The strains of the fiddle were soft and low, and pleasing in the extreme. Compared with the high "*skirling*" tones of many Chinese and Mongol instruments, the sound of this one was more like that of some good piano touched by a skilful hand. The lama was a skilful player, as a few seconds sufficed to show. He had made the fiddle himself, and knew how to use it, and he soon showed that highly artistic effects could be produced from a very clownish-looking instrument.

The lama played a few verses, and it was then evident that it was time to stop him. There was a daughter in the tent, clad only in two garments of common rough

Chinese cloth, but graceful and beautiful in build and feature. She was just reaching womanhood, and her mouth was adorned by a set of milk-white and perfect teeth. From the looks of the mother it was evident she wished her daughter to be asked to sing. We did ask her to sing, and, after the usual amount of refusing

MONGOL GIRLS.

and pressing, she overcame her bashfulness and began. The mother looked on pleased and approving, one or two more struck in, the lama scraped away on his two strings, and we had quite a little concert. The burden of the song was the praises of a maiden named Pinglang, and the words are supposed to proceed from the mouth of a disappointed suitor who is stricken with grief, when the girl finally mounts her horse and rides off in procession to be the wife of a more fortunate rival.

The plan of the song is truly Mongolian. The various birds singing on the temple roof, twittering on the plain, and floating on the lakes, are each asked in turn, and in separate verses, if they have seen the marriage procession of the dear, the beautiful, the friendly Pinglang pass along. Even the rainbow, the five-coloured and the nine-coloured rainbow, is interrogated. The procession itself is described in a series of verses, the burden and refrain of each of which is that the little Pinglang is conspicuous as she rides along solitary in the centre. The song also enlarges on her beauties and graces. Her skin is like cotton or snow, her breath is like musk, even her perspiration is minutely characterised in a manner which to Mongols may be eulogistic, but which would seem ridiculous to foreign ears.

It was a little difficult to start the singers in this song, but it was more difficult to stop them. Different versions seem to have different numbers of verses, and it was not till a long list of them had been slowly gone through that an opportunity could be found to terminate the performance by praising its merits. All the while that the singing went on the fond mother sat with satisfaction beaming all over her pleased face, now casting proud glances at her daughter, now noticing the effect of the display on the visitors. She was quite satisfied with the praise awarded, and the playing and singing were really so good that high commendation could be given without any exaggeration.

The impression of that visit dwells vividly in the memory still. The pleasure derived from it was doubtless much increased by the fact, that after long travelling in arid and parched places, sometimes among shy and unfriendly people, the valley in which that family lived was the first one we had entered, green and luxuriant from the summer rains. After weeks of parching and hot air for ourselves, and burnt and scanty pasture for our travelling cattle, it was delicious to breathe in a moist and kindly atmosphere, and to look with soothed eyes on the cattle, roaming in the soft greenness of fresh pastures. The well also, an essential feature in the landscape and calculations of a traveller in Mongolia, was stone-built, capacious, and full nearly to the mouth with clear cold water.

Behind, the valley ran up into a wedge-point imbedded in a great hill; before, the valley stretched out and away, widening as it went, for miles and miles, till it became a great plain bounded by a lumpy horizon of distant and indistinct hill-tops. Nearer, and to one side, a low ridge was variegated and mottled by the different colours of a drove of some hundreds of horses up there to get coal. If there is a poetical spot in Mongolia, that is it; if there is a comfortably placed and happy family, that seems to be the one. To the passing stranger there seems little left to be desired.

But there is another side to this picture. Of the ten or twelve inhabitants of that place, not more than one or two were free from disease and distress of body in some shape or other, and the mind never reverts to those scenes of beauty without seeing in the midst of it all, the prone form of a young man so severely afflicted by a common and easily curable disease, that the only posture he could assume with comfort was that of resting on his knees and elbows. Beauties of nature are often found in Mongolia, but beauty is only half the scene. No picture of the plains is true to nature or complete without the attendant miseries and distresses which seem to be inseparable from the inhabitants.

CHAPTER XXII.

THIEVES IN MONGOLIA.

A dangerous man. Successful thieves respected. Difficulties of cattle-lifters. Famous locality for thieves. Bold daylight theft. Pilgrim's horse stolen. Strange adventure. A bow at a venture. Hiding cattle. Way of transgressors is hard. A good word for the Mongols. Buddhism does not repress stealing.

ONE evening at sunset, as we were sitting round the tent fire, picking mutton bones, and looking at the millet as it boiled in the pot, an old lama, who lived close by, hobbled into the tent counting his beads, sat down where we made room for him, and, after glancing at the boiling millet, remarked, "A dangerous man came to-day." "Who?" asked my camel-driver. "Why, the lama who came with his son in the afternoon; did you not know him? Bajer, the famous thief." The camel-driver had not recognised him, but, as soon as his name was mentioned, said, "Oh, is *that* the man?" His face he did not know, but he knew him well by fame. After talking a little, the lama noticed that the millet was ready, rose to take his leave, and said that he had come to put us on our guard, as he was not at all easy in his mind when such a man appeared in the neighbourhood. As we went on with our supper, I had a pretty full description of the dangerous visitor from the camel-driver, who seemed to take a delight in going over the many adventures connected with the name of the man against whom we had been warned. This celebrated thief was a lama. He was well known, as were also his thieving propensities, yet he had his cattle and his sheep, his home and habitation, and was allowed to live undisturbed. He had been concerned in many cattle-stealings for years before, but had managed so well that he escaped with little damage. The whole country-side knew him for a thief, but no one could, or would, have him convicted.

In Mongolia known thieves are treated as respectable members of society. As long as they manage well and are successful, little or no odium seems to attach to them; and it is no uncommon thing to hear them spoken of in terms of high praise. Success seems to be regarded as a kind of palliation of their crimes. A man caught in the act, or a man convicted of theft, finds few to speak for him; but a man who can arrange to have thefts performed in a business-like manner by others, while he himself is ostentatiously at home, or at some convivial party, is a good thief, and, it would seem, a praiseworthy man. As for their religion, that does not seem to deter them at all. The reputed thief who visited me was a lama, and he had not lost caste. Another lama, who died a year or two ago, had his funeral rites interdicted by a superior lama, on the ground that the deceased had been in some way concerned in the death of a man. "Had he been a thief," said the superior, "that could have been passed over; but murder is a more serious affair." And so the able and business-like thieves pursue their course brazen-faced and high-handed.

From the nature of the country, the operations of thieves are confined mostly to cattle-lifting; and as force is almost unheard of in stealing, it requires great tact to take them, drive them off, and dispose of them so as to elude detection. Almost anybody, any day or night of the year, could run off with a few horses, or oxen, or camels; that is easy enough; but the difficulty is to convey them safely in a country where every friend and stranger you meet has unbounded curiosity, and asks all manner of questions, and to deposit them safely till a market is found. Some parts of the country, too, afford protection against thieves from the nature of the ground. One district of Mongolia is very sandy; it is in fact a vast billowy sea of sand, with patched vegetation. Stolen cattle could easily be tracked through this; so cattle-lifting is not common there.

Of all places, perhaps temples and their neighbourhoods are the most infested by thieves. The numbers of people coming and going, and the numerous roads diverging towards all parts of the country, make pursuit more difficult. The temple Bandit Gegenae Hcet, which lies away to the north-east of Lama Miao, is the best adapted for Mongol thieves. It stands in a wide plain, which is covered over with sword-grass, tall and high, so that even a horseman in a few minutes can screen himself completely from view. We arrived there one August afternoon. The sword-grass had reached its height, and was beginning to become dry and white. Entering a road that ran winding through the grass, we threaded our way towards the temple, seeing little but its towering roof. We pitched our tent among some other pilgrims on a piece of open ground. We had many visitors, but one was especially noted by us. He was a nondescript lama, had a negative enough account to give of himself, but there was something about him, or his manner, it would be difficult to say which, that marked him out as one to be remembered among many that would be forgotten.

In the evening, a girl, belonging, as her dialect showed, and as she herself said, to a very distant tribe, came into our tent and sat down. After a little she requested us to permit her to sleep in our tent for that night. The camel-driver, who usually decided on such applications himself, referred her to me. I at once told her we could not have her with us, because that would lay us open to the suspicion of immorality, gave her some supper, and sent her off. When she had gone, my old lama laughed at me for giving such a reason for refusing her lodgings, and said there was a much more serious reason for dismissing her. Should anything be stolen within a day or two, and that girl not be forthcoming, we would be held responsible for the thief, and the theft, because we had harboured her.

Next day about noon, some thief or other walked up to a row of about a dozen horses tied in a public place, mounted one and rode off before the eyes of numbers of people; horsemen were mounting and dismounting, arriving and departing, at the time, and the thief ran the greatest risk of being seen by some one who knew the horse; but no one noticed, and the thief got clear off. Who the thief was, no one knew, but we remarked that the girl was no more seen about the temple. Next night, I think it was, a horseman rode up to the tent next ours, where there was a very fine camel tied. The man on watch, pretending to be asleep as before, let him ride quite close up—then challenged him. The horseman said he was looking for a tent that had arrived that day, turned and rode slowly off, displaying against the sky the dark outline of the nondescript lama. He was foiled that night, but he, or some one else, succeeded next day.

A pilgrim who had been to Wu-T'ai and back, and was still a month's journey from home, hobbled his horse and entered a tent to drink the usual cup of tea. Going out again in a few minutes, no horse was to be seen; he had disappeared once for all among the roads screened by the long sword-grass. The pilgrim came, among other places, to our tent to ask if aught had been seen. Some lamas belonging to the temple were with us at the time, and one of them seemed disposed to take an interest in the lost horse, when a companion overawed him and cut the conversation short by saying authoritatively, "*No one here knows anything about it.*" The words themselves were not amiss, but the look seemed to mean that though they knew, they would not tell him. That temple seems to be a paradise of thieves. The Government gets all credit for activity and zeal in attempting to put down stealing, but the friendly screen of the sword-grass is too much for it.

On one occasion we had a strange adventure. We were encamped at a solitary spot away from all dwellings, and had just gone to bed for the night, when we heard voices approaching, evidently those of two men on horseback. They rode up softly, talking quietly as they came. I poked my head out at the tent mouth, and there they were, quite close on us; the camel-driver was in bed outside the tent, beyond the camels, and heard them remark, "There is a head looking out from the tent." He gave a slight cough, and the two men dismounted, hailed us, and entered the tent. They had come to ask me to go to see a sick man close at hand. They described the symptoms minutely, and arranged to bring me a saddled horse before sunrise next morning. Sunrise came, but no horse; we waited, still no horse; loaded our camels and started, still no horse. The affair now looked suspicious, and whether they were thieves or not, I am told that is how clever thieves often do. They ride up talking softly, and throw the watcher off his guard. If he is awake he coughs or speaks; then the thieves come up and talk like honest men. If no one speaks or appears, the probability is that all are asleep, and they have a fair chance of making a haul.

Thieves who visit caravan encampments usually come early in the night, as that is the most likely time to find the people asleep; a good dinner after a hard day in the desert having a soporific effect. A story is told of a Chinese thief who came a little too early. A Mongol had been to China to buy grain, and coming home with it on an ox-cart alone, pitched his tent one evening, and after sunset, set about cooking his dinner. Knowing the place was dangerous for thieves, as he sat by his fire he kept calling out at intervals, "Ah! you thief, you let go that ox!" Once, after shouting, he heard the sound of feet, and looking out, saw a Chinaman running across the plain, leaving the ox he had been just in the act of stealing. The Mongol's random shot had just been in time, and scared the Chinaman, who thought he had been observed.

Another trick frequently put upon travellers is, not

to steal the cattle alt gether, but to drive them off to some place where they would not be easily found. The owners, on discovering the loss, ride about looking and asking for them. Those in the plot volunteer information; the owner follows it up and finds the cattle in some one's keeping, who of course has *found* them and demands the usual finder's fee. The owner knows, the finder knows, everybody knows, they have been driven off intentionally; but the driving off has been so managed as to look like a case of straying; the owner can bring no proof against any one, and, though he knows it is a swindle, has to pay the redemption money. The whole country-side understand the transaction exactly, but, in place of condemning the affair, rather envy the cleverness and success of those who managed it.

The way of transgressors is hard, and the main check on Mongol dishonesty seems to be, the misfortune and disaster which usually follow on the heels of dishonesty. Honest men frequently come to poverty too, but openly dishonest men, such as those who implicate themselves in cattle-stealings, very seldom remain in prosperity; and this, the disaster which commonly follows dishonesty, goes a long way in securing to the Mongols the protection to property that is afforded by the righteous administration of good laws in other countries. Though almost everybody has the *heart* to steal, everybody is not always *actually* stealing. The Mongols know each other and take proper precautions; and with a little care a foreign traveller need not lose much among them.

The alarming thing about Mongol dishonesty is, not the actual amount of stealing that goes on, but the seemingly universal inclination to steal in almost all, and the utter want of public sentiment against it. In favour of the Mongols I must testify, that in my intercourse with them I have lost very little indeed; partly, perhaps, because few things were left lying about in my tent, and my Mongol attendants, considering themselves responsible, and knowing the native weakness, kept a sharp look out. Often when going out, I would be detained by them to put away this, that, and the other thing, which they were afraid people who came in might pick up; and, as far as I am aware, my Mongol servants never stole anything. On one occasion too, I left a parcel of silver in a leather bag for some days in a tent. I trusted more to their ignorance than to their honesty in this last particular, and the silver was safe and sound.

In books, I have read some extraordinary examples of honesty and integrity in Buddhists; stories which, if true, would almost cast the integrity of some Christians into the shade. These stories *may* have been true, but the state of things I have seen among the Mongols, who are extremely pious, makes wonderful stories of Buddhist truth and uprightness hard to believe; and if any one wants to exalt Buddhism as compared with Christianity, the farther he keeps from Mongolia the better. Thieves and stealing abound in Christian countries, but all Christians are not thieves; and known thieves are not regarded as respectable members of society; and it is not too much to hope, that one of the fruits of Christianity in Mongolia will be the creation of a healthy and honest contempt for thieves and stealing, among a people whom even the Chinese regard as personified dishonesty.

CHAPTER XXIII.

A MONGOL COURT OF JUSTICE.

"Have you medicine good for wounds?" Mental tonic wanted. The justice-tent. The court opened. Onlookers. A row of prisoners waiting trial. Punishment. Manner of counting the lashes. Various cases. Conditional confession. The Governor-general. Fatality about confessing. Departure of the judge. Defiant prisoner.

ONE evening after sunset, a Mongol came furtively into my tent, and, after a few commonplace remarks, asked in an earnest whisper if I had any medicine good for wounds. I said I would like to see the wounds before giving medicine for them, and asked what sort of wounds they were and who had them. It turned out that the wounds were not yet inflicted, that the visitor was to be tried for theft next day, and as part of the examination was by scourging, he wanted to be prepared for the worst. In his own name, and that of a friend, he also preferred a very earnest request that I would give him some medicine to make his flesh able to endure scourging without feeling pain! If I could not furnish him with this, perhaps I might give him something to "tighten up his mind," so that he would not confess under torture! After quite a long and confidential conversation as to his guilt and prospects for the morrow, he rose to go, asking me to tell no one of his visit, because he was in custody, and allowed to go about only by the kindness of his keeper. Next morning early, I had another visitor on the same errand; like his neighbour, he wanted something to heal his possible wounds, to harden his flesh, and to brace up his mind.

In the early morning a large tent of blue cloth fluttered gaily in the breeze. It was pitched just beyond the temple limits. The whole half-year's secular business of the tribe had been transacted in the temple buildings, but criminal proceedings could not be taken against culprits within the hallowed ground. Within the boundary it is not lawful to beat and whip men; so the thieves had to be examined outside the little footpath made by devout Mongols, who travel round and round the sacred precincts by way of religious duty. No one appeared to know exactly when the Court would begin; but after a while stragglers seemed to converge towards the conspicuous tent, and the rumour got abroad that the mandarins had gone out to begin business.

The tent was open at both ends, and, with the exception of a contracted space down the centre, was packed full of mandarins of various ranks. Around the mouth of the tent was the disorderly crowd of spectators, who pushed each other about, and talked away among themselves without any seeming restraint. At the tail of the tent was another and smaller crowd, kept in a little better order by the angry commands of "stand back," shouted at short intervals by one or other of the dignitaries sweating under the heat that found its way through the cloth of the tent. The tail of the tent had been opened to secure coolness by circulation of air, but, blocked up by a sweltering crowd at both ends, the circulation amounted to little; and the discomfort of the judges within was only exceeded by that of the trembling culprits who were led up and made to kneel before them. Behind the little table, on which were laid official papers, sat two or three mandarins with buttons of various kinds, but no one appeared to claim higher rank than his neighbours, and no one was seen to be specially presiding. Any one that liked seemed to say anything he liked, and frequently more than one spoke at once; and on more than one occasion a prisoner had to attend to the different sets of remarks made to him by two different mandarins at one and the same time. The noise of the two crowds of spectators outside, and the free and easy way of contemporaneous speaking inside, made it difficult to keep track of what was going on. It was hardly possible both to see and hear; so a good many of those really interested in the proceedings did not attempt to see, but knelt down outside the tent, and with bended head listened attentively through the cloth. Beyond the crowd in front of the tent sat a row of laymen and lamas, all looking very solemn and sedate. These were the prisoners waiting to be tried. No one seemed to watch them, and they were not handcuffed or bound in any way. They simply sat and waited till an attendant came and called them forward.

One case tried was that of two lamas. The reading of some charge of evidence or other could be heard indistinctly amid the hum and bustle, and then the elder lama was led out in front of the tent and lay down in full view of the court. As the crowd fell back, a whip, a couple of rods, and the leather sole of a shoe, became apparent. The lictor asked which he was to use, and on being told to take the whip, proceeded to administer thirty lashes. The whip was really a formidable weapon, and looked alarming; but the whipper stood so close in towards the culprit that almost all the force of the thong was spent on the grass. This was farce enough, but this was not all. One, two, three, five, eight, nine, ten, eleven, thirteen, seventeen, twenty—counted the sturdy lictor, bringing up his whip with great display, and letting it gently down—twenty he counted, and as he counted twenty-one, an official standing near by shouted thirty. THIRTY, with tremendous emphasis shouted the lictor, and then rested his whip, as if his arm had been quite worn out with the great exertion. "*Oi yoi, yoi,*" sighed the victim as he got up, and the whole crowd of spectators laughed aloud; the sufferer joining in the laugh as soon as he got his face turned away from the court. Everybody seemed pleased, and what seemed to please them most was the counting—twenty, twenty-one, thirty. The turn of the younger priest came next, but his was a more serious affair. He was uncovered, and his infliction was with a rod that left a mark at each stroke. The count too was carefully looked to, and when it jumped from three to five, the lictor was ordered to stop and be careful as to how he counted. This lama got his full complement of thirty strokes, and good strokes too.

Another case was that of cattle-stealing. Several men were implicated, but the din and bustle made it impossible to hear whether the accused confessed and were punished for the deed, or did not confess and were whipped to make them tell the truth. Doubtless Mongols accustomed to the proceedings knew all about what was going on, but an unaccustomed spectator, hustled about, could only guess. One of the culprits was an old man with a decent dress and respectable look; and one of the judges inside the tent could be heard shouting to him: "You are an old man, more than sixty, your life is almost past, you should know better by this time than to steal; if you are poor and hungry, beg; begging is better than stealing; if you beg, people will give you food." Then after a little: "After this will you be deterred (from stealing)? Will you be careful? Will you amend your ways?" He was then led forth, and had thirty slight lashes with the whip, without being deprived of the protection of his trousers. Concerned in the same case was a young lama who came next in turn, and was punished severely with the rod. No miscounting,—no laying it on light for him. He was about twenty years of age, and, according to the expressed verdict of the unofficial mob, just the sort of fellow to steal. The officials were evidently of the same mind, and took care that the scourging was no sham. Once they stopped the lictor, and threatened to have *him* whipped if he did not hurt the prisoner more. The young lama got fifty good ones, and seemed to get up with difficulty. Perhaps too he was tenderer than his neighbours, for he manifestly suffered severely.

Then came a complicated business of the theft of a single horse. Four or five prisoners were called up, and a long examination ensued. Several persons were beaten, among them the well-dressed, respectable-looking son of a man of official rank. This young man was the most decent-looking fellow among the prisoners. He had his thirty lashes by way of examination, and might have had more, if another man had not confessed under his torture, that he alone was the thief, and that the decent-looking young man was falsely accused. The man who confessed was the same who had come to me by night for medicine. His confession admitted that he had stolen the horse, and tied it up in the mountains till he should be able to convey it away secretly; but in his absence the wolves had come and devoured it; so he was none the better for his theft! His unsuccessful experiment was the cause of no little mirth to the official and unofficial spectators.

Another case was peculiarly Mongolian. A young lama was brought up accused of causing a prairie fire, which ran for miles and scorched a caravan of Halhas, encamped with their camels and loads of tea in the long dry grass. The accused admitted the charge, but pleaded that it was unintentional; and appealed to the mercy of the court, reminding them that he was a quiet and orderly subject, and the sole support of his father, an old man aged eighty years. The court was evidently satisfied with the explanation, but the law must be magnified, which was supposed to be done when thirty nominal lashes were laid on lightly, not even his coat being removed; and the count being so cooked that though *thirty* was counted, hardly more than fifteen were administered.

Another case elicited rather a curious confession. An elderly man under examination said, that *if his two companions in accusation would not own up*, he would take the responsibility of the loss. The judges seemed well satisfied with the arrangement, asked if he had means sufficient to make good the loss, and dismissed him without corporal punishment.

A few more cases followed, and then the greater part

of the spectators dispersed, remarking that what was to come next was a civil suit, at which they evidently did not expect to see much beating and whipping, which seem to form the main attraction.

It must not be supposed that these beatings constituted the sole punishment of the thieves. Sentences of imprisonment were passed afterwards.

During the course of the proceedings, I had been endeavouring to distinguish the governor-general of the tribe; but in the crowd of mandarins in the tent, no one seemed to claim much higher rank than his neighbours. Returning towards my tent, a fat Mongol in a greasy old dress called me to him, passed salutations, conversed a little, then let me go. He had a couple of attendants hanging around near him, and an old lama came up as we were speaking. Two days afterwards meeting the old lama, I asked who that mandarin was who had been talking to me. It had been the governor-general *incog*. He had deputed his duties to the inferior mandarins; and while they were sweating in the crowded tent, bullying thieves, and speaking down each other, he had been enjoying himself lounging around.

A day or two afterwards, in my tent, I happened to ask an aged lama of some small rank in the temple, if he had been to see the trial of the thieves. Hitching himself round, and looking at me as if he thought I was taking some undue liberty with his dignity, he replied, "No, no, no; do you think that a respectable man like me would go to see thieves tried?" This seemed to be the universal feeling on the matter—that it was an exhibition fit only for the eyes of boys and menials.

Towards sunset I had another visit from the prisoner who, the night before, wanted medicine for his wounds and bracing for his mind. How changed he seemed. He had had sixty strokes, and was to be sentenced to something or other, he did not as yet know what; but he seemed happy and radiant, and smiled all over. The anxiety and uncertainty had gone, he had confessed and been condemned; but had he been acquitted, he could not have seemed much more relieved. Though severely beaten, he had not received wounds, his mind did not now want any bracing, and it was evident that his confession had been an excellent tonic for his mental constitution.

A good many cases of theft were left untried at the close of the day, and how they were settled does not appear. The tent was not pitched again, and next morning early, the governor-general took his departure, conspicuous in his two-horse cart guided by a mounted driver, and preceded by a horseman carrying the seals of office in a box strapped on between his shoulders. This was the signal for a general scattering. Many Mongols had returned to their homes before; those that were left now disappeared, the traders from Peking and other places who had come for the occasion departed to travel round the country; and the temple, which for a week had swarmed with men, and had its pastures adorned with scores of hobbled horses, resumed its normally deserted appearance, not to be again disturbed till the summer sacred festival would attract its crowds of traders and worshippers from the four quarters.

In travelling round the country afterwards, we met several of the prisoners at their homes, and every two or three days were reminded of the court of justice by hearing our Mongol servant counting, in a mock official tone of voice, seven, ten, eleven, fourteen, nineteen

U

twenty-one, THIRTY, as he hammered the tent-pins into the hard ground.

It turned out too that one of the prisoners at least did not get off so easily as the trial we had seen might have led a spectator to suppose. Another prisoner had taken the whole guilt upon himself, and thus freed his neighbour, who, at that time, was allowed to get off rather easily. Some time after, the man thus freed was sent for by the governor-general, and subjected to another examination. The accused was a man of means, and he was now charged with bribing his confederate to confess and take the blame. A severe castigation was administered to make him reveal the truth; but the man stood firm, and though there was a general feeling that he was guilty, he could not be made to confess, and had

MANDARIN OF RANK TRAVLLLING IN SEDAN CARRIED

to be dismissed. The story goes, that after he had received the severe infliction of over a hundred strokes, and the examination was ended, he got up with the bearing of an innocent man, showing his unbroken skin as proof of his innocence. "You have broken several rods on me," said he; "see how I have stood it; are you satisfied now?" The Mongols have great admiration for a man who will thus dare and endure without confessing; and, however objectionable the examining by torture of witnesses may be, it affords good opportunity for inflicting pretty severe punishment under pretence of questioning men who are pretty well known to be guilty, but who cannot be convicted for want of conclusive evidence.

[*From a Native Sketch.*

BY FOUR HORSES AND PRECEDED BY HIS SEAL BEARER.

CHAPTER XXIV.

A MONGOL PRISON.

Deputation from patients in prison. The staff of prison officials. A prison with open doors. Arrival of turnkey with candle. Appearance of turnkey. Chess-playing. Thunderstorm. The dungeon. Mongol prisoners not in danger of escaping. A feast in prison. Parting ceremonials. Irksomeness of confinement to Mongol prisoners.

A LITTLE, stoop-shouldered, one-eyed, stiff-jointed, barefooted, elderly man, after being treated for some disease of his own, said he had come as a deputation from some patients who lived close at hand, and who were anxious that I should visit them. On its being suggested that, if the distance was not great, and the patients not severely afflicted, perhaps it would be better for them to come to me, a young man sitting by said that they could not come; that the men in question were criminals confined in prison, and would not be allowed to come out. Of course I agreed to go, and offered to do so at once, but that would not do for the old man. He must first go back to the prison, put on his boots, and escort me over with proper formality.

He soon came with his boots on, and as we walked towards the place, the old man gave a detailed account of himself, his prison, and his prisoners. He was there on duty for a month only, and was sub-governor. There was a head-governor above him, a turnkey under him, a couple of soldiers to supply any force or do any fighting that might be needed, and six prisoners to be looked after. The head governor did not live in the prison, so that, keepers and criminals, the total of the inmates was ten.

The two soldiers had gone out visiting, the turnkey had gone to buy a candle, he himself was escorting me, and the six prisoners, with open doors, had been left to look after themselves! There they were, the whole six of them, five lamas and one black man, standing staring at us over the low wall that surrounded the "blackhouse," as the prison is called. The turnkey had not arrived with the candle, and the old man was in a dilemma; it was too dark inside the house without a light, so I suggested that we might sit outside. The old man shouted his orders; a commotion was visible among the six prisoners, and by the time we arrived at the little gate in the low mud wall cushions were spread on the ground outside. All the usual formalities of salutation had to be gone through. Though the half of them were invalids and suffering more or less, when asked as to the state of their bodies, they all replied, as politeness required them to do, that they were in perfect health and comfort; and when, also in deference to custom, the condition and prosperity of their cattle were inquired about, they all hastened to affirm that their cattle were fat and flourishing, though the great probability was, that one half of them had not a hoof to their name, and that those who owned animals had not seen them for months.

Salutations over, the prisoners crouched in front of

the cushions, and the patients detailed their afflictions. Meantime the turnkey, holding a candle in one hand, and with his other steadying a couple of water-buckets that hung from his shoulder, came through the low doorway, staggering under the weight of his load. The candle was lighted, and we adjourned inside. The first thing noticeable in the darkness was the candlestick. Candlestick they had none; the beer-bottle, which in a civilised country would probably have supplied such a lack, is a scarce article in Mongolia; but cups and millet abound, so a cup was filled with millet and the candle stuck into the centre. Mongols very seldom have candles to burn, but when they do find a candle, a cup filled with millet is a common substitute for a candlestick. The next most noticeable thing in the house was the turnkey, who still hovered around the newly-lighted candle. The sub-governor wanted an eye; the turnkey was minus the nose, and a most lugubrious man he looked. His affliction interfered with his speech, and the depression in the centre of his face terminated in a dark hole, which gave him such a repulsive yet fascinating appearance, that it was almost impossible to keep the eye from following him and resting on his disfigurement.

Next day this turnkey escorted me to the prison. He turned out to be a government servant there on duty for a month, and so poor that he was glad to get employment at anything. This time it was broad daylight, and we surprised the inmates playing chess. For a board they had taken down one half of a window-shutter, and scratched the form of the chess-board on it. Proper chess-men they had none, but the black man, being a scribe, had written on little flat pieces of wood, *camel, mandarin, child,* and so on, thus indicating the different kinds of men. With this makeshift board and these makeshift men, they were playing quite a keen game; both players and spectators protested against the positions being disturbed, and the chess-board was laid carefully away, that the game might be resumed where it was left off. A few minutes later, a terrible storm of wind, rain, and hail beat against the front of the house. The door was closed. One window had no shutters; the other aperture had no window, but shutters only. The one half of the shutter was under a pile of clothes, keeping them from the damp of the *kh'ang* ;[1] the other was laid away with the game of chess on it; but as the storm beat into the room, the clothes were thrown aside, the chess-men were swept up, the shutters fixed, and with only one small window left, the *black-house* was true to its name.

The storm soon passed over, light was re-admitted, and the place once more became visible. There was little but bare walls to be seen. Two *kh'angs*, one at each end, without flues, and almost destitute of mats; a couple of broken-down-looking fireplaces, a pot, and a couple of water-buckets, comprised nearly the whole of the furniture in the place. All the floor, except two or three feet at each side, was wood. Near the centre was a trap-door with a little square hole cut in the middle. When this door was raised, it disclosed an underground room about ten feet deep, eight feet wide, and fifteen or twenty feet long, with mud floor, plastered walls, and the flooring of the prison for ceiling. This room had no furniture, and contained nothing of any kind. There seemed to be no air-holes or provision for ventilation.

[1] A raised brick platform used for sleeping.

except the seams between the boards of the ceiling, and the little hole, about four or five inches square, in the trap-door. Outside the house there was conspicuous from afar a clumsy Chinese ladder. By means of this ladder, every night at dark, three of the prisoners were let down with their bedding to pass the night in this strong room. It was rather hard lines, even for a criminal, to pass eight or ten hours of the twenty-four in such a damp stagnant hole, which never gets warm all the year round. It was summer time then; but the keeper remarked, " In the morning the men come up shivering with cold."

One thing the dungeon afforded—safe keeping for the prisoners. Once let down into it, and the ladder withdrawn and placed outside the house, the three men were in no danger of getting out. The trap-door was fastened down firmly ten feet above their heads, and to mine themselves out they would have had to work through the solid earth. Experienced breakers of foreign prisons would doubtless have easily devised means of escape, but Mongols were safe enough. Three of the six were not compelled to sleep in the dungeon, but shared the comforts of the upper prison in common with the sub-governor, the turnkey, and the two soldiers.

The most remarkable thing about the prison was the amount of liberty allowed the prisoners. It seemed to be no uncommon thing for the keepers and soldiers to be away at the same time; when the prisoners were left at perfect freedom. It is true that on these occasions the keepers never went far, and kept continually casting glances towards the jail; yet it sounds strange to hear of half-a-dozen criminals left to roam at will inside and outside of the prison and the prison yard. The great distances and the naked solitudes of the country doubtless accounted for this. Suppose a prisoner ran away, where could he go? If he travelled, his track would not be difficult to find; and if he did not travel, where could he lie hid? During the night he might get away and baffle pursuit, but more care was exercised after dark. Another consideration, too, that makes jails easy to guard in Mongolia is this, that an escaped prisoner would doom himself to perpetual banishment. If he returned home at any time, he would be instantly apprehended, and most Mongols would prefer to endure two or three years' imprisonment, to being compelled to skulk for life. The three prisoners that were allowed to sleep in the upper prison had almost completed their term of restraint; a few weeks or months more would make them free men; and in these circumstances they would not render themselves liable to fresh punishment by attempting to escape. The keepers knew this, and were not at all afraid to give them plenty of liberty.

The prison was pleasantly situated on high ground, overlooking a valley lively with flocks, herds, tents, and a couple of large Chinese trading establishments. Close at hand, but round the shoulder of a hill, and just out of sight, but within hearing, was a large temple. The monotony of prison life was much relieved by the sight of all the life and activity in the neighbourhood. People were riding to and fro, carts coming and going, flocks pasturing, horse droves conspicuous on the hill-tops, lamas in state coming to the temple and going off to the country on religious business, and government officials conspicuous with their buttons. These things the prisoners could see from their prison; frequently they stood looking at them over the low mud wall; but more frequently still they were to be seen crouching on the ash-heap in front of the gate. All prisons in Mongolia have not such a good prospect. Some of them are built in quiet situations, and have a wall about ten feet high round them, which shuts out nearly everything but the sky. Even then the fate of the inmates is not so hard as it might be, because in most cases they are allowed to go outside the inclosure.

The last time I visited the prison they were having a feast. They had clubbed together and bought the head and some other parts of an ox slaughtered at the temple hard by, to supply rations to ten lamas engaged on the great summer services. The tongue they had slit and hung up to dry. The rest they were boiling. The pot was much too small for even the moiety they had in hand, but they piled it high above the rim, and kept industriously turning the raw parts down into the water. The fuel too was bad. They had a little argol, but that seemed damp, and was utterly insufficient; so they had gone out to the hills and pulled up by the roots a great quantity of southernwood, and that they used as fuel. The day before, it was blooming in all its August freshness and fragrance; now it was cast into the furnace, blazing a little and smoking a great deal. The Mongols rather like their meat half raw, and on this occasion they seemed to be having their taste gratified to the full. When one potful was pronounced to be *done*, the same half shutter that had before acted as a chess-board was now called into requisition as a trencher, and covered with huge pieces of steaming meat and bone With perfect liberty, fraternity, and equality, prisoners and keepers gathered round and did their best. Knives were "scarce" and the table small, so they had to take it in turns; and one poor fellow was poorly that day, and had to sit apart and look at his companions feasting. His was a hard lot; they had such a feast but seldom; and to think that of all the days of the year he should have been sick on that day!

On the termination of the last visit, the inmates offered hearty thanks for all the attention that had been paid them, and lamented that they had not been able to offer the universal token of Mongol hospitality—tea. Wishing to set them at their ease, I said I would taste their white food, which is the common compromise adopted when it is difficult or inconvenient to get tea. The sour white milk-cake was at once produced, and, in addition, some white flour scones basted in butter, which had come from the temple hard by. Though suffering as criminals, the five lamas had not been neglected in the temple ministrations, but a dole had been sent them as if they had taken actual part in the services.

Prisoners in Mongolia seem to have a good time of it. Perhaps they have, but it is not impossible that the modified kind of restraint to which they have to submit, proves to them as irksome as the severer discipline of other nations proves to more civilised prisoners.

One of the inmates of the prison, when asked how long he had been there, replied with exactness, stating the number of days. This showed how he felt. Mongols usually state time loosely, such as, more than three months, about a month, less than a year. This poor fellow was exact in his statement. He had been wearying and counting the days of his confinement. Our visits, for the time being, helped to relieve the monotony of their days, but this was only a temporary relief.

Months after we left, perhaps most of them were there still, crouching on the ash-heap, watching the riders as they came and went in the valley, and counting the days that must elapse before they themselves could again wander at their sweet will in the open plains.

CHAPTER XXV.

WHISKY IN MONGOLIA.

"Have you caught the mares?" "Is the *airak* good?" The taste of *airak*. The distillation of whisky. Milking of mares not profitable. Leads to drunkenness. Fewness of teetotallers. Behaviour of a *good* man when drunk. Evils of drink. A whisky-loving living Buddha.

"Have you caught the mares?" Travelling in Mongolia, during the summer season, you will often hear your followers address this question to those who come about them. If "No" is the answer, the questioner is a little disappointed. If the mares have been caught, the next question most likely will be, "Is the *airak* good?" Then, perhaps, the man questioned asks the questioner to go and taste it. In Mongolia they catch the mares for the purpose of milking them. Properly speaking, they catch the foals, not the mares; but it comes to the same thing, because when the foal is tied up the mare is secured, as she will not leave her offspring. Camels, cows, sheep, and goats leave their young and go to pasture; but, as the Mongols say, the mare is unable to desert her foal, and stands half the day whisking her tail in patient idleness beside her tethered young. The foal is secured to let the milk gather. During the night and part of the day the mare and foal are allowed to roam over the plains with the drove. The milk that the foal then gets is supposed to be sufficient for its wants; the owner, by separating the foal from the mother, secures a part of the milk for himself. All cattle, or, as the Mongols say, the five tribes of cattle, are treated in the same way.

The Mongols milk anything they can lay hands on: goats, sheep, cows, camels, and mares. The milk of these different creatures has different qualities and is put to different uses. The number of different preparations of milk is great, but, as far as I am aware, mare's milk is put to only one use—making *airak* and *arrihae*. *Airak* is simply soured mare's milk stirred up. In Southern Mongolia they have earthenware jars about four feet high and a foot and a half diameter. In Central and Northern Mongolia there are skin bags of about the same dimensions. Into these each day's freshly milked pailful is emptied, and the whole mass frequently stirred up. Visitors have this served out to them frequently in huge bowls, or basins rather, which they empty rapidly and repeatedly. The drinkers are all right for a while, but if they keep at it long enough they get most decidedly drunk, and have a season of discomfort which arises in no small degree from the large quantity they have imbibed before reaching the goal of intoxication.

At the risk of my reputation as a teetotaller, I on two separate occasions tasted small quantities of this *airak*, and found it very much like "sour milk" (buttermilk is the English name, I believe) which had been kept too long. This *airak* is the mother of *arrihae* or whisky. The *airak* is put into a huge pot, covered with what looks like a barrel with both ends knocked out; a vessel is suspended in the middle of the barrel; a pot kept filled with cold water is set on the top, and after a few minutes' boiling, the vessel inside the barrel is found filled with pure and good whisky. The spirit thus distilled is much milder than that which the Chinese manufacture from grain, but is intoxicating when taken in considerable quantities. In districts where large horse droves abound, the quantity of spirit produced is large, and as it is consumed on the spot, the number of drunk men to be met is proportionately great.

As far as I am aware, this Mongol whisky is never exported; much of it is drunk almost as soon as it is made, and any that is left does not last long. Custom seems to demand that it should be presented to every visitor, and every visitor seems to think that custom requires him to consume all that is set before him. Rich men are proud of their droves, and like to indicate their wealth by the number of the foals tied up to the long rope, which is pinned down to the ground some little distance off, in front of their line of tents. They are proud of their whisky, the produce of their drove, and if you call on them, you come in for no stinted share of it. It seems quite poetical to see the simple-minded herdsmen of the plains drinking the mild whisky of their own making, costing them no money and but little trouble. There are no excisemen, no duties, no smuggling. It comes easily, and goes freely, even to the hangers-on and poor dependents, who, at the season, do not fail to present themselves frequently on imaginary business, or to ask about their patron's welfare. This seems all very poetical, quite Arcadian indeed. Perhaps so, but it has its other side.

The milking of the mares is in no sense a source of profit. The milk they do not sell; and, as far as I know, they do not sell the whisky made from it. It never brings a single cash into the owner's pocket. Neither the *airak* nor the *arrihae* can be called food in any sense; and poetical, primitive, and simple as it may seem, it is a source of disaster and distress to the country. From their youth up, Mongols are familiar with the taste of the native spirit. They acquire a liking for it; a liking which the quantity produced in the country can by no means satisfy. As a consequence, they take to Chinese whisky, which is much stronger, and every ounce of which they have to purchase from Chinamen. It is not only when they go to Chinese towns that Mongols buy Chinese whisky. They do buy it then, perhaps; a Mongol rarely returns from a visit to the "inner country," as they call China, without a jar safely stowed away among his baggage; but, unfortunately, whisky can be got anywhere, any day of the year. Chinese traders on a small scale go about the country in all directions. They have their little stock of goods packed on ox-carts, and move slowly along, going round from one cluster of tents to another, trading mostly by barter, taking skins and produce in return for their wares. Skins and produce do not come handy for exact sums; so in many cases the account has to be adjusted by taking so many ounces of whisky —an article which no trader ever seems to be without. Even when there is not the flimsy excuse of an account to be adjusted, the temptation is too great for the simple Mongol. The pedlar comes into the tent, sits down and talks. At last the Mongol asks, "Have you any whisky?" "Yes." "Good?" "Tip-top." This is more than the

Mongol can stand. "Let me have some," he adds, "and I'll pay it again." So he has it and drinks it, and is in debt for it, and it is just the same old story of inattention to business, things going to wreck, poverty, ruin.

All that the mare's-milk whisky is good for is to give the Mongols an appetite for the stronger and more expensive spirit made from grain. The milk-whisky succeeds in educating most of the Mongols into drinking habits, not excepting even the lamas, who, from their vow to abstain from drink, might be expected to be teetotallers. Teetotallers they are not. Among many hundreds I have met only one who would not take spirits; the common run of lamas drink as much as they can get. I do not remember ever having met a layman who refused to drink; and drunkenness is so common among all classes, that it is useless to make sobriety one of the qualifications in a Mongol servant you seek to engage. Mongols laugh and say, "We all drink," and the only point to be careful about in hiring a Mongol, as far as drink is concerned, is to see that the man you have is not given to violence when he is drunk. "A good man," say they, "when drunk, goes off to sleep; a bad man makes a disturbance." A drunken man is about the only thing to be feared by the lonely traveller in the desert. When sober, a Mongol is good-hearted and friendly; or, if suspicious, he is careful and harmless; but once let his head get inflamed with drink, and he is reckless; friend and foe are alike to him, and his great knife is there at his side, and can be drawn with alarming ease and rapidity. Happy is it for all concerned, when the thoughtful and clever-handed mistress of the tent steals the weapon, and hides it among the furniture when she sees the quarrel coming. Several times I have been among people unfriendly and suspicious, but the only serious trouble or danger I have seen has been caused by men inflamed by drink.

The Mongols themselves are fully aware of its evils. They have instances every day. Gichick goes to a gathering. He has a fine snuff-bottle, and valuable silver ornaments, and rides a magnificent horse. He comes back on foot, his bottle, his ornaments, and his horse gone. Ask him, and he says, "I got drunk, did not know what I was doing, struck Dimbril, wounding him seriously, and here I am." Or a man drinks at a friend's tent, then mounts and rides homeward. His horse arrives riderless, and he is found dead on the plain. "How did it happen?" "He was drunk." Or a man has been rich, the owner of droves, herds, and flocks. Now he is glad to earn his bread as a hired servant. "How does this come about?" "He is fond of whisky." This explains all; no more questions need be asked.

The Mongols are so sensible of the evils of whisky that frequently the lamas in authority, though by no means teetotallers themselves, forbid Chinese traders to come within a certain distance of the temples. I have often heard Buddhism praised, as a religion tending towards temperance. It is not so in Mongolia. One of the living Buddhas of high repute, and much sought after on account of his supposed power to confer blessings, has the reputation of drinking several catties of Chinese whisky daily, and is followed by a crowd of attendant lamas, who pass their lives drinking and quarrelling over the rich offerings brought by the devout to their whisky-loving master. The Mongols as a rule do not smoke opium. They have not money enough for that, but I do not think that I am exaggerating much, if at all, when I say that drink hurts Mongolia just about as much as opium hurts China.

The line of mares in front of the tent, the bustle of milking, the process of brewing, the hospitable welcome, the conviviality of drinking, are picturesque and pleasing, and have a charm to the eye of the cursory observer; but look more closely, and you find that these things are but the gaudy colour on the skin of the deadly serpent, the poison of whose bite brings calamity and death. If Christianity is ever to do any good in Mongolia, it must go hand in hand with teetotalism.

CHAPTER XXVI.

THE MIDSUMMER FESTIVAL.

Summit-spring temple. Worshippers and traders encamped. Carrying sacred books round the temple. Chinese traders. Chinese restaurant. Arrival of worshippers. The *Dault*. My turn comes. The *Ch'am* described. The *Ch'am* is a representation in pantomime of the early history of Buddhism. Passing under the *Sawr*. Carrying forth the *Sawr*. The Babel of dispersion. Thunderstorm. Carrying round Maitreya.

This is the great annual religious festival of the Mongols, and as large numbers of both sexes and all classes resort at this time to the religious centres of the country, we too bent our steps towards a temple. We found the "Summit-spring temple," as it was called, a very good sample both as to itself and its surroundings. There was the usual large worship hall, lofty and resplendent with gilt ornaments that glittered from afar in the sun, two or three smaller and less pretentious chapels, a good cluster of little built houses inhabited by the more wealthy lamas, and on the outskirts of these a number of felt tents, the abodes of the poorer sort of priests.

Behind was a range of hills, at some little elevation, in which rose the spring that gave name to the place;

in front was a typical Mongol lake, small, shallow, half-dried up, and presenting to the eye little more than an expanse of yellow slime; great part of the view was shut in by circular ridges of hills, but in one direction the prospect was unlimited, stretching away across the plain to a far-off dim horizon, affording glimpses of flocks, herds, and Mongol encampments, one cluster of tents standing in the foreground at no great distance from the temple.

Our caravans arrived on the twelfth of the sixth month. As we came near, a great, tall, blustering Mongol came out of a tent—which seemed to be full of women drinking tea—saluted me boisterously, invited me to drink tea with him, and advised me to camp beside him. A little further on we passed through a line of Chinese traders, who recognised our caravan and invited us to camp with them; but, aware of the riot and drunkenness that might be expected at the festival, we went higher up the hill and pitched our tents where no traders or worshippers were likely to come. It was a spot which permitted of a little retirement, yet was within easy reach of any who might wish to visit us, and commanded a full view of the temple, the worshippers, the traders, and all the busy activity of the scene.

Even as early as the twelfth, there was a good deal of coming and going, and riding to and fro, and a number of worshippers were seeking absolution from their sins by walking round the temple loaded, each of them, with quite a heavy volume of the sacred books. The sacred precincts are marked off by a series of little cairns of stones, within which are included not only the temple itself, but the residences of the lamas, the fuel stacks, and even the rubbish heaps. Any one wishing to clear away his sins has only to come to the temple, load himself (or herself, for this seems a method of merit-making specially in favour among the women) with a sacred volume, and, early and late, keep trudging round in the beaten path that runs outside of the little cairns.

The number of lamas, young and old, moving about in the temple garb was considerable. The services, which were to culminate on the fifteenth, had been going on for about two weeks, and, as distributions of money and food are made to all who take part in these services, nearly every lama who had connection with the place put in an appearance, and though the chanting seemed to go on almost all day, there were never wanting numbers of priests who, on some excuse or other, absented themselves from one or more of the meetings.

Throughout the twelfth and thirteenth, Chinese traders kept arriving with their wares, on one, two, or three ox-carts. They drew themselves up in line along the face of the hill, forming a kind of one-sided street. Some had tents, others tilted up their carts, fixed a straw mat or two above, and bestowed themselves and their goods below. Their stock in trade consisted mainly of such things as onions, turnips, cucumbers, apricots, apples, dried meat, confections, black sugar, buttons, thread, needles, thimbles, toys for the children, and whisky for the grown-up.

The other articles of merchandise caused no trouble; but the whisky and the toys proved a perpetual nuisance. Morning, noon, and evening, there were never wanting men in all stages of intoxication, causing all manner of disturbance and trouble; and morning, noon, and evening, during the days that this fair lasted, there never ceased the sound of the *thlimba*, a little section of bamboo about six inches long, furnished with holes like a flute, with a slit in the mouth-piece to act as a reed. Of these some were coloured, some were plain; they cost about a halfpenny or three farthings a piece, and were the heart's delight of the children and young lamas. Mongolian children are very fond of Chinese biscuits and sugar-candy, but whenever the number of cash reached the price of a *thlimba*, it was promptly purchased, and blown with great vigour and perseverance.

Long afterwards, and in far different scenes, whenever the thought reverted to the incidents of that midsummer festival, shrill above the boom of the temple drums, the hum of buyers, the trampling of horsemen, and the shouts of the drunken, would come the squeak of the *thlimba*, and the very temple itself seems to have become inseparably associated in the mind with the piercing sound of this little harmless-looking musical instrument.

One of the Chinese trading arrivals consisted of an eating-house complete in all particulars. There was one cart loaded with tent, utensils, and provisions; another with fuel; and behind both came a couple of men driving a small flock of sheep. Soon after their arrival the tent was set up, the cooking-range established, the carcass of a sheep hanging from the shaft of a tilted-up cart, and tripe supplied to all comers at three farthings a basin.

This establishment drove a thriving trade, combining as it did the threefold business of the butcher, the dram-seller, and the restaurant-keeper.

By dawn of the fourteenth, the tale of traders' encampments was complete, and about eight o'clock that morning the worshippers began to arrive in force.

Solitary and in companies, men and women, young and old, lamas and laymen, respectable men and notorious thieves, on horseback and in carts; dressed, some well, some poorly, but nearly all gaudily in yellow, blue, red, white, or green, their garments in many cases contrasting strikingly with their horses; along roads, across plains, over ridges, from mountain gorges, came the ever increasing crowd of worshippers; some riding rapidly, some riding cautiously, but all converging on one centre, and many of them ending up with a furious gallop, to show their fine horses at their best. Rich men of consequence, and mandarins of rank, for the most part came in carts with a train of outriders, swollen by the joining on of all and sundry mounted persons of their neighbourhood, and any others whom they happened to fall in with on the road.

For an hour or two after arriving the visitors hunted up their friends, looked in on the temple service which happened to be in progress, went the round of the traders asking prices, and perhaps drinking a little whisky, and in many cases drew up at my tent; such as knew me greeting me in a friendly way; all eager to see my Bible-pictures, most of them willing to listen to what I had to say, some of them ready to discuss the differences between Christianity and Buddhism, a few finishing up by buying a tract or two.

On a sudden the crowd gave way for two men, who entered and sat down opposite to me. Each held in his right hand an iron frame about two and a half feet high, hung all over with sacred scarves, from among which could be seen a framed picture of Buddha and other sacred things. At a glance I recognised the visitors as two begging lamas, and knew I was "in for it." I protested vigorously, but, as I had expected, in vain; the men were immovable. After sitting for a little while motionless, they suddenly, one after the other, shook the *Dault*, as the iron frame is called, and jingled a multiplicity of iron rings hung all about it. Meantime the spectators were all reverence and attention, and, after a few more shakes and jinglings of the rings, one of the lamas started off with a sing-song recitation which began by detailing one of the adventures of Buddha.

The recitation lasted some minutes, and when lama number one had finished, lama number two began. When number two had finished, they both joined in a chant, and when the chant was ended, they requested alms, displaying a large cup which hung from their belt, and about the bottom of which, when the lid was raised, were visible traces of butter, a delicate means of suggesting the kind of offering that would be most acceptable.

As soon as the ceremony was over, all the Mongols present in the tent in turn reverently inclined their heads, and were touched on the brow by the lama with the *Dault*, as a king might touch a suppliant with a sceptre.

The eyes of all were now turned to me, to see what I would do. I began by asking them what good they supposed the repetition was calculated to effect. They said it would make my flocks and herds prosperous. On reminding them that I had neither flock nor herd, they said it would bless me in all my concerns both of body and soul. I told them that I sought blessings from quite a different quarter and by quite different means, and beginning from this went on to explain to them Christ and Christianity, and I think I seldom saw a more attentive audience.

After a time, some one suggested that the *Sawr* was doubtless by this time set forth, and young and old trooped off to pass under it.

A little later, it was reported that the *Ch'am* had begun, and immediately all the tents were deserted. Flocks and herds were left to care for themselves, and I soon followed the multitude.

Arrived at the main court of the large temple, where the sacred dance was going on, I found a large circle of spectators sitting three or four deep, and outside of them a second circle standing, also three or four deep. Inside the circle were two or three lads, in fantastic dresses and immense head-coverings resembling skulls, armed with short batons, keeping order and preventing the spectators from encroaching too much on the open space. Outside of the sitting and standing spectators were, here and there, groups of women holding private conversations, the interest of which seemed so absorbing, that they paid no attention to anything else.

This festival is the great meeting time for the women. Occasionally during the year Mongol women frequent marriage festivals and other ceremonies, but this midsummer gathering is the only opportunity during the whole twelve months that the women of a tribe have of meeting each other in one great assembly. It is only too probable also that this day is the solitary holiday that many of them have all the year round. It is not to be wondered at then that considerations of worship and piety form only part of the attraction that draws women together on this occasion, and it is not strange that the interchange of friendly conversation

THE YELLOW TEMPLE, PEKING.

should draw away the attention of many from beholding the performance of the religious dance. With a few exceptions Mongol women are soft-hearted, and some of them, on seeing each other at this annual reunion, break down altogether, and for a time are unable to express their feelings except by sobbing and tears.

But whether the spectators talk apart in groups or attend, the religious dance goes on. Ever and anon two or more figures in uncouth masks, for the most part resembling the heads of different animals, and gaudy dresses, issue forth into the court and prance about in the circle to the sound of music. The step is a kind of stately leap from one foot to the other, and the whole exhibition soon becomes monotonous in the extreme, so much so, that Chinese masons and labourers who reside at the temples every summer, building and repairing houses and courtyard walls, seldom think it worth their while to go and see it.

At some parts of the performance quite a number of actors appear simultaneously, and at one stage of the proceedings a grey-headed old man comes out and fires off crackers. The antics of this individual are received with shouts of laughter, which may be heard at a distance over the plain.

One part of the exhibition is curious. A dough-made miniature figure of a man is produced, and with great solemnity cut to pieces. It is said that this little image—to make the resemblance of the execution more complete—is supplied with entrails, and it is also further affirmed that this model is made some days before, and has prayers read over it, to make it alive as it were. The explanation given of this proceeding is that it is in memory of an enemy who opposed Buddhism in the ancient times.

Ask a hundred Mongols what is the meaning of the performance of this religious dance, and the vast majority can give no reasonable explanation; but the learned few who are conversant with the more recondite things of their religion explain it to be a representation in pantomime of the early history of Buddhism, the various actors who take part in the exhibition being representations of eminent men, friends and foes, who helped or hindered Buddhism in its early struggles.

But the great finishing solemnity of the day is the escorting of the *Sawr*. The *Sawr* seems to be a triangular pyramid of dough, fixed on a frame of wood. The dough is coloured red and moulded to represent flames. On the top, as crown, is the representation of a human skull. In the 'fore part of the day the *Sawr* stands in the temple while a service is being held, and before it is carried out, young and old crowd to pass under it. By passing under it, men are supposed to escape from disease, disaster, misfortune, calamity, or trouble, that would otherwise befall themselves, their enterprises, their cattle, or their country. After all have passed under it, and the sacred dance has been finished, the dancers, still wearing their masks and robes, led by the head lama of the temple, in his most imposing ceremonial costume, form themselves into a solemn procession, and followed by the whole mass of devout worshippers, and less devout pleasure-seekers, drawn together by the events of the day, issue from the sacred precincts, and lead the way to an erection of bushes, straw, or other inflammable material, prepared and set up on the plain a short distance from the temple. The procession moves slowly along to the sound of two immense trumpets ten or twelve feet long.

Arrived at the spot selected, which seems almost uniformly to be beyond the south-east angle of the temple grounds, the chief lama takes his stand, the other performers crowd around, the great body of the temple lamas, and the spectators generally, close up behind, and a service consisting of the chanting of prayers and the blowing of trumpets is gone through. Sometimes the chief lama, at a certain stage of the service, waves repeatedly a black handkerchief towards the skull-crowned pyramid. Sometimes this part of the ceremony is not performed. After a time, at a signal from the chief lama, the pile of brushwood is lighted. As it blazes up, the pyramid is thrown headlong into it, a man, who has been standing ready with gun in hand, fires off his piece at it, the attendant lamas gather round their chief to congratulate him, and he replies, "It has become fortunate for the many." This is the signal for the dispersion, and the whole crowd of lamas and spectators hurry off without waiting to see the doomed structure consumed.

The ceremony is impressive, but there is only one step from the sublime to the ridiculous. While the others are hurrying off as fast as they can, a single lama may be seen poking about the fire: he is trying to rescue from the flames the few inches of board on which the pyramid stood, probably with the hope that it may serve again on the next occasion, and after this lama has gone, two or three dogs lie down and wait quietly till the fire subsides, when they fight for the possession of the scorched dough.

The whole ceremony is solemn and suggestive, and seems intended to avert evil on the vicarious principle. The doomed pyramid is set forth in public, prayers are chanted, and people pass under it, and thus, it is supposed, the evils of country and inhabitants are concentrated on it; it is carried forth to the desert, the black handkerchief of the officiating lama seems to wave maledictions towards it, and it is thrown into the fire and shot at, as a thing accursed and to be destroyed.

Immediately on the conclusion of the ceremony, a rush is made for the booths of the traders, and all over the temple grounds a perfect Babel of sounds arises. Men, women, and children are hurrying about and calling to each other, confusing and confused. Not a few have yet to buy at the traders' tents the Chinese biscuits, which all Mongol children left at home expect to receive from parents, friends, or neighbours who have been to a fair or a Chinese town.

On this particular day the hurry and bustle of the scattering was much intensified by a thunderstorm, which, after threatening and growling for some time at a distance, finally drew near and sent down dashing showers of rain. Most of the Mongols covered their gaudy garments with old weather-stained rain cloaks, those who had no rain cloaks turned their more valuable clothes inside out, and thus looked a good deal less picturesque at their departure than at their arrival. The storm, however, hastened their movements, and made the riding of drunk men and sober more furious and precipitate than it had been in the morning. It was wonderful to see how far a drunken man could lean over his horse without falling off, and women and very small children, as they urged to still greater speed their already galloping steeds, showed a horsemanship that would have done credit to grown men.

The next day, the fifteenth of the sixth month, was a repetition, to a great extent, of the same scenes, but the concourse of visitors was much smaller. The ceremony consisted in carrying the image of Maitreya round the temple grounds. The idol was brought out in state, a grand procession formed, flags carried aloft, drums beat, musical instruments sounded, lamas chanted sacred liturgies, and all the men, women, and children who had come to worship turned out in their most striking costumes and swelled the numbers of the great crowd. By a strange similarity this day's proceedings were also brought to an abrupt close by a thunderstorm. Next morning we were early astir, and before the sun was very high, not only we, but most of the traders, had packed up and gone off to other scenes, and the temple lately so full of people and life subsided into its normal quietness.

CHAPTER XXVII.

MONGOL TOILET.

Difference between the dress of men and women. A Mongol's robe is his room. Slovenly appearance of women's dress. Dressing. Washing. Mongols do not bathe. Snuff-bottle. Women's hair ornaments. Men's dress very becoming.

THE dress of both sexes, as far as shape is concerned is much alike. The main difference is that the men gird themselves with a belt, while the women allow their long garments to hang loose from shoulder to heel, and hence it comes that the common word for "woman" in Mongolia is "beltless." The outer garment of both sexes is a wide roomy coat which reaches down to the ground, with sleeves so ample that the arms can be withdrawn from them and reintroduced at pleasure, without disturbing the buttons.

This coat forms the blanket under which the wearer sleeps. Surrounded by this ample covering, the Mongol, withdrawing his arms from the sleeves, finds himself for all practical purposes inclosed in a little private tent from which his head only projects. Shrouded by it he rises from his couch in the morning, covered by it he sinks to rest at night, and the less happily situated foreigner cannot but envy the facility which this robe affords its wearer of dressing and undressing in perfect privacy, though surrounded by the crowded inmates of a full tent.

Mongol women on rising in the morning button up their coats at once, and commence household duties. The long wide robe hanging loose gives them a very slovenly appearance; in milking and cooking the great part of the gown lies about on the dirty ground, and in general the women appear slatternly in the extreme. The loose gown once appeared to advantage. A traveller crossing the desert in a camel-cart, was for a time puzzled one forenoon to know what the woman, who, mounted on a camel, led his cart camel, was about. Her hands disappeared, and inexplicable leanings and movements were seen about the shoulders, till at last the gown slid off and revealed another, more suitable to the increasing heat of the day. The girl had managed to change her dress while riding her camel and leading the cart, and had done it so adroitly and modestly, that it was impossible to tell what she was about till the process was complete.

Men on rising usually crouch down close to the fire, open their coat and sit lazily warming themselves and smoking. After a while they look about for a short cotton garment which is worn under the coat, and which might by extension of courtesy be called a shirt. The production of this garment is usually the signal for the most unpleasant sensation that a foreigner is conscious of in connexion with Mongol dressing, as the shirt was probably new or washed six months ago, and has been constantly worn since!

Washing is another sight. The Mongols wash once a day. A little water is poured into the ever-present wooden cup, from which it is either emptied little by little into the hand, or taken into the mouth and squirted out as needed. Washing is usually confined to the face and hands; neck and everything else not being regarded as standing in need of water. The washing itself is not so bad, but the "drying" is a little out of the way. With his ordinary want of forethought, a Mongol usually begins to think how he is to get his face dried only after he has got it washed. As he looks round, dripping, most probably the first thing that catches his eye is the "shirt" aforementioned, and it is pressed to do duty as a towel. A more provident Mongol has a handkerchief which is but a slight improvement on the shirt. There is another method in vogue, mostly among girls. When the washing is completed, the hands are rubbed slowly over the face, gathering the moisture, which is sucked from them as they pass over the mouth. The sound and the idea are not pleasant, but it is undoubtedly the cleanest method of wiping the face, and as such perhaps the least disagreeable to the beholders.

Feet are never washed except by accident, as when herding sheep in the rain, or crossing a stream on foot. Bathing is not customary. Said a Mongol, "It is too cold in winter; in summer the flies bite." This is of course the sluggard's excuse. If they were alive to the importance of it, nine-tenths of them could secure a bath with very little trouble. I once met an invalid, who, being a doctor, prescribed hot-bathing for his disease, and had fitted up a gem of a little bath in his tent. He had sunk into the ground a tub about three feet deep and big enough to sit in, and hung from the roof of the tent two felt curtains. All he had to do was to get inside, close the curtains, and then he was at liberty to dress and undress in complete retirement; and this is probably the shape the Mongol bath will take, when the Mongols are persuaded of its utility as a preventive against disease.

The dress of the poor is wretched. Men and women go about in rags, tatters, and filth, shivering in the cold. The rich dress impressively. The men have beautiful robes lined with the finest lambs' skin, and hang a profusion of massive silver ornaments from their belt. They are also great on fur caps, and one may sometimes meet a man wearing a cap worth as much as all the rest of his clothes put together. But the true criterion of a Mongol's wealth and standing is his snuff-bottle; and as custom requires him to hand it on introduction, one can make a good guess as to the position of any man he may meet. These bottles come from Peking, and range in price from a few cents to eighty taels. The cheap ones are made of glass; the valuable ones are beautiful stones skilfully hollowed out and nicely finished. Women do not usually carry a snuff-bottle, but on ceremonial occasions they also produce it from the box where it is stowed away. Women's bottles are almost uniformly small, thin, flat stones, with scarcely any capacity; and, as far as I have yet seen, always empty. The being empty does not matter. It is handed with due ceremony and form, and the recipient, too polite to see that it is empty, smells it deliberately, and returns it with dignity.

But the most remarkable parts of Mongol costume are the hair ornaments and headdresses of the women. Even a poor woman, if married, has a profusion of silver ornaments and fittings on her head and hanging from her hair, which contrasts strangely with the dirt and squalor of her general appearance. The precise nature and shape of these ornaments vary with the tribes; and any one well up in this species of heraldry can tell a woman's tribe at a glance. But though they vary, they all agree in being cumbersome—perhaps a Mongol would say impressive—and in necessitating a style of dressing the hair, which, when once performed, will most likely be allowed to stand undisturbed till growth disarranges it and demands fresh attention. Perhaps one may think a head not dressed for a month would look untidy. Not at all. Though the hair from which the pendants hang is not undone, the upper hair can be dressed so as to look quite neat. *They smear it with glue,* and if one does not know and does not examine too closely, it looks well enough.

Some of the tribes have hanging ornaments, which are suspended from a band running round the head, and kept in place by a hook in the ear. As these pendants are heavy, it is quite painful to see how the lobe is distended when the head is bent forward; and the unpleasant feeling is increased by noticing that many of the elder females have had their ears rent open, some of them more than once. One tribe I am acquainted with has a headdress for its matrons which projects up and makes it impossible for a cap to sit on the head. On occasions of ceremony, such as formal introductions, or the meeting of friends after absence, a cap must be worn. It is placed above the ornaments and tied on, remaining all the while clear of the head, and looks so absurd that it requires an effort to receive the lady's snuff-bottle with becoming gravity.

The everyday gear permanently worn is sufficiently cumbersome, but on gala days a perfect curtain of beads is superadded; and when a crowd of women arranged in flaming dresses and rich fur caps, enveloped almost to the waist in strings of red coral beads, and flashing with the sheen of silver ornaments, take their stand together in the veranda of a temple, the effect is striking. In the presence of such a sight, none but the blind and the prejudiced would refuse to admit that the beauty of these women is enhanced by their ornaments. Mongol women, on seeing foreign ladies, are struck by the absence of head-gear; and we are in the habit of trying to persuade ourselves that beauty is, when unadorned, adorned the most. Mongol women when young are often beautiful, but always look best in their ornaments; and perhaps their foreign sisters might gain something, as far as mere look is concerned, by an impressive headdress, though coral beads and glue would hardly do. The difference between them and us is this: the Mongol woman's field of attraction is confined to her face and appearance, while we estimate a lady's worth, not so much by her looks, as by her mental qualities. The Mongol woman is scarcely taught that she has a mind at all, and it is not strange that, having nothing else to recommend her, she should strive to excel us in making the most of her face.

The dress of the men also is more becoming than ours. To be convinced of this, you have only to glance at a foreigner in his tights and short coat, and a Mongol in his ample robe flowing down to his heels. Let us not grudge him his looks. If we had as little to do as he, we might dress as well.

CHAPTER XXVIII.

ÆSOP IN MONGOLIA.

The hare and the lion. The tortoise in the well. The seven lice and the flea. The trader and the madman. The crow and the lama. The parrot and the king. The reformed cat. Pebbles for jewels. The mouse and elephant. The pearl-borer. The bad-tempered monkey. Fox and bird. The painted fox. Strain at a gnat and swallow a camel. The frog and the two geese.

THE following fables are selected from a number which a Mongol teacher dictated, in his attempts to familiarise me with the language. It will be seen at a glance that most of them are not native to the country, but come from a land abounding with sights and scenes unknown to Mongolia. The teacher afterwards committed them to writing; but whether he copied them from a book, or merely wrote them from memory, and added the "Morals" "out of his own head," it is impossible to say.

I. *The Hare and the Lion.*

There was a lion that used to vary his diet by eating in turn one from all the kinds of the beasts of the field. One day it was the hare's turn, and the lion looking sorrowfully at the animal said: "A poor meal for me to-day. You're not worth eating; you won't even fill up the chinks between my teeth. Little use in eating you." The hare replied, "Do please condescend to eat me, I have just had a narrow escape from being eaten by an animal as terrible-looking as you." The lion, in a rage, demanded: "Where is there any animal like me, let me see him!" The hare led him away to a well and told him to look down. Look down he did, and there sure enough saw a beast that twisted his face, looked daggers, set up his mane, and showed his teeth as fiercely as he did. The lion could not stand this, and leaping down to fight his rival, perished in the water.

Moral. If a man has good intellectual powers, don't despise him though his bodily strength may be small; and since powerful enemies can be overcome by mental power, seek to develop the powers of the mind.

II. *The Blind Tortoise in the Well.*

A blind tortoise lived in a well. Another tortoise, a native of the ocean, in its inland travels happened to tumble into this well. The blind one asked of his new comrade whence he came. "From the sea." Hearing of the sea, he of the well swam round a little circle and asked: "Is the water of the ocean as large as this?" "Larger," replied he of the sea. The well tortoise then swam round two-thirds of the well and asked if the sea was as big as that. "Much larger than that," said the sea tortoise. "Well then," asked the blind tortoise, "is the sea as large as this whole well?" "Larger," said the sea tortoise. "If that is so," said the well tortoise, "how big then is the sea?" The sea tortoise replied: "You having never seen any other water than that of your well, your capability of understanding is small.

As to the ocean, though you spent many years in it, you would never be able to explore the half of it, nor to reach the limit, and it is utterly impossible to compare it with this well of yours." The tortoise replied, "It is impossible that there can be a larger water than this well; you are simply praising up your native place with vain words."

Moral. People of small attainments, who cannot conceive of the acquirements of men of great abilities, and who pride themselves on their own learning and talent, are like the blind tortoise in the well.

III. *The Seven Lice and the Flea.*

A hermit had seven lice in his coat, which used to interrupt his devotions to such an extent, that, at last, he made an agreement with them, that if they would not bite him when he was at his exercises, he would not banish them for biting him in his times of leisure. This arrangement did well enough till a flea arrived. "Ha, comrades," said the flea, "you are snug here, I'll stay with you." The lice informed him of the compact and asked him to observe it. The flea replied: "He has bargained with you, he has not bargained with me, devotions or no devotions I don't care, here goes." The lama felt him biting. "Ah," said he, "the lice have not kept their word." So saying he interrupted his devotions, and opened his garment, whereupon the flea jumped out and escaped. Seeing the lice all there the lama reproached them with their bad faith. They related to him the whole of the circumstances, but thinking they were deceiving him, he caught them and threw them far away.

Moral. Warned by this disaster brought upon the

seven lice by the wicked flea, beware of bad companions.

IV. *The Trader and the Madman.*

A trader travelling alone, as he toiled up a mountain pass, meeting a madman, asked if there were any dangers on the other side of the hill. The madman replied: "On the other side are fire and water, weapons and robbers, from which there is no escape." The trader, hearing this, turned back without accomplishing his purpose. The madman's foolish words were no good to himself, and were hurtful to the trader.

Moral. Avoid foolish words.

V. *The Crow and the Lama.*

A lama was in the habit of giving a handful of food to a crow daily, when he drew his rations at noon. One day the crow did not come. Next day, when noon came, the bird expected double rations, but did not get them, and, enraged at the lama, went off to some robbers and said that the lama had a large number of gold coins. Among the robbers was a man who understood the language of the crows, so, hearing this report, the robbers went to the lama and demanded his gold money.

The lama denied having gold in his possession, and asked who told them that he had such wealth. Hearing that a crow told them, the lama related the whole circumstances of the case, and the robbers perceived that the lama had no gold, and that the crow was a poor foolish creature. After this the crow got no more food from the lama, and had to live on short rations.

Moral. Don't quarrel with your bread and butter.

Also; If a man can thus, by learning, understand the language of the lower animals, how much more will not he understand human language!

VI. *The Parrot and the King.*

Long ago a certain king went a hunting and caught a parrot that could speak. The parrot said to the king, "O king, don't go a hunting, a chieftain has meantime murdered your wives and your children, and plundered your palace." "Evil words hast thou spoken," said the king, then, having killed the parrot, he went off to the abode of the chieftain, slew a number of men, and returned to his palace to find that there was nothing the matter.

Finding all quiet and peaceful, he then discovered that the words of the parrot had been false, and felt extremely sorry for what he had done.

Moral. False and idle words are disastrous, so beware of them.

VII. *The Reformed Cat.*

A cat was in the habit of stealing many things from a lama, and last of all stole his rosary. The lama gave chase and seized the animal by the tail just as it was entering a hole. Pulling lustily the tail gave way, and the cat, in pain, and destitute of food, was soon reduced to great straits. With a view to improve her condition, she hung the rosary on her neck and went out to a convenient place on the plain. By-and-by a field rat saw her and was about to flee, when the cat hailed her and said, "Don't be afraid, my child, I am a cat that has taken holy orders, I don't destroy life, I do nothing wicked. I exhort you to lead a holy life like me."

The news spread among the rat tribe, and they gathered in great numbers to hear the cat chant prayers (purring). At the conclusion of the service, the cat told them to form in a procession, march round her from left to right in single file, and depart one by one to their several holes. The last one she devoured.

This continued some length of time, and the rat tribe gradually decreased till it became a subject of remark, and suspicions were excited. The leader of the rats, taking a companion, contrived to keep a watch, and finding hair and bones, their worst suspicions were confirmed. Next day, after service, the leader of the rats asked the cat, "O teacher, on what sort of food do you deign to live?" "I live on dry leaves and grass," the cat replied. The leader next called a mass-meeting of the rats, related to them his suspicions, and gave orders to have a bell and a rope stolen from the abode of some man. The bell would be suspended from the neck of the cat, and if on any occasion after a service the bell should be heard to tinkle, they were all to turn back and see what was up. The bell was procured, and at next service the leader of the rats, in a complimentary speech, presented the teacher with an ornament, and, suiting the action to the word, hung the bell from the cat's neck. After the close of the service, as all were going home, suddenly the bell sounded, and hurrying back, the cat was seen in the act of devouring a rat. The leader thus addressed her: "O teacher, you have fattened, but we have become few, and have not flourished under this religion. We now invite our teacher to return to your own place, but before you go tell us how it happens that, though you eat grass only, there are so many traces of bones and hair." The rats then left for their own abodes, and the cat, taking it to heart that all the trouble arose from carelessness, took to wiser ways.

Moral. Murder will out.

VIII. *Pebbles for Jewels.*

A set of half-witted people went to the sea to gather precious stones. Not being well able to discriminate between true and false stones, they took for precious a lot of common pebbles, thinking they must be good because they were of bright colour and heavy. The really precious stones, being of uncertain colour and light weight, they rejected as worthless.

Moral. The generality of people make the same mistake with regard to religion. Wealth, fame, honour, look brighter and better and are preferred to the fruits of religion, but in reality those who reject religion for worldly things are rejecting diamonds and choosing common pebbles.

IX. *The Mouse and Elephant.*

A mouse fell into a pit and could not get out. An elephant hearing its little piteous voice, looked into the pit, and, seeing a mouse, lowered down his tail, which the mouse laid hold of, and thus reached the surface. The little animal thanked his great deliverer and said he would never forget the kindness he received. The elephant said he had helped him only because he had been moved by pity, and disclaimed any hope of being repaid for his trouble, and dismissed the mouse with a benediction.

Years passed by, and the same elephant, old and infirm, fell into a ravine too narrow to permit him to rise. This same mouse, seeing his distress, collected all the mice in these parts, and scraped away one side of the ravine, making it wide enough for the elephant to rise.

Moral. Be helpful to others and you will be helped yourself.

X. *The Pearl-borer.*

A lad learned to bore pearls, and priding himself on the attainment learned nothing more. Other lads, his companions, learned many things, and succeeded in life to such an extent that he who could bore pearls before they could do anything was left far behind them, and was glad to hire himself out to them as their servant.

Moral. Don't be too proud of any attainment, and always be diligent to learn more.

XI. *The Bad-tempered Monkey.*

A sparrow had its nest half way up a tree, in the top of which dwelt a monkey. After a heavy rain, the sparrow, snug and dry in its nest, saw the monkey shaking his dripping body and addressed him thus: "Comrade, your hands are skilful, your strength great, your intellect clever, why do you live in such a miserable state? Can't you build a snug nest like mine?" The monkey, angered at the complacency of the sparrow, replied: "Am I to be mocked by an evil creature like you? Your nest is snug, is it?" So saying he destroyed it and threw it down.

Moral. Don't talk with a passionate man.

XII. *Fox and Bird.*

A fox and a bird made friends and lived together. While the parent bird was away searching for food, the fox used to devour one of the young birds. This continued till all the fledgelings were gone. The mother bird, then aware of the fate of her young, resolved to be avenged, and, finding a trap set, decoyed the fox to it and saw him caught.

Moral. Beware of an evil-intentioned man.

XIII. *The Painted Fox.*

A fox finding a deserted dyer's sink containing blue colour, painted itself all over of a beautiful azure hue, and went and showed itself to the other animals. They did not recognise him, and asked him: "Who are you?" The fox replied: "I am the king of the beasts."

The lions and other creatures then all did him homage, and the fox, when he travelled, rode on the lion's back, lording it over all classes of animals generally, but carrying it with an especially high hand in the assembly of the foxes. After a time the fox sent provisions to his mother, who, hearing the whole tale, sent back word to her son not to trouble himself about her, but to occupy himself with the affairs of his kingdom. The messenger foxes hearing this, filled with envy, went to the other beasts and said: "This king of yours is but a fox after all; if you honour him, why don't you honour us? he is just like us."

"Like you," said the other beasts, "why, he is a different colour altogether." The foxes replied: "As to the colour, wait till the first month of spring. In that month, on the night of the star called Bos, we foxes howl. If we don't howl our hair falls off. On that night you can decide the question and know whether or not your king is a fox."

When that night came all the other foxes howled aloud, and the blue fox, afraid lest its hair should fall off, howled in a low voice, but still loud enough for the other beasts to hear him. They thus knew that their pretended king was but a fox after all, and the lion, enraged at being deceived, killed him with one stroke of his paw.

Moral. Though you attain to high rank, don't oppress your inferiors.

XIV. *Strain at a Gnat and Swallow a Camel.*

A traveller noticed a parrot clearing the water with his wing, and asking what it meant, the parrot replied: "I clear the water to avoid drinking flies, and thus destroying life." The parrot flew off, and a little further on the same traveller saw the same bird perched on a wall saying his prayers. Taking a liking for such a pious bird, the traveller went up to where he was, and found him busily feasting on worms.

On the same journey the traveller entered an abode, and found the master of the house feasting a priest whom he had invited to perform services. On the ground, in front of the priest, was a piece of gold. The priest slyly stuck a piece of wax on his praying sceptre, and thus, unnoticed, picked up the gold, and put it into the bosom of his coat. As the priest left the house he happened to see a piece of thread sticking to his dress. This thread he pompously returned to the master of the house, saying that it would be sinful in him, a priest, to take anything out of the house that had not been given him.

Moral. Don't be a hypocrite.

XV. *The Frog and the Two Geese.*

Two geese, when about to start southwards on their annual autumn migration, were entreated by a frog to take him with them. On the geese expressing their willingness to do so if a means of conveyance could be devised, the frog produced a stalk of strong grass, got the two geese to take it one by each end, while he clung to it by his mouth in the middle. In this manner the three were making their journey successfully when they were noticed from below by some men, who loudly expressed their admiration of the device, and wondered who had been clever enough to discover it. The vainglorious frog, opening his mouth to say, "It was me," lost his hold, fell to the earth, and was dashed to pieces.

Moral. Don't let pride induce you to speak when safety requires you to be silent.

CHAPTER XXIX.

MONGOL STORIES.

The recluse. The good king and the bad king. The wizard. The painter and the joiner.

I. *The Recluse.*

WHEN the Mongols want to encourage any one in a life given up to the pursuit of the higher things of their religion, they sometimes tell the following story, which is, of course, the popular version of one of their multitudinous religious legends.

A lama once gave himself up to meditation, prayer, and study, on a mountain side. For three years he prayed assiduously, hoping that Borhan [1] would reveal himself to him, but the three years passed and no vision came. Disheartened, worn out, and impoverished, he quitted his mountain abode to return to the haunts and occupations of men. On his way he came to the foot of a precipitous hill of rock, where he beheld a man sawing away at the hill with a hair. "What are you up to?" asked the lama. "I am going to saw through this hill," replied the man. "What," said the lama, "with a hair? It is impossible!" "Ah no," said the man, "it is not impossible; patience and perseverance will enable

[1] Buddha.

me to cut through this hill with a hair." At this the lama wondered much, and turned away musing thus: "This man is content to sit and work away at the hopeless task of sawing through a hill with a hair. I should not then be discouraged. I have striven for three years to have a revelation of Borhan, and am discouraged because I have not yet succeeded. Compared with this man's case, my three years are nothing. I am ashamed of myself for being discouraged. I'll go back, and try for other three years."

Back he went, and had another three years' trial, with all its many hardships, and still no revelation. Again discouraged, he gave up the attempt, and set out to return to the world. On his way he came to a hill where he saw a man with an enormous cauldron, into which, every now and then, a drop of water descended from a rock.

"What are you doing?" asked the lama. "Filling my pot with water," said the man. "What," said the lama, "fill such a pot with a stray drop of water that falls now and again?" "It's a slow process," said the man, "but it will fill in time."

At this the lama wondered, and mused thus: "I have spent six years striving for a revelation of Borhan, and am discouraged because I have not got it. If this man can contentedly wait till his pot is filled by this slow process, I ought not to be discouraged because I have waited in vain six years. I'll go back, and have another three years at it."

Back he went; three years passed, and still no revelation. Utterly disheartened, he gave up the whole thing finally, and took his way back to the world. At the foot of a mountain he saw a poor female dog covered with sores, which swarmed with worms. The lama stopped and considered what he was to do. If he freed the dog from the worms and cast them on the ground, *they* would die. If he did not free the dog, *it* would die. In this dilemma he conceived the idea of giving half the flesh of his own thigh to the worms and half to the dog. He was just in the act of doing so, when, above him, there appeared a glory and an apparition—it was Maitreya Borhan appeared to him at last! Looking towards the dog—it was gone; it had only been an apparition.

Maitreya asked the lama who and what he was. The lama complained, that though an earnest seeker, he had been left in the dark and without any vision or revelation for nine long years. Suddenly the splendid dress of the apparition changed in appearance, and Maitreya said, "Foolish man that you are, I have never been more than two inches from you all these years. Look, don't you see how your spittle and snuff have bespattered all my robe?" Thus spake Maitreya, and the lama suddenly and at once attained to the status of Borhan.

II. *The Good King and the Bad King.*

When they wish to encourage virtue and discourage vice they tell such stories as the following:—

There was a good king, who was liberal to the poor and to begging lamas. He was liberal to every one, and gave away so much that, latterly, he had little left. He had one only son, whom on his death-bed he instructed to follow his example, and do as his father had done. As long as he had anything at all he was to be careful to give to those who had nothing.

The father died, and the son succeeded to the kingdom. His inheritance was a poverty-stricken one, and, by following his father's precepts, the young king was soon reduced to the most abject poverty. His father's instructions were explicit. "If you have a yard of cloth, and meet a man who has none, give him half. If you have two cups of millet, and meet a man who has none, give him one." Following these instructions, the young king had at last only ten cash left. A begging lama came, and to him he gave five cash. Having now only five cash left, he proposed to follow the fortunes of the begging lama. The lama was well pleased, and the two set out together.

There was a bad king who, by continual oppression and robbery, had amassed great wealth. He had three sons, and on his death he charged them to continue his policy of robbery and oppression. He had grown rich by it, and by it they would keep rich, as their father had done; they followed their father's advice and example, and kept on increasing in wealth.

The poverty-stricken son of the good king, following the fortunes and hardships of his master, arrived at the court of the three sons of the bad king, and was an object of curiosity and scorn to them all. They said among themselves, "Our father was right to warn us against the policy of the king whose son is now reduced to the state of a beggar." So they called their father wise and themselves happy. Meanwhile, an idea struck the youngest, and he said to his two elder brethren: "Suppose I join the lama for a frolic, and travel with him, to see the suffering of the penniless king! Do you approve or disapprove?" "Capital," they said; "by all means do so, and come back and tell us all about it, that we may divert ourselves with the story of his sufferings." So the youngest brother joined himself to the lama, and the party of three, the lama and his two disciples, set out on their travels. They had the usual hardships and consolations of such a lot—hunger and thirst, and sore travel; eating, drinking, hospitality, and rest. Finally they came to a great mountain, at the foot of which was a single tent, poor, ragged and black. The only inhabitants of the tent were two old people. There the travellers put up and rested. The old people, having no children of their own, begged the lama to give them one of his scholars. The lama ordered the son of the good king to remain. To this the youth would not agree. He had given himself up as a scholar to his master, and from his master he would not part on any account. The son of the bad king, tired of the roaming life, consented to remain there, and, leaving him behind, the lama and his disciple began to ascend the mountain. They had already gone a good way when the lama said: "Ah, I have left my rosary in the tent, it is on the west side; go you and bring it; don't enter the tent, but stand a good way off outside and call for it."

After a while the scholar returned to his master, trembling and pale. "What's the matter?" asked the teacher. The scholar replied, "Oh, I saw the old man and the old woman transformed into horrible creatures, sucking the blood of the son of the bad king." "Just so," said the lama; "he came here to see your distress and in place of that you saw his."

Arrived at the top of the mountain the lama said, "I must now go away and leave you." The scholar was in great grief, and begged his teacher to wait and teach him something before he left. The teacher consented, and spent some days in instructing his disciple, and teaching him, among other things, the art of flying.

After he had made good progress in the art of flying, his teacher said: "Go away there to the eastward, see what that is, and come again." The disciple went and saw. It was a huge place, colder than cold, in which people were being frozen hard, then broken across, this process being repeated unceasingly on the same persons. Among the sufferers he recognised the bad king being put through his tortures. "Fly away now in the other direction," said the teacher, "see what that is there, and come again." The disciple went and saw a place full of trees and green grasses, and flowers, and fruits, and delights. He also saw his parents seated in yellow sedans, borne along in state, followed by a crowd of adoring lamas. He called to his father, but he would not regard him; he addressed him, but he would not answer. He recognised them well enough, but they would accord him no token of recognition; so, having waited till he was satisfied with seeing, he returned to his master. "Yes," said the lama, "you have seen your parents enjoying the reward of their virtuous and meritorious life on earth. For their good deeds they have attained to the state of Borhan, and are enjoying the happiness you saw." "But why," asked the youth, "would they not recognise me nor speak to me?" "Because," said the lama, "you have not yet changed this body of yours." Thereupon the lama left him. The lama was not the mere begging priest he seemed, but Sakyamuni.

III. *The Wizard.*

When they want to impress any one who is sceptical as to the power of their wizards, they tell such a story as this:

The merits of a famous wizard were being discussed, when a rash young man remarked that perhaps the wizard had great power, and perhaps he could deceive others, but he could never deceive him. The wizard, hearing of this boast, had his fine saddle put on his splendid black horse, and rode to the abode of the rash young man. The conversation soon turned to the supposed powers of the wizard, and the youth rather wished to put them to the test. The wizard said that was all right, but that meantime he was in trouble and wanted to get out of it. A Chinaman had come to his house, and refused to stir from it till an old debt of ten taels was paid up. Failing the money, the Chinaman would be content with nothing less than the handsome black horse, but he, the wizard, was unwilling to let an animal worth thirty taels be sacrificed to clear a debt of ten taels, and so had come to offer to sell the animal for twenty taels to the young man. The wife was just in the act of pouring out three cups of tea, one for the wizard, one for her husband, one for herself, when the husband went out to have a look at the horse. As he looked at it he suddenly became unconscious, did not know where he was, and wandered about in a land without inhabitants, till, finally, he came to a single hut at the foot of a mountain not far from the sea-shore. The hut proved to be that of a lone woman who could give no account at all of herself. The young man also found that he too could give no account of himself, but remained a day or two under her roof.

When the time came for him to go he did not want to leave; had, in fact, nowhere to go to, and proposed to marry his hostess. They did marry, and between them managed to make life more endurable. The woman gathered fuel on the mountain, drew water, and busied herself with household concerns, while the husband went a-hunting and kept the house in provisions. In due time a child was born, to the great delight of the parents. "Ah," said they, "we are three now, and don't need to fear." Other two years passed away, and another child was born. "Ah," said they, "we are four now, and may live at ease." Six years in all elapsed, when one day, as the father returned loaded with a deer, and the mother was nearing the house with a bundle of fuel, the youngest of the two children was seen creeping towards the sea, and suddenly fell in. Trying to save him, the elder also fell in, and the mother, distracted, trying to save her two children, fell in also. The father threw down the carcase of the deer, and rushed to the scene of the disaster, but he was too late, it was all over, and he was all alone. For a month or two he had rather a hard time of it. If he went for venison he had no fuel; if he went for fuel he had nothing to cook. Eventually he found himself unconscious, and uncertain as to his whereabouts, but saw a tent like his own with a horse tied before it, and was recalled to consciousness by his wife asking him, angrily, if he did not mean to drink his tea before it cooled.

The truth flashed upon him. He had been under the power of the wizard, and had experienced the joys and sorrows of six long years and more, all in less time than a cup of tea takes to cool.

IV. *The Painter and the Joiner.*

When they wish to deter a man from plotting evil against his neighbour, they tell such a story as the following, to show the danger a schemer runs of falling into his own snare:

At the time of the accession of a certain king to the throne there were among his subjects a painter and a joiner, between whom there was a bitter feud. One day the painter went to the young king and said, "Your royal father having taken a new birth, sent for me, and when I went to him I found him in the enjoyment of power beyond all imagination, and he gave me the following letter." The letter was addressed to the young king his son, and ran as follows: "Now that I am in heaven I am happy. I am about to build a temple here, so, my son, send me from your city, Universal Joy, the joiner. I will rejoice in the prosperity of the kingdom under your rule, and from here will help you in your endeavours for its good."

The young king was rejoiced at the contents of the letter, and having called the joiner, said to him, "My father, having been born into heaven, has sent for you to build him a temple," and handed him the letter. The joiner, seeing the letter, thought thus within himself: "This is altogether absurd; this painter is always plotting mischief." Thinking thus within himself, he asked the king, "How am I to get to heaven?" The king asked the painter, and the painter replied, "Place the joiner and his tools in the centre, pile up fuel sprinkled all over with oil, then, to the sound of drums, cymbals, flutes, and fiddles, set fire to the pile, and the joiner will go off on a smoke horse, so says the king your father." The joiner replied, "Before I go I want to make a few preparations. I'll be ready to start in seven days." He then went home and told his wife all about the mischief the painter was plotting against him, and, as a means of escape from the evil, dug a subterranean passage from the inside of his house to the place where he was to be burned, terminating the passage with a stone, which again he covered with sand.

On the seventh day, the king, that he might send the joiner to his father, exacted of all the people a basket of fuel and a bottle of oil. This was all piled up, the joiner and his tools placed in the centre, and fire applied. The drums beat, the cymbals clashed, the flutes whistled, the flames leaped up, and the joiner, under cover of the smoke, entered the subterranean passage and went home with his tools on his back. The painter, pointing to the thick volumes of smoke that rose into the air, exclaimed, "There goes the joiner," and the spectators dispersed joyfully, remarking, "The joiner has got to heaven."

For the space of a month the joiner lay quiet, washing himself daily with milk to make his person white. When the month was over he appeared before the king robed in silk, and bearing a letter purporting to be from the old king to his son. The letter was as follows: "I am much pleased with your pious management of the realm. Universal Joy, the joiner, having built for me a temple here give him a suitable recompense for his labour; and as the temple wants decorating, send me up Eternal Joy, the painter, in the same manner as you sent the joiner." The king asked, "When you got to heaven, was my father glad to see you?" The joiner answered in all respects as if he

IN HIS OWN TRAP.

had been to heaven. The young king was delighted, and giving a handsome reward to the joiner, sent for the painter, who, seeing the white skin and silk robes of the joiner, really supposed that he had not died, but had been to heaven and back. Imagining that his rival had really gone to heaven on a smoke horse, the painter signified his willingness to go after the lapse of seven days. The hour came and the man. The painter with his paints and brushes was placed amidst the oily fuel, fire was applied, the smoke rose, the flames leaped upon him, in agony he plunged about and yelled aloud but, drowned by the sound of the drums, cymbals, flutes, and fiddles, his cries were unheard, and he was burnt to a cinder.

CHAPTER XXX.

WOLVES IN MONGOLIA.

Sometimes not seen for a long time. Adventure. Wolves fear Mongols. Wolves attack Chinamen. Encounters with wolves. Wolf hunts. Oxen heading off a wolf. Wolves in the fold. Wolves called "*wild dogs.*"

SOME travellers expect to see wolves as soon as they enter Mongolia. Wolves there are, but a traveller may go from Kalgan to Kiachta and never see one. Sometimes, again, wolves are heard and not seen. A foreigner was once travelling in winter with a single Mongol attendant. The tent-cart broke down, and had to be exchanged for a common open cart. On one occasion, when the caravan was standing still, a sound was heard; the cart camel pricked up his ears and started at full speed, carrying the foreigner away on the cart, but leaving the Mongol and the other camel behind. It was the sound of wolves that raised the alarm, and the camel, panic-struck, sped away and away. The foreigner, watching his opportunity, seized his pillows and leaped from the cart as he was crossing some ice, when the camel, uncertain of foot, went more slowly. The foreigner, escaped from one danger, began to think that he had fallen into another; what if the wolves should attack him! Out in the dark wood, alone and helpless, what was he to do? By and by a sound as of something approaching was heard; the luckless traveller stared among the trees, expecting to see the wolves appear, when to his great relief up rode the Mongol on his camel. The fugitive camel and cart were found standing beside a tent.

The traveller's fear was superfluous; for wolves do not attack men in Mongolia. It is said they do attack men in Russia; and I knew of a Buriat who died of bites inflicted by a wolf which he brought to bay in his fold at night. In China also there are numerous stories of men being bitten, and of children being carried off by wolves. Chinamen travelling and trading in Mongolia have a great dread of wolves. Mongols hate wolves, and dread their ravages on their flocks and herds; but they never seem to dream of personal danger. When a Chinaman sees a wolf, he runs away from it; when a Mongol sees a wolf, he runs at it gesticulating, shouting, screaming, and generally frantic. Sometimes in the stillness of the afternoon, a terrible uproar and clamour arises suddenly among the tents. Everybody knows what it is, and rushes out to join in and swell the uproar. A wolf is among or making for the sheep. Systematically treated to such a terrible reception wherever they approach man, it is not strange that the wolves acquire habitual dread of Mongols, and run even from a boy.

The reason for the difference between the Russian and Chinese wolves, which are said to eat men, and the Mongolian wolves, which do not eat men, is, perhaps, that the Mongol wolves are never driven to extremity. All the year round they can get a lamb or a sheep abroad on the plains by day, or inside a badly defended fold by night. Failing a sheep, which animal is the most advantageous speculation, inasmuch as a single wolf can perform the capture, the disappointed wolf can join a hungry band of disappointed comrades, and compass an ox, or a camel, or a horse, or as many oxen, or camels, or horses, as may be necessary for the requirements of the pack, and have a good feast. Why then should they eat men?—And they do not eat them.

The Mongols boast themselves not a little on their superiority to the Chinese in showing a bold front to wolves. They even say that the wolves know and distinguish Chinamen from afar, and do not hesitate to pursue them. It is true that a practised human eye can tell whether the diminutive outline of a man seen afar on the plain, is that of a Chinaman or a Mongol. There is something very different about the dress and bearing which is manifest a long way off. Whether the wolves notice the difference or not I cannot say; the Mongols affirm most stoutly that they do. If men in blue wadded jacket and trousers invariably run away, and allow themselves to be eaten when overtaken, and men in long skin robes rush up howling like madmen, and break the heads of any wolves their horses may be swift enough to overtake, it would not be at all beyond the bounds of credibility that wolves should note the difference, and treat the two sorts of men differently.

The Mongols have many pleasant stories of conquering wolves which have proved the terror of mean-spirited Chinamen. Here are samples.

A Mongol had been down to China trading. Riding up towards home again, he saw a wolf lying on the top of a wall, lashing its tail and ready to spring down into a court where a number of Chinese children were playing. Undoing his gun from the baggage, he aimed, fired, and killed his prey. The Chinese had not seen the animal, and were not a little startled at hearing the report of a gun, and seeing a huge wolf fall dead into the yard. Learning how it happened, the Chinese were profuse in their thanks, entertained their preserver to an impromptu feast, and loaded him with presents.

On another occasion, a threshingfloor on the border between Mongolia and China was frequented by a huge wolf, which had already destroyed several men. It raised such a panic, that men could not be got to carry on the work of cleaning the harvested grain;—no Chinaman would go near the place. In the nearest government town was a Mongol on *yamen* duty, who was noted for his bravery, and was a good shot. A deputation of farmers, shopkeepers, and country people generally, waited upon him and begged him to help them to rid the country-side of this terrible wolf. Inducement offering, he was nothing loth to go and have a shot at a beast he heartily despised. He went and slept on the floor among the grain. The wolf appeared as usual to eat his man; but somehow finding a man who would not run, the wolf ran off, and would not give the marksman a chance, Chinese guns handled by Mongols being rather slow affairs. Several nights he tried, but the cowardly beast would not stand fire. At last he declared he would give up the attempt except some Chinamen watched with him. When the wolf appeared again, the whole of the Chinese took to flight, stumbling and falling all about in their headlong trepidation. Now was his chance. Standing his ground, when the wolf came up he was ready and shot the creature dead on the spot.

A number of Mongols were on their way to Peking one autumn. At night they put up at an inn at the foot of Cock-crow Hill. Starting next morning with the early dawn, one of the number saw a shepherd and flock of sheep in full flight, the sheep scattered all about. The shepherd was a Chinaman leading a flock of fat sheep to the Peking market. The practised eye of the Mongol took in the situation at a glance. A wolf had caught a sheep and was tearing it. The shepherd was in full flight, afraid, as the Mongol said, of being eaten himself. With the Mongol, to see and understand all this was the work of an instant; at once his blood was up, and, as if he had been on his native plains, howling and gesticulating frantically, he urged his horse towards the wolf. It turned out to be an extra large and fierce animal, and he had no weapon but a small whip. But no weapon was needed; the bold front and terror-inspiring cries put the beast to flight. Dismounting, he took possession of his prize, strapped the carcase on behind the saddle, and sold it for a good sum at the first town he came to.

A Mongol once related to me an adventure he had with a wolf. He was a lama, and was at the time mounted on a camel, carrying a mail over a very desolate part of the country. Suddenly his camel became alarmed, and soon after a wolf of the largest size showed itself and kept abreast of him a little way off. Such a companion was rather uncomfortable at that particular time and place, and the lama for a time pretended to take no notice of the beast, hoping it would slink away. Then, I think, he resorted to the usual method of shouting and gesticulating, but that would not do. The lama began to think he had fallen in with one of the very few wolves that are spoken of as having attacked men; and, as he had no weapon but a light riding-whip, felt but poorly able to defend himself should he be actually attacked. He kept his wits about him, however, and making his camel kneel took a stone and kept on striking it hard on his iron stirrup. The hard metallic ring was quite a formidable noise; and the wolf slowly and with evident reluctance drew off. Had this lama been mounted on a horse and had a stick five or six feet long, he would have treated the wolf very differently.

There are such things as wolf hunts in Mongolia. On large plains, a rider on a good horse can harass a wolf pretty severely; and even when near hills, a couple of horsemen, one to hunt, and one to head off, can be pretty sure of killing their game. There is one tract of country where the plains are wide, and good horses numerous; and woe betide the wolf that shows himself rashly in the daytime. The ready natives throw themselves into the saddles of the horses, which stand ready at their tent doors, and armed with the "horse catcher," soon hem in their victim. The "horse catcher" is a strong fishing-rod looking apparatus, ten or twelve feet long, and fitted with a large thong loop strong enough to hold a wild horse by the neck.

Winter is the best time to hunt wolves on horseback. The snow hinders the wolf much more than it hinders the horse, and a hard ride does not tell so severely on the horse as it would in hot weather. This wolf hunting is not by any means a common pastime. The Mongols have plenty of horses, but are too careful of them to chase wolves unnecessarily; if, however, they think their flocks are in danger, they do not spare their steeds.

One day we were encamped beside the tent of a wealthy Mongol. Suddenly his whole drove of oxen, which should have been grazing at a distance, were seen running along in a compact column. "They are chasing a wolf," said the serving men. The master was called out to see, and at once ordered his men to mount and pursue the beast. This order made every face radiant with joyous excitement; and in a few moments the retainers were galloping over the plain, trailing their great "horse catchers" behind them. It was evidently a great treat to the poor fellows, but they were disappointed after all. The sly old wolf seeing them coming, put on speed and got into the hills before he could be intercepted. Once into the hills, pursuit was impossible. The master was a little annoyed at missing the wolf, as he had suffered a good deal from the ravages of these animals; they having come one night in force and devoured a camel tied not far from his tent door.

The wolves in their ravages are not very fierce or formidable, and rely more on not being seen than on their strength or courage. Very few instances can be quoted of wolves destroying cattle which were properly tended. Sheep are often thus destroyed, but the wolf here relies on his own swiftness and the carelessness of the shepherd. The shepherd is in a tent drinking tea, or sitting on the ground holding his horse, and looking in some other direction; or he has ridden away a few hundred yards to look at something or other; this is the wolf's chance. Running with great speed, he is among the sheep before he is noticed, and in the few minutes it takes the shepherd to come up, two or three sheep have been torn, some blood sucked, and perhaps a few fragments of the fatty tail devoured. The shepherd comes up, frequently followed by most of the near inhabitants; the torn sheep are examined, and opinions expressed as to whether they will live or die. Meantime, the wolf has withdrawn himself to the nearest mountain, or over the horizon of the plain, followed by all the dogs of the neighbourhood.

People sometimes imagine that wild beasts make one of the dangers of Mongolia, but personal danger from wild beasts seems never to enter the head of a Mongol about to travel. The wolf is the only formidable animal that abounds in those parts of the country with which I am acquainted; and, as may be seen from what is said above, he is glad to keep clear of men. I never heard of them banding together into the large and fierce packs that are said to appear in Russia at times; and only once have I heard of any place where wolves were said to have attacked man.

Perhaps when the Mongols become as careful of their cattle, and as painstaking over their folds as the Russians and Chinese are, the wolves may be starved into more fierceness. Meantime they feed easily and behave well to man; and if they would only refrain from eating their cattle the Mongols would not much object to them. But on account of their destructive ravages, the Mongols do dread them, and superstitiously refrain from pronouncing the word *wolf*. The term in common use is *dog*, which is shortened from the full expression *wild dog*. I was once pulled up sharply for venturing to say the proper word for *wolf* after dark; and, once reprimanded, was careful always to speak of wolves as *dogs*.

The only redeeming feature about the wolf is his skin. The skin makes capital winter clothing, much too fine and expensive for common people and every-day wear; but it is not the finest nor most expensive fur worn by the wealthier classes. It keeps out the cold well, and makes a respectable-looking garment. It is most commonly used for a short jacket worn outside all the other clothing, and has a comfortable look on a horseman braving the dry blasts of winter.

CHAPTER XXXI.

THE MONGOLS IN PEKING.

Attractions offered to Mongols by Peking. Resident lamas. Temples in Peking. Book-shops. Mongols come to Peking on Government duty, on pilgrimages, and to trade. The Wai Kuan and the Li Kuan. Christian books. Duration of the Mongol season.

To the Mongols Peking is the city of the great king. As the seat of the Government and the residence of the Emperor it is an object of great reverence, and as the largest city they know, it is regarded with wonder and awe. Many of them during the course of their lives visit it, either summoned by Imperial mandate to perform Government duty, or attracted to it as a religious centre by considerations of devotion; while not a few resort to it as a mart where they can sell most advantageously the products of their native country, and purchase best and most cheaply materials for clothing and the many other appliances of civilisation for which they are dependent on China.

Very seldom does a Mongol come to Peking on only one errand. Now and again pilgrims come whose sole object is to worship at the celebrated shrine of the Chan T'an Ssŭ, but devotees like these are rare. In most cases those who come to worship take the opportunity to do a stroke of trade, and those who come to trade do not neglect to make the round of the temples when their secular business is finished. Those who come to perform Government duty find opportunities for both traffic and devotion.

There are some fifteen hundred Mongols permanently resident in the capital. There are priests, lamas, who are distributed among a number of temples both inside and outside the walls. They come for the most part to Peking in early youth, and in language, diet, and habits, so adapt themselves to the Chinese civilisation around them, that it is sometimes difficult to be sure that they are Mongols at all, and even at a distance they can be readily distinguished from their up-country visitors when walking together on the street. Some of these city lamas are said to be supported by funds contributed by their native tribes, but most of them seem to hold offices to which are attached revenues derived either directly from the Imperial exchequer, or accruing from endowments bestowed upon the temples by the piety of former ages.

These Peking priests have Government duty to perform, part of which is to chant prayers for the prosperity of the country, and for the happiness of the departed souls of deceased members of the imperial family When an emperor or an empress dies a temple of straw mats is erected, lamas are invited, and services for the benefit of the dead kept up for two or three months. This so course brings the lamas an additional revenue.

Sometimes they are asked out to chant prayers in rich families recently bereaved, when they may be seen going along the street resplendent in yellow coats and faultless hats; but notwithstanding all this most of

MONGOL TENTS AND CAMELS.

them are very poor, arising in great part from the fact that the poverty of the Government has made it necessary to curtail the imperial allowances granted to these agents of religion. Many a lama who has nominally a sufficient income never receives much more than the half of his due, and has yet to be content with what he gets.

Some of the temples in which Mongol lamas reside in Peking have acquired a considerable reputation for sanctity, and are resorted to by pilgrims. The most famous is the Chan T'an Ssŭ, round the main buildings of which is a path worn out in the pavement bricks by the feet of devout worshippers, who walk round these halls as a meritorious duty.

One great attraction which Peking offers to the religious Mongol is its book-shops. In other places, such as Urga and Wu T'ai, there are books published, but the great majority of sacred books used by the priesthood and laity of Mongolia are produced in Peking. In close proximity to two of the lama temples are two publishing establishments conducted by Chinamen, which have always on hand a stock of the most popular books of the Buddhist religion both in the Mongolian and Tibetan languages. They are always ready also to cut blocks for and print any book that may be desired.

Some Mongols prefer to use editions of the sacred works transcribed by hand, and the lamas resident in the Peking temples are only too glad to eke out their scanty allowances by undertaking contracts of this kind. They tell with satisfaction the story of a Mongolian prince who ordered, or, to put it as the priests would, supplicated for, an extensive work of this kind, paid a princely price for it when it was finished, and carried it away on a train of white camels, he himself in person leading the first camel, as a token of respectful reverence to the sacred treasure he had obtained.

Those who visit Peking in response to the summons of the Government are usually of the higher ranks, are mostly summoned in winter, and come attended by a train of followers. They receive a settled allowance per head per day. Some of the princes summoned annually to Peking have residences of their own at which they put up during their stay in the capital, but those of lower rank hire lodging-places from the Chinese.

The Government duty they have to perform seems to be purely formal, the princes attending the emperor in the early morning receptions given at the palace, the Mongols of lower rank lending dignity to their superiors by attending them to and from the palace. One set of Mongols who visit Peking say their claim to be summoned to the capital rests on the fact of their being the lineal descendants of Genghis Khan, and that as such they are admitted to feast with the emperor. The feast, however, is only formal, consisting, according to their own account, of a few eatables and a large quantity of imitation viands, made of clay or some such base material, and painted to look like real food. It matters little to the guests whether the food is imitation or real, etiquette requiring them to remain motionless at the board, as if it would be presumption to eat in the presence of the emperor. They say that though they dare not eat in the emperor's presence, they manage to hide in their sleeves and bring away with them some of these real or sham viands as mementoes of the honour conferred upon them.

After dancing attendance on the court for a month or

two they receive their dismission, are paid their Government allowance, and within a few days are expected to settle up their affairs and return to their remote abodes, from which they are not again summoned to perform this formal court service for a year, or perhaps two.

The great majority of Mongols, whose appearance lends picturesqueness to the Chinese crowds that swarm about the busy centres of Peking in winter, belong to the trading class; some few come with ox-carts, some on horses, but most come with camels, trains of which, numbering sometimes as many as sixty, may be seen making their way along the crowded streets, the camels taking fright at the, to them, unusual sights of the city, and blocking up the roadway by crowding their unwieldy bodies and loads together when panic-struck. The Peking carters, seeing them come, good-humouredly revile them, and give place till the caravan passes, for though the Mongol is despised as ignorant, dirty, stupid, and thievish, he is everywhere welcomed as a customer with whom a Chinaman can trade profitably. In Peking there are two principal lodging-places of the Mongols, the Halha Kuan, situated about a mile beyond the north wall of the city, hence called also the Wai Kuan, or outside lodging, and the Li Kuan, or inside lodging, close behind the British Legation.

If any one wants to see Mongol life without going to Mongolia, the Li Kuan is the place to see it. In the open space that forms the market are seldom wanting a few tents, standing at the door of which a spectator may see the inmates boiling their tea, cooking their food, washing their faces, and sitting about all in true Mongol style. Round the tents are placed creels of frozen game and poultry, and outside these again are ranged the

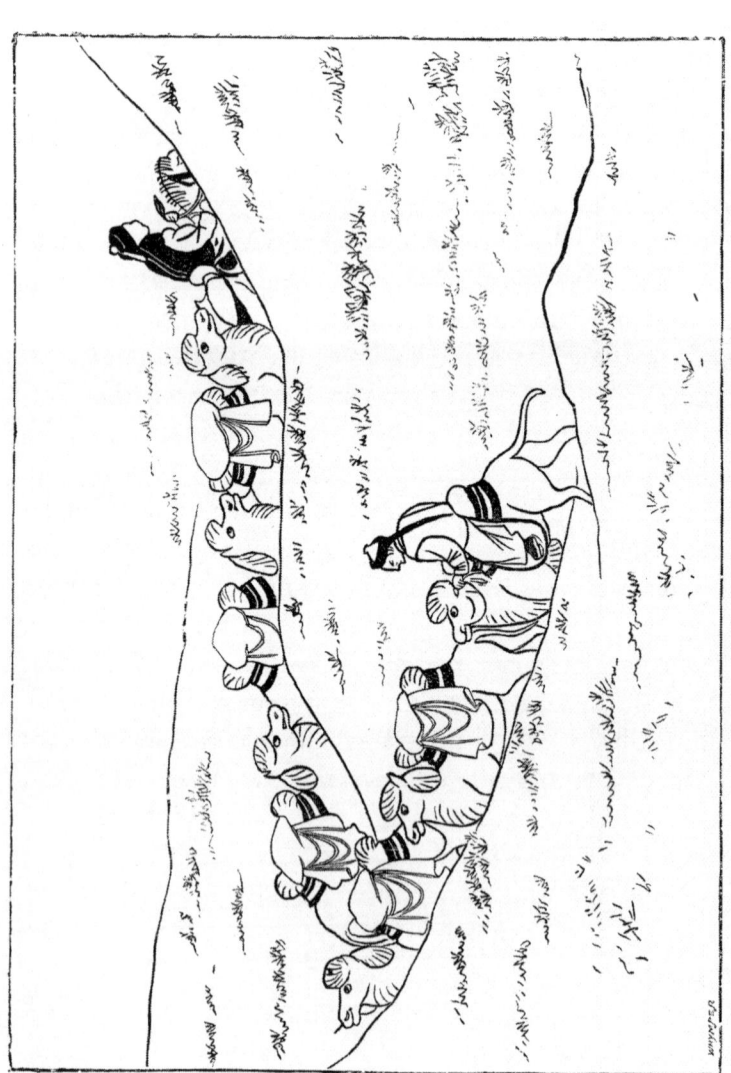

CAMEL CARAVAN EN ROUTE. [*From a Native Sketch.*

camels, or oxen and carts, which formed their means of conveyance. A small crowd of Chinese idlers and petty traders usually surrounds the tent door, and one member and another of the tent's company keeps going and coming to and from "*the street*," as the busy part of the market is called.

The Li Kuan with its miscellaneous crowd of Mongols hailing from almost all parts of their wide country, is a good place to sell Christian books, which, carried home by the travellers on their return, can thus penetrate to remote and outlying places. Any one engaging in this kind of bookselling will often find his customers destitute of cash, and have to take in payment numerous and strange articles of barter.

For two months in the winter the Wai Kuan and the Li Kuan are lively with buyers and sellers. For a month before and a month after the two busy seasons there are a few buyers and sellers, but for eight months of the year both places look deserted and dead. The Mongols, disliking the heat of Peking, have retired to the colder and more congenial *habitats*, and the Chinese have either betaken themselves to other industries, or, if of an adventurous spirit, have made up a stock of goods and gone out to the plains on a summer trading venture.

THE END.

RICHARD CLAY & SONS, LIMITED,
LONDON & BUNGAY.

Printed in Great Britain
by Amazon.co.uk, Ltd.,
Marston Gate.